A Cognitive
Psychology of
Mass Communication

COMMUNICATION
TEXTBOOK SERIES
Jennings Bryant—Editor

Mass Communication
Alan M. Rubin—Advisor

HSIA • Mass Communications
Research Methods:
A Step-by-Step Approach

HARRIS • A Cognitive Psychology
of Mass Communication

"A Cognitive Psychology of Mass Communication"

RICHARD JACKSON HARRIS

Kansas State University

LEA LAWRENCE ERLBAUM ASSOCIATES, PUBLISHERS

1989 Hillsdale, New Jersey   Hove and London

Lawrence Erlbaum Associates, Inc., Publishers
365 Broadway
Hillsdale, New Jersey 07642

Library of Congress Cataloging-in-Publication Data

Harris, Richard Jackson.
    A cognitive psychology of mass communication.

    (Communication textbook series. Mass communications)
    Bibliography: p.
    Includes index.
    1. Mass media — Psychological aspects.   I. Title.
II. Series. [DNLM: 1. Cognition.   2. Communication.
3. Mass Media.   P 96.P75 H315c]
P96.P75H37   1989   302.23   89-7805
ISBN 0-8058-0094-8

Printed in the United States of America
10 9 8 7 6 5 4 3 2 1

Contents P
96
P75
H37
1989

Preface

This book evolved from developing and teaching a course "Psychology of Mass Communication" at Kansas State University yearly since 1981. I am grateful to the students in this class over the years for their enthusiasm, inspiration, and challenge; their ideas and responses to my material have affected the book throughout. Some research on the cognition of deceptive advertising in the late 1970s originally challenged me to think seriously about mass media consumption as information processing. Thanks are due to Tony Dubitsky and Kristin Bruno for contributions to this research. The support of the Psychology Department at Kansas State University during the writing has been tremendous. I also greatly appreciate the Fulbright Visiting Lectureship I held in Belo Horizonte Brazil in 1982; this experience gave me an internationalist perspective which I have tried to bring to this book.

Particular thanks are due to John Bechtold, Sherry Wright, Jean Peters, and Ty Callahan for their helpful reactions and conversations about this material. Jennings Bryant and the reviewers for Lawrence Erlbaum Associates have made exceptionally helpful comments which have improved the book immeasurably. Working with them on developing the manuscript could not have been more helpful and pleasant.

Finally, I thank my parents E. R. and Helen Harris for modelling such effective media use in the home I grew up in. I am sure that many conversations over the television or the evening newspaper provided some intellectual seeds that bear some fruit in this book.

Richard Jackson Harris

Introduction

As long as I can remember, there were lots of magazines around the house I grew up in. Even before we went to school, a highlight of every weekend was sitting up on Dad's lap while he read us the funnies from the Sunday paper. Then one gray day when I was six years old, the magic box entered our home for the first time—television. Life was never the same again.

A contemporary Brazilian story by Millôr Fernandes (1978) tells of a man who comes home from work one day and starts bemoaning his troubles to his young child. It's been the most terrible day of his life. He's lost thousands of dollars, his office building has been torn down, his car has been towed away, and his secretary has quit. At the end of this lament, the puzzled child turns to his father and says, "But, Daddy, when it's this way, why don't you just change the channel?"

A second anecdote, this one a true story, tells of a young BBC news reporter sent to cover the Vietnam War in 1969 (Bogart, 1980). Not being very experienced or knowledgeable about what he was observing, he led off his first televised report of an American attack of a Vietcong stronghold in Hue with "My God! It's just like watching television." Instead of television being a more or less accurate reflection of some other reality, it has in both of these stories *become* the reality against which the real world is compared. The media view of the world has become more real than the real world itself.

Finally, a 13-year-old boy, Robert Call, of suburban Kansas City, died instantly after shooting himself in the head with a .357-caliber Magnum handgun while he and a friend were re-enacting a scene from *The Deer Hunter,* a film depicting American POWs in Vietnam being forced by their Vietcong captors to play Russian roulette. Call and two friends had recently seen the 1978 Oscar-winning film. He had later taken the handgun from under his father's bed. The county coroner ruled the death accidental. As of 1984, 31 people were known to have died reenacting that climactic scene from *The Deer Hunter.*

These three stories concisely suggest a major theme of this book, that our experience with the media is the basis for building our knowledge about the world. We may call this a *cognitive* approach to mass communication because the emphasis is on the way that our minds create knowledge, indeed, create a reality about the world based on our experience with the media. This mental reality then becomes the basis for all sorts of behaviors and has numerous effects on our lives.

Mass communication in the form of print media has been with us almost since Gutenberg's invention of movable type and the printing press in 1456. However, the nature of mass communication, indeed of life in general, has been radically changed in the 20th century by the advent of broadcast media, especially television. Television has transformed the day-to-day life of more people in the last 40 years than has perhaps any invention in human history. Radio and the print media have been greatly changed by TV as well. In a recent U.S. poll (Handler, 1987) 68% reported that watching television was their main source of pleasure, followed by spending time with friends, helping others, and taking vacations. Besides changing the way we spend our time, television has also revolutionized the way we think and the way we view the world. These effects on our perception and our cognition are particular emphases of this book. The media are not only our "magic window" on the world but also the way we learn about the world.

Media are far more important than merely serving as conduits of knowledge, though that is no trivial role. The act of transmitting that knowledge may itself become the event of note. When Dan Rather and Vice President George Bush engaged in a mutually accusatory shouting match in an interview on the "CBS Evening News" during the 1988 Presidential primary campaign, the interview itself, more than the content discussed, became the news story in all media the next day. The media were not merely communicating the news; they had become the news.

We have come a long way from Gutenberg to the 1657 daily newspapers, 1611 television stations, and 10,128 radio stations in the United States in 1987 (Friedrich, 1987). See Box 1.1 for some further background on print and broadcast media. In this chapter we will introduce the notion of perceived reality and a cognitive perspective. Then we will discuss how researchers have approached the study of media. Before we look at the scientific study of media, however, let us briefly examine the general nature of mass communication.

WHAT IS MASS COMMUNICATION?

What makes mass communication *mass*? First of all, the audience is large and anonymous, often very heterogeneous. Individual viewers, listeners, or readers or even groups of individuals can be targeted but only with limited precision. Secondly, the sources of the communication are institutional and organizational. Some, such as television networks or newspaper chains, are among the largest and richest private corporations. Third, and perhaps most importantly, the basic economic function of most media in Western and Third World nations is to attract and hold as large an audience as possible for the advertisers. In one way or another, advertising pays 100% of the costs of commercial broadcast television networks like the "Big Three" of the United States (CBS, NBC, ABC), and even public television and government-subsidized networks like the British Broadcasting Corporation (BBC) are far from immune from commercial pressures. In spite of all the high-sounding rhetoric about serving the public, the bottom line of commercial mass media is money, which comes from advertisers at rates directly determined by the audience size or readership, which in turn determines the content (see Box 1.2). This is not to say that editors and programmers have no real concern about responsibly meeting the needs of the public. They do, but such needs must necessarily be considered within the constraints of the economic realities of the media industry. Print media also have the pressure of numbers. Newspapers and many magazines receive a majority, though not all, of their income from advertising. There are economic pressures, as well as sometimes political and ideological ones, to control the content of media. These are explored in Box 1.3.

In spite of its mass nature, there is more than *mass* to mass communication. There is also *communication,* and communication implies a reciprocity, some kind of response from the audience. Although the TV viewer is often characterized as being extremely passive and mindlessly absorbing the program content, this book argues that such

BOX 1.1   A PRIMER ON BROADCAST AND PRINT MEDIA

Mass media are of two basic types: print and broadcast. Print media (newspapers and magazines) provide information through the production and distribution of copies. In contrast to broadcast, print media tend to be more permanent (at least before the advent of widespread video and audio taping) and are dependent on the literacy of the audience. There are also no channel limits in print media. Although there are only a finite number of possible television channels, there is no inherent limit to the number of newspapers that may be published. Print media also lend themselves better to detailed treatment of subjects than do broadcast media. Although the number of daily newspapers has sharply declined in the United States in the last two decades, they remain essential sources of local news, sports, and advertising. Magazines, on the other hand, are less often localized regionally but more often are segmented by interest (e.g, *Runner's World, Apartment Life, Modern Photography*).

In contrast to print, broadcast media (radio and television) are technologically more recent, less permanent, and less dependent on formal literacy or accessibility to urban infrastructure. This last point becomes especially crucial in the isolated regions of Third World nations. One can have a portable radio without any access to electricity, schooling, or urban life. Because of the limited channel capacity, radio and television tend to be easier to control centrally than are print media. From its beginnings in a Pittsburgh garage in 1920, radio grew substantially in its first decade in a manner parallel to the rise of television in the 1950s. Upon the advent of television after the Second World War, however, the character of radio changed drastically, away from prime-time programming to music/news formats and later to more specialized (especially FM) stations like country and western, classical, gospel, or all news.

Because of its use of the public airwaves, which are sharply limited in capacity, radio and television typically are regulated by governments much more tightly than are print media. The assignment of television channels by the U.S. Federal Communications Commission (FCC) is an example of such regulation. In more authoritarian societies, it is relatively easy for the government to step in and take over radio and (especially) television in times it deems to be unduly threatening.

Although television networks, both private and government-owned, tend to be national in scope, they often have influence far beyond their country's borders. Because broadcast signals do not respect political boundaries, most Canadians are able to receive U.S. television and most East Germans can watch West German television. Beyond this, however, telecommunications is a major export business. The four largest networks in the world (CBS, NBC, and ABC in the United States and TV Globo in Brazil) export their programs to dozens of other nations.

BOX 1.1. continued

Millions of people around the world may know virtually nothing about the United States besides what they see on such programs as "Dynasty." Conversely, many Americans' impressions of British people are unduly colored by televised imports like "Masterpiece Theatre" or "Fawlty Towers" on PBS. Mexican television programs from the Televisa network are seen throughout Spanish-speaking Latin America and the United States, as well as in Spain. How we learn about other groups of people from media is the subject of Chapter 3.

a picture is far from accurate. The meaning of a particular program certainly depends heavily on the content of that program, but not entirely so. It also depends on what is in the mind and experience of the viewer. A TV movie dealing with rape will have a very different effect on, indeed a different meaning for, a viewer who has herself been a rape victim than someone with no such personal experience. A violent X-rated video may incite one man to sexual violence because of the way his mind interpreted and interacted with the content of the video, whereas another man seeing the same video may have no such antisocial response.

The nature of the media consumption experience must also be considered. Watching television or listening to the radio may be done alone or in small groups. Reading newspapers or magazines is typically, though not always, a solo activity. Though this is not always a concern of the communication source, it can greatly affect the psychological experience of using the medium. For example, consider the difference between watching an exciting ball game by yourself or with a group of friends. Consider the difference between watching a horror film with someone who either shrieked in fun, cried in severe distress, laughed, or made no obvious reaction at all (Zillmann, Weaver, Mundorf, & Aust, 1986).

MEDIA AS PERCEIVED REALITY

The Reflection Myth

Often people think of the media as vehicles for reflecting the world around them. News stories report what happened in the world that day. TV sitcoms reflect the values, lifestyles, and habits of their

BOX 1.2. THOSE ALL-IMPORTANT RATINGS

The Nielsen ratings are the all-important thermometers used to measure the audience size for network television programming in the United States. It is on these ratings that programs, careers, and even broad social trends rise and fall. The A. C. Nielsen Company has for many years selected around 1700 American homes to have "Storage Instantaneous Audimeters" hooked up to their TV sets. This machine measures when the set is on and what channel is on and relays this information back to a Nielsen computer. It does not measure whom, if anyone, is watching the set, how intently they are watching, or what else they are doing at the same time. Another sample of homes, frequently changed, keeps weekly diaries of programs watched.

In the late 1980s the method of data collection of Nielsen ratings began to change dramatically. The advent of the new technology of "people meters" promised to give Nielsen more accurate information on exactly who is watching when the TV is on. The people meter is a remote-control-like device whereby the viewer punches in the exact time of beginning and ending of viewing and information on who is watching. When this device has been completely phased in to replace the audimeters and diaries, it should provide more accurate information on viewing than merely a global on-off measure. Some questions have been raised, however, as to whether Nielsen families, especially children, are actually entering all the required information. Some early evidence suggested an over-reporting of viewing commercials and an under-reporting of young children's unsupervised viewing.

The Nielsen "ratings" are in fact two types of information. The rating proper is the percentage of the potential audience that is viewing a program, for example, a rating of 30 reflects that 30% of the homes with TV have that program on. The "share" compares that program's performance with the competition on at the same time. In the United States, commercial programs with much less than a one-quarter share are very ripe candidates for cancellation. Network advertising charges are usually based primarily on the Nielsen ratings and shares measured during the three 4-week "sweeps" periods, usually in February, May, and November. For this reason networks frequently throw their blockbuster miniseries and other highly promoted programming on during these weeks.

Advertising charges are based primarily on the number of homes reached by an ad, ranging all the way from very modest charges for a spot on a local late-night show to well over a million dollars for a 60-second national spot on the Super Bowl. Charges of over $100,000 for a 30-second prime-time spot were not unusual in the late 1980s. The cost for a 30-second spot on the Super Bowl rose from $125,000 in 1975 to $600,000 in 1987. The even more lucrative 15-second spot typically sells for 55% to 60% of the 30-second price. Most U.S. networks or TV stations sell around 9.5 minutes of advertising per hour

BOX 1.2. continued

during prime-time (8–11 P.M. Eastern time zone) and 16 minutes other times, with charges per minute typically much higher for the prime-time slots. Even the third-place network in the United States is a highly profitable business, though the recent growth of cable stations has diminished this significantly.

It also matters who is watching. An audience of 18 to 49-year-old upper-middle-class viewers is worth more to advertisers than one the same size consisting largely of the elderly, the unemployed, and children. In this sense one of the most successful talk shows on American TV is the "Late Night with David Letterman" (Jamieson & Campbell, 1988). So-called "yuppie shows" like "Thirtysomething" can survive the modest Nielsen ratings because of the buying power of their upscale audience.

society. TV dramas and magazine fiction reflect the concerns and issues that viewers are struggling with. The presence of violence and offensive stereotypes merely reflects the ugly reality of an imperfect world. The commercials reflect the needs and wants that we have. Media, in this view, are a sort of window on reality.

This is not the only way to view mass communication, however. It may be that we think certain events and issues are important because the news tells us they are. Sitcoms may portray certain values, life-styles, and habits that are then adopted by society. TV dramas deal with certain issues, which then are considered and dealt with by the viewers. Stereotypes seen on television implicitly teach young viewers what different groups of people are like, and the presence of much violence on TV teaches that the world is a violent place. Advertising convinces us that we have certain needs and wants that we didn't know we had before. In this view, media are not merely reflecting what is out there in the world. Rather, they are constructing a world that becomes reality for the consumer. This world may be accepted by TV viewers, who are often unaware of such a process happening, while they feel they are only being entertained. Soon the world as constructed by media may become so implanted in our minds that we cannot distinguish it from reality, as in the case of the little boy who asked his father why he didn't just change the channel to get rid of a bad day at work.

Do the media reflect the world or create a new reality? Certainly media do in many ways reflect what is out there in the world. However, they also choose what to tell us about what is out there in the world

BOX 1.3. THE ISSUE OF CENSORSHIP

A major philosophical and legal issue in regard to media is censorship. This obviously varies greatly across different societies. Although prior censorship, that is, requiring approval of all content before broadcast or publication, occurs in some totalitarian societies, other more subtle forms of censorship exist in all nations. Even in the United States, whose First Amendment guarantees freedom of speech and press, such freedom has never been absolute. It operates within certain constraints upheld through numerous court challenges. For example, one may not advocate armed overthrow of the government or print libelous aspersions on people. One may not broadcast material that has been classified, incites people to violence, or that infringes on copyright laws. Also, broadcast of content deemed obscene may not be permitted. Of course, exactly what constitutes defamatory or obscene content has been the object of considerable debate in and out of the judicial system for years and no doubt will continue to be.

In the case of television, the Federal Communications Commission (FCC) has a degree of control over broadcast content unlike any governmental body. Because of the limited nature of the public airwaves (unlike the unlimited nature of paper for print media), the FCC assigns channels and issues licenses. Although they have the power to deny renewal of licenses, less than 150 radio and TV renewal licenses (out of 70,000) have been rejected in over 50 years of operation. The FCC also insures application of the Equal Time rule (and until its demise in 1987 the Fairness Doctrine as well) to insure that opposing points of view on controversial issues and political campaigns are aired.

There are other pressures toward censorship, though it often is not called that, especially in the United States, where "censorship" is a very dirty word. Even its most vigorous proponents do not call it "censorship." The National Association of Broadcasters (NAB), a professional organization of radio and television stations, has a fairly rigorous ethical code, which it expects its members to adhere to, although court challenges and appeals, an atmosphere of deregulation, and changing social standards in the eighties weakened adherence to the NAB code. Some content which may not be illegal *per se* may nevertheless not appear on television because it is not in accord with NAB guidelines or because broadcasters fear legal challenges or public outrage, for example, very graphic and explicit sex, violence, or surgery. Also, certain words (e.g., "shit," "fuck," many racial epithets, and religious expletives stronger than "Oh, my God!") seldom occur on American primetime network television. Incidentally, these standards change; 30 years ago we did not hear "damn," "hell," or "pregnant" either, though we may have heard "nigger" in early days of radio.

Real or feared reaction from advertisers is another subtle source of self-censorship. Television networks and stations are very loath to risk offending those who pay the bills for their livelihood. Though in-

BOX 1.3. continued

frequent, advertisers occasionally threaten to withdraw their ads in protest. For example, in 1979 General Electric was unhappy with ABC's Barbara Walters plans to interview Jane Fonda about her antinuclear activism and pulled their ads in protest. However, ABC still aired the interview. Some media scholars have argued that network news reporting regularly plays down corporate and commercial abuses for fear of advertiser wrath, but such a claim is hard to either substantiate or discredit.

A democratic government may exert influence even in cases where it has no formal censoring authority. For example, the British government requested the BBC not to run a scheduled documentary on Northern Ireland in August 1985. This documentary included extensive interviews with two extremists, one Catholic IRA member and one Protestant extremist. The government argued that this gave those whom it called "terrorists" an undeserved platform and hearing. After extensive discussion, BBC management decided to honor the government's request, though this decision evoked a one-day strike by BBC employees in protest.

Concern over the public's reaction may be another source of self-censorship. In 1985 two of the three U.S. commercial networks refused to run an antismoking public service announcement, which showed a fetus smoking a cigarette in the womb. Similarly, before about 1987 we did not see ads for contraceptives on U.S. television, though they have appeared in many popular magazines for years. In fact, commercials are the most conservative component of television. Advertisers are extremely reluctant to offend viewers, with the possible exception of insulting their intelligence.

Such extreme concern about public reaction may or may not be well-founded. In the 1950s, U.S. television producers and advertisers feared that using Blacks in commercials would offend and alienate whites. When this practice changed as part of the civil rights movement of the 1960s, this concern proved to be totally without foundation. Through most of the history of television there has been a similar reluctance by networks to use openly homosexual characters in prime-time series programming, although there are increasing cautious exceptions in the late 1980s. From a commercial perspective, the worst sin a broadcaster can commit is to air something that causes viewers to turn the set off.

and we accept that interpretation, which then becomes part of our memory and our experience. In this book we will examine how television and other media *create* a world which then *becomes* our reality. This cognitive perspective will focus on the mental construction of reality that we form as a result of our contact with print and broadcast media. This constructed reality often differs significantly from objective reality in ways that are not always appreciated. The plan of this book will be to examine various content areas from a cognitive psychological perspective, while focusing on this theme of how media create a reality.

The Study of Perceived Reality

Within the scientific study of communication, there are several theoretical approaches to studying this perceived reality created by media. Although these are discussed more fully in treatment of specific content areas later in the text, we will briefly introduce these approaches here. As we will see throughout the book, each has something important to say about the perceived reality we cognitively construct through interaction with media.

Social learning theory (Bandura, 1977; Tan, 1986) examines how media provide models whose behavior and attitudes are imitated by viewers. This approach has its roots in behaviorist (S-R) psychology, as extended to social issues. Social learning theory has been particularly useful in studying the process of learning violent behavior from media and, as such, is considered in more detail in Chapter 9.

Agenda-setting (Berelson, 1942; McCombs, 1981) focuses on the way that media "set an agenda" by telling us what is important and what to think about (though not necessarily what to think about it). Our attention is directed toward certain areas and, by extension, away from others. This approach has been used in examining news and politics. For example, by virtue of their heavy coverage, the news media set an agenda and tell us that the quadrennial U.S. Presidential primary campaigns are very important. Certain types of news stories tend to be more heavily covered than others (Jamieson & Campbell, 1988). Agenda-setting will be discussed further in Chapters 7 and 8.

Cultivation theory (Gerbner, Gross, Morgan, & Signiorelli, 1986) looks at media, particularly television, as a socializing agent. Through extensive interaction with television, children's developing perceived social reality approximates more and more closely that which is presented on the screen. This approach has had wide usefulness across content areas but has been particularly studied in regard to violence in media (See Chapter 9).

The uses and gratifications approach (Blumler, 1979; Palmgreen, 1984; Rubin, 1983, 1986; Windahl, 1981) focuses on examining the reasons that people consume media and the benefits they receive from that consumption. Recently there has been a trend to more closely connect this research to an examination of the effects of media (Rubin, 1986). This is a particularly useful approach to use in studying new technologies in communications, such as VCR use (Box 1.4).

The Construct of Perceived Reality

The perceived reality from the media is actually a more complex concept than it may first appear (Hawkins, 1977; Potter, 1988). At least three components are involved (Potter, 1988). The central factor in perceived reality is what has come to be called *magic window*. This is the belief in the literal reality of media messages. This reality can either be conveyed at the level of style or content. The style of news reporting, for example, may convey a message of factual correctness more strongly than a style of an entertainment program (Altheide, 1976; Lippmann, 1922; Tuchman, 1978). The content of action-adventure shows presenting a world that is very dangerous may cultivate a view that the world is also like that (Gerbner et al., 1986).

A second component of perceived reality is sometimes called *utility* and refers to the perceived applicability of the media to one's own life. For example, a viewer with a strong belief that soap operas present very real-life situations would expect more application to their own life than another viewer who felt soap operas present wildly unrealistic and purely escapist content (Rubin & Perse, 1988).

The third component of perceived reality is *identity,* which refers to the degree to which a viewer feels that a character is active in the viewer's real life. Sometimes a media character becomes a significant person in the viewer's life; the involvement with that character is called *parasocial interaction* (Levy, 1982; Rubin & McHugh, 1987; Rubin, Perse, & Powell, 1985). See Potter (1988) for further discussion of the construct of perceived reality.

There are many ways that this perceived reality we infer from the media may be studied scientifically. Now let's turn to look at some specific research frameworks used in the scientific study of mass communication by social scientists.

MEDIA RESEARCH FRAMEWORKS

As well as being of great concern to the public, the media are also objects of considerable study among both commercial interests and scientific researchers. Much of that study is done by TV networks,

BOX 1.4. STUDYING THE VCR REVOLUTION

One of the major video revolutions of recent years has been the rapid growth of the VCR industry and the near-record-time penetration of this appliance into homes. Starting from their slow introduction into the U.S. market in 1975 (5 years later less than 1% of U.S. homes owned a VCR), growth took off in the early 1980s, until over half of U.S. homes owned one by 1987 (Rogers, 1988). Today many shows are routinely recorded for later viewing ("time-shifting"), with the most-recorded genre of TV shows being soap operas, which the VCR has now opened to viewing by those who work regular hours (Hickey, 1988).

Though bitterly opposed to videotaping at first, Hollywood studios have now joined forces to forge a very symbiotic and lucrative relationship between movies and VCRs. Cassette sales and rentals have helped bring additional income and interest to the movie industry, making 1984 and later 1987 as the biggest-grossing years ever for the major studios (Hickey, 1988). The widespread renting of movies on cassettes has raised some new ethical and legal issues. Although the U.S. film rating system (G, PG, PG-13, R, X) can have some force in theaters, it has very little in rental stores, where 13-year-olds generally have no trouble renting an R-rated movie. More recently, increasing numbers of films are being produced solely for cassette distribution, bypassing both theaters and the need to have a rating.

One segment of television still distressed by VCRs is advertising. The capability of time-shifting by taping TV shows and watching them later while zipping through the ads has encouraged a new creativity in the ad industry, in an attempt to produce ads that viewers will be reluctant to fast-forward by (Harvey & Rothe, 1986; Yorke & Kitchen, 1985). There are also increasing attempts to create ads whose highlights can be noticed while fast-forwarding.

Because of the relative newness of widespread VCR ownership and use, there has been relatively little empirical research on VCR use (see Levy, 1987, for a discussion of the issues). There have been a few preliminary studies of VCR use in the uses and gratifications tradition (Gunter & Levy, 1987; Levy, 1980; Williams, Phillips, & Lum, 1985).

publishers, corporations, or ad agencies for commercial purposes. For example, the Nielsen ratings or marketing research studying the public's taste in colas increases profits of a corporation. The other general type of scientific study is usually performed by independent scientists with a goal of explaining the effects of media and studying their role in society and in people's lives (Davis & Baran, 1981; Lazarsfeld, 1941). For example, studies of the effects of TV violence or analyses of the so-called sexist content of ads are generally done

with no commercial motivation. It is such noncommercial research
that is the primary focus in this book.

Looking for Effects

There are different perspectives that are used in studying media
(Lowery & DeFleur, 1983; McGuire, 1985; Roberts & Maccoby,
1985). Probably the most common general perspective is a search
for the *effects* of exposure to mass communication. The crudest form
of a theoretical effects model is the theory of uniform effects. This
model argues that individuals of a mass society perceive messages from media in the same fashion and react to them strongly
and very similarly. Media messages are thus "magic bullets" pierc-
ing the mind of the populace. Such a model has been used since
World War I to describe propaganda effects. Lasswell (1935)
suggested the "hypodermic" model of media; that is, viewers
were "injected" with some dubious message that brought out their
worst behavior and thoughts. The assumption that media pur-
veyors are evil thought controllers that manipulate a passive and
helpless population is largely seen today only in strident popular
media critics (e.g., Key, 1974, 1976, 1981; Mankiewicz & Swerdlow,
1978; Winn, 1977).

We still believe that media can have substantial effects, but often
they occur only under certain conditions and in less dramatic form
than imagined by the strongest critics. This is a theory of selective
influence based on individual differences. Different people perceive
the same message differently and respond to it in varied forms. For
example, a violent TV program probably will not incite all of the
viewers to go out and commit mayhem themselves, but it may reinforce the already existing violent tendencies of a small sample of the
viewers and slightly dull the sensitivities of many others. The fact that
the effects are not uniform is not to denigrate the importance of such
effects, however. Because of the huge size of the TV audience, even
an effect on .01% of the viewers may still impact on 4000 people out
of an audience of 40 million.

In considering the effects of media, we need to bear in mind that
these may vary as a function of how the consumer uses the media and
what gratifications he or she receives from that media use (Rubin,
1986). Effects of the media do not occur as a transmission from the
medium to the person, but rather through the person's experiencing
the medium. The experience of one person with a given TV show, for

example, may be very different from the experience of another, and for this reason the effect on the two persons might be substantially different.

Behavioral effects.   There are three general classes of effects that can be measured. Probably the type most people think of first are behavioral effects, where somebody *does* something after seeing someone else do it on TV; for example, acting violently, buying a product, voting in an election, or laughing at a comedy. This is the emphasis of social learning theory (Bandura, 1977; Tan, 1986). Although these are in some ways the most obvious type of effects, they are in fact often very difficult to measure and definitively attribute a causative role to the media. For example, we can know if somebody sees a certain commercial, and we can check to see if they buy that product, but knowing for sure that they bought the product *because* of seeing the ad and not for other unrelated reasons is very difficult to demonstrate. Even in a case like the deaths of young teenagers playing Russian roulette after watching *The Deer Hunter,* it is very difficult to *legally* and *scientifically* demonstrate a cause-and-effect relationship between seeing the movie and a subsequent tragic death.

Attitudinal effects.   A second general class of effects of media are attitudinal effects. For example, an ad might make you think more highly of some product or candidate; whether this attitude would be followed up in actual buying or voting behavior is another question. Although part of an attitude is the intellectual component (e.g., reasons that you favor one candidate's position over another's), much of the psychological dynamic in attitudes is emotional (e.g., liking one candidate more than another). Positive feelings about products or candidates may be taught through the process of classical conditioning, whereby a conditioned stimulus of a product is associated with an unconditioned stimulus that naturally elicits some positive response. For example, a beautiful model paired with some product may teach us positive attitudes toward that product. The precise processes by which this occurs are discussed in more detail in Chapter 4.

Media may teach us a whole constellation of attitudes on a given subject. For example, a dramatic TV movie or documentary on AIDS may sensitize people to the problem and make them more sympathetic to AIDS victims. Seeing soft-core porn where women appear to be sexually aroused by being raped or assaulted may lead viewers to believe that women derive some secret pleasure out of being victims of sexual violence (Donnerstein, Linz, & Penrod, 1987). Attitudes are easier to measure than behaviors and sometimes are of great importance, as they can influence behaviors that may follow.

Attitudes may have influence beyond one's opinion on a particular subject. Sets of attitudes may form a sort of mindset through which we view the world. These attitudes color our selection of what we perceive in the world and how we interpret it. The interaction of this knowledge gained from media with our experience in the world can lead to what is called *cultivation* (Gerbner, et al., 1986). For example, if we accept the cop-show reality of large cities being very dangerous places, that knowledge colors our attitudes about cities but also can affect cognitions and behaviors indirectly in ways that are difficult to measure experimentally, though methods have been developed to test such effects.

Cognitive effects. The third class of effects are cognitive, that is, changing what we *think.* The most straightforward example here would be learning new information from media, for example, facts about chimpanzees from a *National Geographic* special. There are other more subtle kinds of cognitive effects, however, and they overlap with attitudes. Simply by choosing what news stories to cover, for example, media set the agenda. By covering Presidential primary campaigns much more thoroughly than complex but abstract economic issues like the Third World debt crisis or the shift from domestic to export agriculture, media are telling us that the political minutiae of all those primaries is very important, while the other issues are less so.

Different media may stimulate different types of cognitive processing. In a fascinating series of studies comparing cognitive effects of radio versus television in telling stories, children produced more original endings for incomplete stories heard on the radio than they did for stories seen and heard on television. This offers some research support for the intuitive claim that radio stimulates the imagination more than TV. Children remembered verbal information from radio better but visual, action, and overall information better from television (Greenfield & Beagles-Roos, 1988; Greenfield, Farrar, & Beagles-Roos, 1986).

Physiological effects. The fourth class of effects are probably the least often measured but nonetheless are still important. These are the physiological changes in our bodies resulting from exposure to the media. For example, sexual arousal resulting from viewing pornography may be measured by heart rate, skin resistance, penile tumescence, or vaginal lubrication (e.g., Malamuth & Check, 1980a). Watching a scary movie or exciting ball game results in physical changes like rapid breathing and heart rate.

Looking at Content

There are other ways to study media besides looking for effects, however. One way is to study the content. For example, there are studies counting the number of characters of different racial, ethnic, or gender groups in TV shows. If we are going to argue, for example, that television ads or shows are sexist, we must carefully define what we mean by "sexist" and then study the ads or shows to see if they in fact are. Studies of the effects of sex or violence make use of content-analysis studies to provide data as to the prevalence of such themes and changing trends over time.

One research approach to examining content is the use of discourse analysis from linguistics, anthropology, and text analysis (van Dijk, 1985a,b). This careful investigation of the message communicated through media has often been neglected because of the traditionally stronger connection of mass communications research to social, rather than cognitive, psychology. A more cognitive emphasis in this book may help restore some balance here.

Looking at Exposure

A third general way to study media, other than looking at their content and effects, is to study the amount of exposure; see Webster and Wakshlag (1985) for a review of methods of measuring exposure. Who reads how many newspapers or watches how much TV and when? Demographic information about different groups of people watching different programs comes from this type of study. This type of information is useful, but purely measuring exposure is a gross measure. Just because the television is on in the same room is no assurance that one is devoting much attention to it or being affected by it. Often people are simultaneously doing something else while watching TV. Sometimes they leave the room altogether for some periods, especially during commercials. To understand the cognition of experiencing media, it is crucial to take seriously the amount and nature of attention devoted to the medium.

OVERVIEW OF THE BOOK

This chapter has introduced the theme of the way our cognitions create a perceived reality from media. The next chapter explores the *psychology* of mass communication in a general sense. The rest of the book is topically organized to explore the basic theme of media creating reality in several different content areas.

Chapter 3 explores the issue of group portrayals in the media. The emphasis here is on how media, especially television, portray various groups of people and what the effects of such presentations are. We will see that media's portrayal of groups may become a stereotyped reality in the minds of the public, especially in cases where the viewer has limited real-life contact with members of that particular group.

Two groups to be examined are men and women. Are they portrayed in stereotyped fashion? What are the effects of such portrayals on the socialization process of children? A second group to be examined are Blacks, whose portrayals throughout the history of television have been more carefully studied than any other group. The portrayals of Hispanics, Arabs, the elderly, and various occupational groups will also be examined. What are the effects of unrealistic or essentially nonexistent portrayals of such groups on the public's perception of these groups?

Chapter 4 examines the world as created and presented by advertising. We will view advertising as a type of information to be processed, one very important way that we learn about the world. Techniques of persuasion are examined, focusing on various types of psychological appeals, especially as they involve persuasion through the creation of a new reality that then becomes real for the consumer (e.g., a reality full of danger where one needs to buy locks and weapons, a reality where most people are very thin and suntanned, a reality of status-conscious people that one has to continually impress with one's dress and manner). The issue of subliminal advertising is also discussed, to see if it is possible to unconsciously persuade through subtle messages or embedded sexual implants.

Part of our media-created reality involves values. Chapter 5 looks at values communicated by television and other media, and examines how these values affect society. Some values at issue involve such areas as materialism, authority structures, conflict resolution, and sexual values. Television will be studied for changes in values over the last 40 years. Contrary to the popular belief that looser moral values and permissiveness are rampantly increasing, we shall see that, although some values are clearly becoming less strict (e.g., profanity, sexual explicitness), others are actually becoming more strict (e.g., racism, sexism, violence toward women). Many traditional values, such as family solidarity, patriotism, and abstinence from drugs, continue to be stressed.

Chapter 6 on sports and media examines how television not only transmits results and play-by-play of sports but also influences and changes the ways these sports are played. We will look at ways that rules and practices of sports have been changed by the demands of television coverage, and also at the effects of media coverage on the public interest and tastes in sports. Finally, the psychological fulfillment of viewing sports on television will be explored.

Chapter 7 examines how the media's coverage of news affects our understanding and attitudes about events in the world. This is perhaps the area where people are most likely to believe that media merely reflect and report the reality that is "out there." The argument is made that such is not the case, that in fact news reporting is by no means such a "reality transmission," but is necessarily a somewhat "distorted" interpretation of that reality. Simply by choosing what to cover and what not to cover, media are setting an agenda. This necessarily involves only a partial presentation of reality, but this partial reality becomes the basis of our knowledge about the world and even affects foreign policy.

Chapter 8 examines ways that a politician can manipulate media coverage to convey his or her intended reality. As practically all of our information about political candidates and officeholders comes through the media, the importance of mass communication in this area can hardly be overstated. Such issues as image-building and the necessity of an "electronic personality" will be discussed. A second topic in politics and media concerns the appeals and effects of political advertising. It is compared and contrasted to product advertising, covered in Chapter 4. Types of appeals in political advertising and its effects on attitudes and voting behavior are examined.

In Chapter 9 we look at media violence, perhaps the most emotional and heavily researched issue of the book. Different effects of televised and filmed violence are examined, including modelling, catharsis, reinforcement, desensitization, and cultivation of paranoia. In addition, we will explore different factors that may interact with media violence to enhance or lessen its impact. The question of the effect on children of viewing violence turns out to be more complex than is frequently admitted by partisans on both sides of this controversial issue.

Chapter 10 studies the character and effects of sexual content in media, focusing both on mainstream media and what is commonly called pornography. The creation and transmission of sexual values through media, as well as the socialization about sexuality are addressed. Recent research on and concern about effects of sexual violence will be considered, with the conclusion that viewing sexual violence may be far more damaging than viewing either sex or violence by itself.

Chapter 11 examines media that are specifically designed to teach skills or persuade people to change attitudes and/or behaviors in a more health- or safety-oriented direction. One section will discuss children's prosocial television (e.g., "Sesame Street," "Mister Rogers' Neighborhood"), while another will focus on the media's role in multistrategy campaigns to increase prosocial behaviors like stopping smoking, exercising more, or wearing seat belts. Public-service announcements (PSAs) and other such prosocial media face greater obstacles in many ways than does commercial advertising.

Finally, Chapter 12 ties together themes from the entire book and explores how a greater knowledge about media and its impact can help you gain more from television and other media without having your reality distorted in destructive ways. Some ways that we may influence the media and skills for becoming a more critical media user are discussed.

Psychology of
Mass Communication

I'll never forget the most moving film I ever saw. Though the lead character was experiencing life events completely different than anything I had experienced, his modes of responding to those events were very much like my own and touched me extremely deeply, so much so that my body felt limp and I could not even speak for some time afterwards. I felt as though the director had crawled inside my soul and made a movie about what he found; he knew more about my deepest feelings than I did. Not only did he know all about them, but he put them all up there on the screen for everyone to see!

Our relationship with the media is so profound precisely because it meets some of our deepest psychological needs and contributes naturally to our ongoing psychological development. In this chapter we will further explore this cognitive psychological perspective on how we experience the media. The way that we process the information in the media and the way that we process the media themselves will determine the nature of the reality we construct from that experience. Just how this reality is constructed and perceived will be examined in each topical chapter throughout the book, but this chapter will look at some basic issues cutting across the different topics. The two major areas examined are emotions and cognition, as applied to media.

In terms of both the level of public interest and the amount of social science research on media, there is far more study of television than of radio and print media. Many of the psychological issues discussed in this book apply equally well to all media, though most typically have been specifically studied in regard to television. To better understand this reality constructed from television, let us look more closely at who watches television and why.

TELEVISION USE

How Much Do We Watch?

Although experimental sets existed in the 1930s, television was practically unknown among the general public at the end of World War II in 1945. Five years later about 10% of American homes had a set. Ten years after that (1960) almost 90% had one! In the 1980s televisions were found in over 98% of American homes, with most of the remaining 2% abstaining due to choice rather than economics. In much of the world, the most decrepit hovels often sprawl beneath a maze of TV antennas. Although most of the programming over the years has been by networks or local stations, the rapid growth of cable and satellite technology in the 1980s has greatly expanded the offerings. How networks and their affiliates deal with this challenge may dramatically alter the face of television in the 1990s.

The major reason for the bulk of mass communications research being about television is that we spend so much time watching television. A TV set is on in U.S. households over 7 hours a day (over 8 hours for homes with cable and subscription services), with the typical adult or child watching 2 to 3 hours per day, more time than they spend on any other activity except working and sleeping. The average child sees 20,000 advertisements per year, 360,000 by age 18. He or she also sees 9000 scenes of suggested sexual intercourse or innuendo on prime-time TV each year and has witnessed 11,000 televised murders by age 14, still years away from being old enough to drive, vote, or drink beer. Frequently an infant's first coherent sentence will be an advertising jingle learned from television.

Group differences. The amount of television viewing changes somewhat as we grow older. It rises sharply between ages 2 and 4, from about 15 minutes to 2.5 hours. It then levels off until about age 8, rising again to a peak of around 4 hours a day by age 12. It then starts to fall, especially during the high school and college years and young adulthood. There is another rise, however, in older adult years after one's children are grown. In fact, the elderly are some of the heaviest viewers of television. Other relatively heavy viewing groups are women, Blacks, and lower socioeconomic classes. It is interesting that many of the groups that watch the most television are the same groups that are the most underrepresented on TV programs, where characters are disproportionately middle-class, white, male, professional, and affluent. We will return to this issue in the next chapter.

Time-of-day differences. Television also changes sharply throughout the day. Typically the largest audience in the United States is in the "prime-time" hours of 8 to 11 P.M. Eastern and Pacific time (7 to 10 P.M. Central and Mountain). These are the hours of highest advertising costs and greatest investment in programming efforts. The most obvious pinnacle of such efforts may be seen in the prime-time "sweeps" weeks in February, May, and November, where Nielsen audience size is used to calculate advertising charges for the next several months. These are the weeks when the networks outdo themselves presenting blockbuster miniseries, specials, and landmark episodes of top-rated series.

What Else Is Going On?

Merely measuring when the television is on is not really enough to tell us how much is being understood or what influence it is having. A big question in the study of television is how much attention viewers are paying to the tube at any given time it is on. Clearly the TV is often on when it is receiving less than total undivided attention. Research studying videotapes of people watching television show that the typical older child or adult attends to the TV about 70% of the time it is on (Anderson, 1985), depending on the time of day and the program. For example, early morning news shows receive less attention and weekend shows such as sports and children's cartoons receive more attention. Sometimes we may not be looking at the screen very much but may nonetheless be monitoring the sound for items of interest and can redirect our vision toward the screen if necessary.

The nature of mass communication, especially broadcast, is such that we typically must select some information to attend to and process and neglect other information (Zillmann & Bryant, 1983, 1985). Although there are many ways, some very sophisticated, of measuring exposure to media (Webster & Wakshlag, 1985), attention must also be paid to what is being cognitively processed from those media. It is simplistic to assume either that viewers are fully processing everything that they hear on radio or TV or that it is not affecting them at all if they are not paying full conscious attention. Serious attention to cognitive processes is particularly crucial in interpreting television exposure data.

Why Do We Watch?

People watch television for many reasons. The uses and gratifications research perspective (Blumler, 1979; Blumler & Katz, 1974; Palmgreen, 1984; Rubin, 1986) has focused on studying such reasons. Although the motivations to be entertained and to be informed are perhaps the most obvious reasons, they are not the only ones. The television is often turned on more for company than for any other reason. With radio, this is an even more common reason than for television. A person is home alone and wants somebody to listen to, even if not to talk to. We think of Bryant Gumbel and Jane Pauley more as our breakfast companions than as news spokespersons. Dan Rather is a regular dinner guest, not merely someone who reads the news. It is not unusual for people to respond audibly to a greeting from the tube, as in responding "Hi, Tom" to news anchor Tom Brokaw's greeting to start the evening news. Such parasocial interaction is a significant aspect of our relation with television. See McGuire (1974) and Rubin (1981, 1984) for discussion of psychological motives in uses and gratifications research.

We may watch television for many other reasons as well. Perhaps it is to avoid studying or some other activity. Perhaps it is to escape into a fantasy world or get turned on by a particular sexy star. Maybe it is to find out what "everybody's talking about" on some popular show. Maybe it is to conform to others who are watching. Sometimes we will watch a program we strongly dislike simply to have some conversation and make us feel less alone. For most solo drivers, the radio is their constant traveling companion. Fenigstein and Heyduk (1983) argue that most of the research about television has focused primarily on the effects of TV and much less on the attraction of TV. What draws different people to consume different types of media may be a critical issue, for example, factors that cause some people to watch violent pornography.

The relationship of media use to mood and personality variables also bears on the issue of reasons for media use. For example, does heavy TV viewing cause one to be escapist, or do factors of temperament and personality cause one to seek escape through heavy TV viewing? Kubey (1986) investigated this issue and concluded that heavy TV viewing is more likely an effect rather than a cause of mood and personality factors. We have uncomfortable and unpleasant feelings and seek an escape from these through television.

One of the most basic experiences that we have in regard to media use is emotion. Part of being entertained is becoming emotionally involved with the content and the characters of a story or TV show. Let's turn now to looking at emotions as applied to media.

THE EMOTIONS OF MEDIA USE

What is Emotion?

We can't observe emotions directly; we don't see anger or hear happiness. We see violent behavior and infer anger; we hear laughter and infer happiness. Emotions themselves are internal states and must be inferred from behavior. Sometimes such inferences are unwarranted. We may see someone crying over a TV movie and infer that they feel sad, when in fact they might be crying for joy, or for that matter, they might have an allergic condition with the crying not reflecting emotion at all.

Emotions are an integral part of the appreciation of media, especially television, most notably sports, action-adventure shows, soap operas, game shows, and comedies. What we feel while watching these shows is a central part of the whole psychological experience. If we don't feel the usual way on some occasion, we seem to be missing an important part of the experience.

There are two components of emotion—the physiological and the cognitive. When we are aroused, there are certain changes in our bodies, such as increased heart rate, sweating, and change in skin resistance (GSR). We also *think* about our feelings and attribute causes and interpretations to them. For example, if we feel very "hyped up" just after being offered a new job, we would interpret the same state of bodily arousal differently than we would if we had just consumed ten cups of coffee or just escaped from the clutches of a crazed killer. Thus the emotions we feel are a product of both our bodily state and our cognitive interpretation of that state (Schachter & Singer, 1962; Zillmann, 1983).

Media as Vicarious Emotional Experience

Watching a crime show on TV allows us to experience some of the emotion felt by the characters without putting ourselves in any physical danger. Thus we can become aroused safely through this vicarious experience. This allows us to focus on the excitement of a police show or the humor of a sitcom. If we actually experienced those situations in real life, the danger or embarrassment might overpower the positive aspects and they wouldn't be nearly as much fun as they are on TV (Tannenbaum, 1980).

Other types of emotions are enjoyable to experience vicariously. Many comedies show people in embarrassing situations that are more humorous when happening to someone else. TV characters may do things we would like to do but have moral or ethical proscriptions against. We can, however, with a clear conscience, watch them have extramarital affairs, verbally insult others, or drive recklessly. One type of programming where participants are particularly encouraged to be highly expressive emotionally is the game show; see Box 2.1 for some examples of game shows around the world that allow vicarious expression of emotions.

Suspending disbelief.   Like movies or theater, television involves the social convention of the *suspension of disbelief* (Esslin, 1982). We know that Bill Cosby and Phylicia Rashad are not really married to each other, but we agree to suspend our disbelief of that and accept them as husband and wife for a half hour every Thursday night. Because of the continuing nature of television series (often several years for a successful show), this suspension of belief is a far more enduring fantasy than it is for a 2-hour movie or play. Producers in the early days of television may have doubted the ability of the public to suspend that much disbelief. Many of the early series featured real-life spouses playing TV partners (Lucille Ball and Desi Arnaz, George Burns and Gracie Allen, Ozzie and Harriet Nelson). This phenomenon has been rare since the 1950s, however.

Sometimes disbelief has been suspended so long that the fantasy–reality distinction is blurred. Young children clearly have difficulty understanding the difference between actors and characters they portray (Dorr, 1980). This problem is not limited to children, however. As any series actor can tell you, adult fans frequently ask an actor playing a doctor for medical advice or hurl epithets at an actress playing a villainess on a soap opera. Such fantasies are covertly encouraged by spinoff series, where the same character moves from one series to another (e.g., George and Louise Jefferson originally were supporting characters on "All in the Family.") Children's cartoon characters like the Smurfs may reappear in commercials, toys, and special meals at restaurants, all of which contributes to a belief in their reality outside the show.

Sometimes a piece on television may provide such a salient exemplar of an unpleasant reality that it is difficult to maintain reality in suspension. The strong emotions engendered may then have a variety of behavioral effects. Box 2.2 explores the feared and actual effects of a much-hyped TV movie on nuclear war.

Identification. The emotional involvement that we have watching a TV show will depend in part on how much we *identify* with the character. It is easier to identify with characters with whom we have more in common. This is not a prerequisite for identification, however. There is a certain universality in most good drama. For example, a huge number of Americans, few of whom had ever been in slavery and most of whom were White, watched the landmark miniseries "Roots" in the late 1970s. Apparently the basic humanity of the characters was portrayed so well that viewers could identify emo-

One of the most hyped television events of all time was the ABC TV movie "The Day After," the drama of the aftermath of a nuclear attack on the American Midwest aired on November 20, 1983. Its anticipation became such a media event in itself that competing CBS' *60 Minutes* took the unprecedented step of covering "The Day After" hype as one of its feature stories one hour before the movie's airing. It also became a political event. Antinuclear groups encouraged people to watch it, while conservatives decried it as an unfair move in the battle to mold public opinion on arms control issues. Mental health professionals worried over its impact on impressionable young minds and warned people to watch it only in groups and to not allow young children to see it at all. All of the heavy media coverage of course insured a large audience, which numbered over 100 million viewers, the largest to date for a TV movie.

Psychologists Janet Scholfield and Mark Pavelchak (1985) decided to study exactly what impact this controversial film's airing had actually had. Contrary to some fears or hopes, the movie actually did little to change attitudes about arms control and related issues. Arguments such as the possible failure of a deterrence through strength policy had been widely discussed in the media and were not really new ideas to most viewers. Many viewers reacted that, horrible as it was, TDA's portrayal of the effects of a nuclear attack was actually milder than hype-weary viewers expected and in fact was somewhat akin to many disaster and horror movies.

The movie did have its effects, however. Viewers were more likely to seek information about nuclear issues and become involved in disarmament activities, and they reported thinking about nuclear war twice as often after seeing the film as they had before.

tionally with the characters at some level without having experienced similar situations themselves. The perceived reality of media is greater if our identification with the characters is such that they become significant persons in our own lives (Potter, 1988).

Empathy.   When we feel what the characters feel, we experience empathy. Empathy may be seen as emotional identification, and it is a very important factor in the enjoyment of media. We enjoy a comedy more if we can feel something of what the characters feel. We enjoy a ball game more if we have played it ourselves and can relate to the tense feelings of being at bat with two outs in the bottom of the ninth and our team down by one run. Our empathy is diminished somewhat by the relatively omniscient position we occupy relative to the characters. We generally know more of what is going on that they do. If we know the final outcome, it is often difficult to become as emotionally involved as if we were in the dark as much as the character. Such enjoyment varies a lot depending on the genre, however. Audiences for reruns of nighttime soaps like "Dallas" or "Dynasty" are traditionally far lower than the original broadcast, while audiences for reruns of comedies and some dramas hold up quite well. Apparently the loyalty to the characters and show and the empathy and degree of parasocial interaction with them are crucial factors (Tannenbaum, 1980).

Empathy may be divided into cognitive and emotional components. Cognitive empathy involves the ability to readily take the perspective of another, while emotional empathy involves readily responding at a purely affective level. Davis, Hull, Young, and Warren (1987) showed that the level of both of these types of empathy influenced emotional reactions to viewing the films *Brian's Song* and *Who's Afraid of Virginia Woolf?*, but that each type of empathy influenced reactions in different ways.

Suspense. The suspense we feel in an adventure or drama is maximal if some negative outcome (hero is about to die) appears to be *highly likely but not absolutely certain*. Everything points to disaster with just a slight hope of escape. If the negative outcome is either not very likely or is absolutely certain, there is not much suspense (Zillmann, 1980). We feel the most suspense if our hero appears to be about to be blown up by a bomb, with just a slight chance to escape. The emotional and physiological excitation of suspense is relatively slow to decay and may be transferred to subsequent activities (Zillmann, 1971, 1978, 1980, 1984).

Emotional Expression and Media

North American and Northern European societies often discourage direct expression of emotions. Television, however, sets some new rules with greater flexibility. It is more acceptable to yell and shake your fist at a referee in a ball game on TV than to do the same at your boss. Although sports is one of the few arenas where adult men may show physical affection toward other men without intimations of homosexuality, some of the same license is transferred to viewing sports on television. Thus two men may playfully slap each other or even embrace after watching a spectacular play in a televised ball game.

The social situation of watching TV also makes a difference in our cognitions and experience. Watching a ball game or scary movie might be very different by yourself versus at a party with friends. There might be more expression of emotion in the group. The scary movie might be scarier alone and funnier with the group. Even though the stimulus of the TV show is the same in both cases, the *experience* of it, especially in terms of emotion, may be quite different. The social experience of teenagers' going to a horror film together is often very different than one might predict purely from considering the content of the film (Zillmann, Weaver, Mundorf, & Aust, 1986).

Children may learn from TV how to deal with emotions they feel in various situations. Young children learning to play tennis may curse and throw their racquets in imitation of John McEnroe, whose antics on the court are carried on TV as a model for dealing with frustration in sports. In an even more serious case, if TV regularly portrays men who feel frustrated with women as expressing such feelings through violence (battering or rape), children may learn that these antisocial ways of dealing with those feelings are acceptable.

In a more productive vein, media may teach us how to deal positively with emotions in difficult situations. A child who has been a victim of incest may learn from a well-made TV movie on that subject something about how to deal with feelings about that experience, as well as concrete steps which may be taken to handle the situation.

Humor in Media

One particular type of emotion that we can feel while consuming media is the good feeling that comes from enjoying something funny (Brown & Bryant, 1983). But what makes something funny? Why is one line of comedy so hilarious and a very similar one not at all funny, and perhaps even offensive?

Most comedy involves some sort of incongruity, inconsistency, or contradiction, which is finally resolved, as in the punch line of a joke (Long & Graesser, 1988; McGhee, 1979). Neither the incongruity or resolution by itself is usually very funny. Consider the following:

1. Two elephants got off the bus and left their luggage by the tree.
2. Two soldiers got off the bus and left their trunks by the tree.
3. Two elephants got off the bus and left their trunks by the tree.

Although statement 1 is incongruous, it is not particularly funny because there is no resolution. Statement 2 has a resolution, but it is not very funny either because there is no incongruity. Only statement 3 has both.

The best jokes offer some intellectual challenge but not so much that we cannot "get it" or have to work too hard to do so. Some of the most satisfying jokes are very esoteric "in-jokes" involving knowledge from our particular group, such as a profession. What is an adequate challenge for one person may not be so for another. For example, many children find certain very predictable, even "dumb," jokes funny, while adults do not. They are simply not novel enough or challenging enough for adults.

Another important concept in understanding media humor is the notion of *catharsis*, the emotional release of tension we feel from expressing some repressed feelings. For example, if you are very worried about some problem but talk to a friend and feel better just for having "gotten it off your chest," what you are experiencing is catharsis. Humor is often seen as a healthy and socially acceptable outlet for dealing with some of our darker feelings. For example, we may be able to deal with some of our own hidden sexual or hostile impulses by listening to a caustic comedian or talk-show host insult people or brazenly ask someone about their first sexual experience. We wouldn't say those things ourselves but might secretly want to; hearing someone else do it partially fulfulls our need to do so. Catharsis is often invoked to explain why people appreciate racist, ethnic, or sexual jokes. It is also frequently put forth as a socially beneficial function of sexual or violent media, though research has failed to confirm such a conclusion (see Chapters 9 and 10).

Social factors can make difference of how funny something on television is. Sometimes the presence of others watching with us enhances our enjoyment, particularly for broader, more raucous humor. Consider watching a film like *Animal House* or *The Rocky Horror Picture Show* on the late show by yourself or in a group. The presence of others may genuinely enhance our enjoyment, or we may outwardly appear to enjoy it more due to peer pressure to conform; if we are in a room full of people laughing uproariously at some TV show, it is hard to avoid at least a few smiles, even if we are not at all amused. It may also be important who is telling the joke. A joke making fun of Hispanics may be much funnier and more acceptable if told by a Chicano than if told by an Anglo or a Black.

There are individual and cultural differences in appreciation of humor. Some people prefer puns, other prefer physical humor or practical jokes, still others prefer sexual or ethnic jokes. Cultural standards change over time. In the very early days of television (early

1950s), *Amos 'n' Andy* could make fun of Blacks being slow-witted; a few years later Ralph Kramden could threaten his wife with physical violence on *The Honeymooners* and everyone roared with laughter. Now we have the chance to laugh at more sexual innuendo on TV than we could then, but Andy and Ralph somehow don't seem quite so funny.

Different cultures find different themes and approaches funny. In North American society, for example, certain topics are off-limits or very touchy, at least for prime-time humor (late night TV is a little more permissive). Jokes on U.S. TV about racism, feminism, or religion are risky; such humor does exist but people are likely to take offense and thus producers and comedians are very cautious. A popular Brazilian TV commercial for a department store chain during a recent Christmas season showed the three wise men walking in Bethlehem. Suddenly, to a rock beat, they threw open their ornate robes and started dancing in their pastel underwear for sale at the store. It seems unlikely that such an ad would be aired in the United States.

One function of television humor is as a sort of leavening in the context of a more serious offering. A little so-called "comic relief" in the midst of a serious drama is much appreciated, though if done badly, it runs the risk of being in poor taste and thus offending people. If done well, it can increase motivation and interest and make the characters seem more human. If done too well, it may distract from the major content. This is particularly a concern with commercials. Some of the funniest and more creatively successful TV commercials have not been too effective at selling because the humor overshadows the commercial message. People remember the gag but forget the product.

Sometimes we hear the concern voiced that there is too much humor in shows dealing with violence and the result is to trivialize the violence and suggest it is less serious than it really is. This criticism is especially made of the "light-hearted" detective shows like "Moonlighting." These shows often have some gruesome (though seldom grisly or very explicit) violence, yet the overall tone is almost comedic, often with a lot of "romance" and "chemistry" between the opposite-sex sleuths. Whether this violence embedded in a happy context can desensitize us to its darker effects will be further explored in Chapter 9.

Now let's turn to the issue of learning from the media by focusing on cognitive processes of constructing interpretations of what we experience in the media.

THE CONSTRUCTIVE NATURE OF MEDIA COGNITION

An important general cognitive principle is that information processing is constructive; that is, people do not literally store and retrieve
information they read or hear in the media (or anywhere else).
Rather, they modify it in accordance with their beliefs and the context
in which it is received. The way we comprehend a program we watch
on TV is through a constant interaction of the stimulus of the program and the knowledge already in our minds.

The Schema

What guides the comprehension and any later memory of the information are *schemas* (Brewer & Nakamura, 1984; Rumelhart, 1980;
Thorndyke, 1984). The concept of schema refers to knowledge structures or frameworks that organize an individual's memory of information about people and events. The schema is a general construct
that acts on all forms of information, irrespective of the mode—visual
or auditory, linguistic or nonlinguistic—to which it is exposed. A
person holds mental schemas based on past experiences. One consequence of this for information processing is that the individual is
likely to go beyond the information actually presented to draw inferences about people or events that are congruent with previously
formed schemas (Harris, 1981; Singer, 1984). For example, someone
with a very negative schema about Hispanic Americans might respond very differently to a new TV show set in Chicano East Los
Angeles. Schemas are typically culturally specific. The schema that
members of one culture may hold may cause them to interpret the
same story very differently than members of a different culture
(Harris, Schoen, & Hensley, in press). Cultural differences must be
carefully considered by TV producers in international programming
sales (See Box 2.3).

Learning from Media: Scripts

One of the many types of information that we learn from media is
how to do things. Borrowing a concept from computer science and
experimental psychology (Bower, Black, & Turner, 1979; Schank &
Abelson, 1977), we may speak of learning *scripts* from television
(Janis, 1980). *Script* here refers to a schema about an activity and is *not*
the same as the usual meaning of pages of dialogue. For example,

---

BOX 2.3 AMERICAN TELEVISION IMPERIALISM: FACT OR FICTION?

The rapid diffusion of American movies and television throughout the world in the last few decades has been well documented (Lee, 1980; Read, 1976; Tunstall, 1977). Although the United States is the world's largest exporter of television programming ($1 billion a year) (Mele, 1987), whether those media completely dominate local sources is considerably more questionable. Recent studies (Cantor & Cantor, 1986; Schement, Gonzalez, Lum, & Valencia, 1984) suggest that no country is able to dominate media today, if indeed they ever were.

The United States is a market as well as a producer. Cities with large Hispanic populations receive channels from the Spanish International Network (SIN), which is a satellite export from Mexico. Mexico's Televisa earned $4 million in 1986 exporting its soap operas, 70% of the sales going to the United States (Michaels, 1988). British television, notably the BBC and Granada TV, have exported programs to PBS for years.

Some countries, like Japan and Brazil, formerly imported much more American TV than they do today, when most of their programming is locally produced. Indeed some foreign producers are major exporters. Brazil's TV Globo, for example, earned $12 million in profits in 1987 selling its popular soap operas (novelas) throughout Latin America and Europe, in spite of the fact they are produced in Portuguese, which is spoken few other places (Michaels, 1988). Sometimes the television empires fall along linguistic lines. For example, Francophone Africa and French Canada generally buy television from France. American and other non-French sources typically must go through Paris to dub their programs in French before selling to French-speaking markets.

---

when we watch a TV movie about a woman who discovers she has breast cancer, we may acquire a script for dealing with that particular situation. The viewer may learn specific activities like breast self-examination, how to tell her husband about her illness, how to seek out information about possible treatments, and how to cope with a mastectomy in terms of her own self-image and sexuality.

Scripts are acquired from the media, among other sources. Through exposure to samples of activities following some script, that abstract script is inferred and gradually becomes a part of our permanent memory. This skeleton structure of some activity is then used to interpret future instances of that activity.

The importance of learning scripts from media becomes especially clear when we consider a situation for which readers have little prior knowledge or scripts. For example, suppose a child's knowledge of dealing with muggers has resulted from watching TV adventure heroes trick and overpower the robber. If that child were to try that script on a real mugger by attempting the same moves as seen on TV, the result might be considerably less happy than the same action done by MacGyver. For another example, consider a TV movie dealing with incest. A preteen in the story is being sexually molested by her father and is sufficiently troubled to mention this to a school counselor, a revelation which sets in motion a sequence of events that eventually but necessarily brings this event "out of the closet." Because this subject has been so taboo until quite recently, most viewers, including those who are currently or were formerly victims of incest, may have no mental script for how to handle it. In this sense such a movie, if done sensitively yet realistically, could help such people come forth and seek help. It could provide information on how one may expect to feel about that experience, where to seek help and, through the context of the drama, could offer a scenario of what the effects of such a revelation might be.

In a more general sense, media fiction may use very abstract scripts such as "overcoming adversity." This implicit knowledge may be reflected in a story about a slave escaping from servitude in the antebellum South, a child learning to cope with alcoholic parents, or a burned-out police officer coming to terms with a vicious crime syndicate (Janis, 1980).

The Narrative Script

There is also a very general script for stories in Western culture (Kintsch, 1977). This "narrative script" is learned implicitly from the earliest days of a young child hearing stories from parents. This narrative script says that stories are composed of episodes, each of which contains an Exposition, Complication, and Resolution. That is, the characters and setting are introduced (Exposition), some problem or obstacle develops (Complication), and that problem or obstacle is somehow overcome (Resolution). We grow up expecting stories to follow this general script. The children's stories (e.g., fairy tales) that we hear tend to do so very explicitly ("Once upon a time there was a. . . ."). More adult stories also follow the script but often in a more complex fashion, for example, some of the complication is introduced before all of the exposition is finished or there are two sub-episodes embedded in the resolution of a larger episode.

Television and print media fiction also draw on the narrative script to make their stories more readily understandable. Children's cartoons follow the script most explicitly. Most TV sitcoms and action–adventure shows do so as well, although perhaps in a bit more complicated fashion, for example, two interwoven episodes (subplots), each with its own narrative structure. Soap operas traditionally hold an audience by breaking for the day just before the resolution. Because we have this sense of our narrative script being incomplete, we return the next day or the next week to complete it. This was used in some of the most spectacularly successful marketing techniques in the history of prime-time TV. The producers of "Dallas" left viewers hanging a whole season to find out "Who shot J.R.?" in the early 1980s. In 1985 the entire cast of "Dynasty" was apparently wiped out by a terrorist attack on a wedding on the last show of the season. Such prime-time soaps, as well as shows like "Hill Street Blues" or "L.A. Law" regularly leave critical complications unresolved at the end of the week's show.

Even many ads draw upon the narrative script. For example, a nice young fellow is ready to go out on a date (exposition), but alas, he has "ring around the collar" (complication). But his mom and her amazing detergent come to the rescue to wash the shirt in time (resolution). Because of our familiarity with the narrative script, we are able to comprehend such a commercial readily, which is all to the advertiser's advantage. Also, because it fits the story structure of many programs, it seems more entertaining and is thus more likely than a traditional sales pitch to hold viewers' attention. The narrative script is a deeply ingrained knowledge structure; Esslin (1982) goes so far as to argue that the 30-second story of an unhappy hemorrhoid sufferer has the same dramatic structure as classic Greek tragedy (i.e., the narrative script)!

CONCLUSION

The meaning that something in the media has for us, at either a cognitive or an emotional level, depends on how that information is processed during our experience of interacting with the medium. There is much more that can be said on the psychology of experiencing the media. However, we will discuss further psychological issues in the context of looking at the particular topics of the rest of the book. The media create a reality for us in many different areas, drawing on different psychological processes as they do so. Now let us turn to the first set of those perceived realities created by media, namely, our knowledge of what different groups of people are like.

Group Portrayals

Growing up in urban Appalachia, my knowledge of farmers and agriculture was limited to the poor mountain farmers we saw from the car
window when traveling and to the media rural folk on "The Beverly
Hillbillies" and "Green Acres." When I moved to the Midwest U.S. as an
adult, I finally set foot on a farm for the first time in my life at age 28. It was
amazing to meet a farmer who had a master's degree and was intelligent!
Then I realized; my reality of farms and agriculture had been the media
country hick stereotype.
While writing this book, I had occasion to sit in a courtroom at a child
custody hearing of a friend. My overwhelming reaction after walking in
was "Oh, this looks different than Perry Mason." Then I realized, at age 41,
that I had never been in a real courtroom before; all of my knowledge of
them had come from television.

One of the major perceived realities that media help create for us
involves information about groups of people. Through TV and other
media we are exposed to a much broader range of people than most
of us would ever encounter in our own lives. Not only are media our
introduction to these people, but often they are practically the only
source of our information about them. Sometimes *everything* we know
about some kinds of people comes from television. Many rural white
Americans have never seen any Blacks or Jews in person. Many urban
Americans have never met a real farmer. Most people of the world
have never met someone from the United States. In such cases the TV
portrayal of blacks or farmers or Americans *is* reality for them. Even
in a study done many years ago, children reported that most of their
information about people from different nationalities came from
their parents and television, with TV becoming increasingly important as the child grew older (Lambert & Klineberg, 1967).

In this chapter we will examine primarily the U.S. media image of a variety of groups of people and look at the consequences of such portrayals. The concerns in some of the areas are widely known and discussed (e.g., women, Blacks), and, in the case of some minorities, have been widely examined in research (e.g., Graves, 1980; Greenberg, 1986; Greenberg & Atkin, 1982). Similar concerns about portrayals of other groups have received relatively little attention (e.g., farmers, Arabs, police officers). Although the issue is relevant to all media, television is the primary medium of concern, both in programming and commercials.

Now let's turn to look at just how media portray various groups of people. The focus here will be on television of the United States, though the same principles, if not all the same specifics, hold true for any nation's broadcasting. Before looking at minorities, let us focus on gender portrayals. What do TV and other media say about what it means to be a man or woman?

PORTRAYALS OF THE SEXES

The View of Women

We have heard a lot in recent years about stereotyping of women by the media (e.g., Baehr & Dyer, 1987), but what, exactly, are the concerns about the way women are portrayed? Some of these concerns are very familiar, whereas others are more subtle but just as serious. For a review of content analysis studies of the image of women in advertising, see Courtney and Whipple (1983).

Perhaps the most basic disparity is that there are too few women. Content analyses of characters on television shows in the 1970s and early 1980s have shown about three times as many men as women in prime-time dramas and four times as many in Saturday morning children's shows (Greenberg, 1980; Kimball, 1986). This situation may be due to the far greater numbers of men than women among writers and producers or to a belief that women find the opposite sex more interesting to watch than men do.

There is some evidence that a better balance is emerging. Until such mid-1980s shows as "Cagney and Lacey," "The Golden Girls," "Designing Women," and "Kate and Allie," shows with all-women leads were largely nonexistent in United States, with very infrequent exceptions like the popular "Charlie's Angels" of the 1970s. Virtually all-male shows have never been unusual, however (e.g., "Barney Miller," "My Three Sons," "Simon and Simon"), and most shows had predominantly male casts. The commercial success of several all-female shows has probably insured the existence of at least some such programming for the foreseeable future.

Still, all is not equal. Although actresses are almost as common as actors in commercials, the voiceover announcer, a sort of authority voice, is still a male 83% of the time (Ferrante, Haynes, & Kingsley, 1988), virtually unchanged from the early 1970s (Dominick & Rauch, 1972). One of the newest forms of media, the music video, shows at least twice as many males as females (Brown & Campbell, 1986; Sherman & Dominick, 1986). On radio, disc jockeys, newspersons, and band singers all are still overwhelmingly male, although increasing numbers of female voices are being heard. A minority of news anchors and weathercasters are now female, though almost no sportscasters are.

Another concern is that women are too often portrayed as youthful beauties whose duty it is to stay young and attractive to please their men. Once a woman is no longer so young and attractive, she becomes an object of ridicule. Support for this criticism comes especially from all the subtle messages that a women must not allow herself to age, a message transmitted especially, though not exclusively, by advertising. Wrinkles, gray hair, or a "mature" figure are to be avoided at all costs. At least until recently, women obviously over 30, and especially those over 50, have been grossly underrepresented on television and, when they were present, were often seen as stereotyped "old folks" that no one would want to grow up and be like (Davis & Davis, 1985). Women in TV ads were disproportionately younger than men (70% versus 40% under 35, respectively), in ratios unchanged from the early 1970s (Dominick & Rauch, 1972; Ferrante, et al., 1988).

Media women are disproportionately seen as homemakers and mothers, with their business, professional, and community roles minimized or nonexistent. This is especially true of advertising (Culley & Bennett, 1976; Knill, Pesch, Pursey, Gilpin, & Perloff, 1981; Schneider & Schneider, 1979), though there is some evidence that the range of occupational roles for women in ads is increasing (Ferrante, Haynes, & Kingsley, 1988). In the early days of television, women almost invariably worked at home; today this is much changed.

A fairly recent concern is directed specifically at a relatively new media portrayal that has arisen to represent modern women more accurately and fairly. Most TV series women characters are employed full-time (64% in the new shows of the 1986-87 season), 61% of those in professional or managerial positions, compared to only 23% in such positions in real life (Kalter, Jan. 30, 1988). Many, most notably sitcom moms, are also mothers. Although characters like Clair Huxtable ("The Cosby Show"), Maggie Seaver ("Growing Pains"), and Elyse Keaton ("Family Ties") are positive role models of professional women as lawyer, journalist, and architect, they seem to handle the demands of career, wife, and parent with amazingly little stress and difficulty. Real women in two-career families need such positive role models, but they also need some acknowledgment from TV that the great difficulties they experience balancing all those responsibilities are not abnormal. Clair Huxtable and her sitcom counterparts ("supermoms") make it all too easy. Viewers for whom that life is not so easy may feel inadequate (Maynard, 1987; Murphy, 1986), though this relatively recent issue deserves more careful study.

The superwoman myth is also reinforced by some advertising. For example, one perfume ad says that a women can "bring home the bacon, fry it up in a pan, but never never let him forget he's a man." In other words, a woman can (or at least should) work outside the home all day, come home and cook dinner for her husband, and still have enough energy left to be sexy for him that evening! Are these realistic messages to send to young girls about what it means to be a woman in today's society?

Another concern is that women are seen as dependent on men and needing their protection. Even relatively egalitarian TV families like the Huxtables or the Keatons generally show the wife deferring to the husband more often than the reverse, although the behaviors showing this are much more subtle than those of 10 or 20 years ago. Women are not seen making important decisions or engaged in important activities as much as men. Advertising often portrays women as terribly perplexed and even neurotic about such matters as dirty laundry or yellow floors. Women squeezing toilet paper or berating others about soiled clothing also make this point. Old sitcoms showing women playing bridge or gossiping with neighbors all day also illustrate this concern. Newspaper cartoons, particularly strips like "Blondie" or "The Girls," also frequently show women primarily preoccupied with trivial concerns. Some of the most heavily sex-typed TV shows are children's cartoons, which are very heavy on the male characters, with few females, often one rather frilly and wimpy female character like Smurfette who mainly seems to nurture and support her male colleagues (Canzoneri, 1984).

Sometimes the power that women do exercise is used in very underhanded and conniving ways, often directly or indirectly involving sexuality. The night-time soap businesswoman who sleeps her way to the top is a good example. There are subtle messages that it is not ladylike to confront men (or even other women) directly, but it is perfectly acceptable to deviously trick them. Portraying sexuality as a weapon of power subtly de-emphasizes and even degrades its tender and relational aspects. A woman like Alexis in "Dynasty" may at first appear to be a very strong and nontraditional role model because she is a powerful executive. However, a closer examination of where her power seems to come from and how it is used suggests a very different situation from that seen in her male counterparts on the tube (Fiske, 1987). Female uses of power are not confined to adult media; the cartoon Peanuts' Lucy dominates the boys through intimidation (Canzoneri, 1984).

A final concern is that women are subtly linked with violence, especially as victims of male violence. Some commercials or programs playing on the seductiveness of women also suggest she is an animal to be tamed, something wild to be brought into line by a man. A high fashion ad selling negligees by showing a scantily-clad woman being playfully attacked by two men, or an auto magazine ad showing a woman in a bikini chained inside a giant shock absorber subtly link sexuality and violence.

Although we may not find Ralph Kramden of "The Honeymooners" threatening his wife with violence ("One of these days, Alice, pow! Right in the kisser!") as amusing in syndicated reruns as we did in 1955, more graphic instances of violence toward women are common, especially in the so-called "slasher" films (*The Texas Chainsaw Massacre, Friday the Thirteenth, Nightmare on Elm Street,* and *Halloween* series) aimed at teenagers and in violent pornography aimed at adults. Association of women with violence is a lesser concern on most network television series, though it does occur. When Luke and Laura on "General Hospital" fall in love and marry after he rapes her, this may send a message to men that, when a woman says no, she may really mean yes. The sex-violence link is also a major concern on rock videos shown on MTV and other cable channels (Brown & Campbell, 1986). Possible desensitization effects of such portrayals (e.g., Donnerstein, Linz, & Penrod, 1987) are examined in Chapter 10.

Now let's turn and look at the criticisms of the portrayals of men on television. Though these have received less general attention and scientific research than portrayals of women, the stereotyping is very real here also.

The View of Men

Men are seen as calm and cool, self-confident, decisive, and emotionless. Although this may be a positive in many ways, it sends the message to young boys that this is what men are supposed to be like and if one cannot, or chooses not to, deny his feelings, he is therefore not a real man. The Marlboro Man is the quintessential TV man, but many classic TV fathers come in a close second. Who could imagine Ward Cleaver or Jim Anderson shedding a tear? This picture has changed some; modern TV dads like Cliff Huxtable ("The Cosby Show"), Jason Seaver ("Growing Pains"), or Stephen Keaton ("Family Ties") are allowed to cry occasionally, although even they are generally somewhat embarrassed and ashamed to do so.

Men are still portrayed as high achievers and dominant over women, though the domination today takes more subtle forms than previously. While J. R. Ewing is obviously domineering over his women, so is Dr. Cliff Huxtable, though much more benignly and sensitively. He is clearly a stronger personality than his lawyer-wife, who very frequently giggles and acquiesces while her husband expresses his opinions and makes the important decisions. Men with "subservient" jobs like housekeeper Tony on "Who's the Boss?" or the English butler on "Mr. Belvedere" are frequently the object of some ridicule (See Box 3.1).

Like women, men are portrayed as young and attractive, but the rules are a little different. It is not quite as bad for a man to age on TV as for a woman (Davis & Davis, 1985). A little gray hair may make a TV man look "distinguished" or possibly even "sexy," whereas it is to be avoided at all costs by women. John Forsythe's gray hair is distinguished but Joan Collins' gray (if she has any) must be colored over. It is not unusual to see a man with some gray hair giving the news, sports, or weather, but seeing a woman with gray hair in these roles is highly unusual.

In spite of this, the message to stay young is still a strong one for men. One example is baldness. Though a sizable proportion of men lose their hair to greater or lesser degree starting in their twenties, few sympathetic leading male characters in TV series or even in commercials ever have even the slightest receding hairline. A bald character, when he does appear at all, is usually an object of at least subtle ridicule (e.g., the pompous George Jefferson, Harry the stupid husband who needs his wife to find him the right laxative), or at best a "character" like the eccentric chap who doesn't believe oatmeal really could have all that fiber. Baldness in a TV series character is an indication of villainy, unfashionable eccentricity such as Yul Brynner's King of Siam, or at best a sort of benign asexuality such as Captain Stubing on "Love Boat" or Burger King's elusive customer Herb. Even middle-aged or elderly male characters usually have full heads of hair. The occasional one who wears a hairpiece ("Today" 's

BOX 3.1   THE MALE TV HOUSEKEEPER

There have been from time to time some very nontraditional men on the tube. Some male domestics appeared on early television like "My Three Sons" (1960–72), where William Frawley and later William Demarest played crotchety older men taking care of a widower and his three sons. The Asian housekeeper on Bachelor Father was another such example. However, these characters tended to be older or at least desexualized to permit them to fit into these emasculated roles, which never really allowed them to be fully rounded characters.

The mid-1980s introduced several shows starring male housekeepers. "Charles in Charge" starred Scott Baio as a college student earning his way through school by taking care of three children of a couple of wealthy but dim-witted yuppie parents. Charles' relationships with the kids was interesting and fairly believable, but the show was cancelled from network TV after one season. "Mr. Belvedere" features a stately English butler who holds together a family of incompetent parents, sultry teenagers, and an obnoxious brat. "Who's the Boss?" drew the highest ratings of this group and starred the ultra-macho Tony Danza working as a housekeeper for a divorced executive. Charles, Tony, and Mr. Belvedere were allowed to be strong males even in these traditionally female occupational roles. It is only too bad that all three were surrounded by pathetically stupid families.

Willard Scott) is the butt of tired old toupee jokes. Even the few apparent exceptions like Kojak and some of Ed Asner's characters are clearly middle-aged if not older.

Although men are generally portrayed as competent professionally, they are often seen as bungling nincompoops in regard to housework and child care. TV fathers of year-old infants often do not know how to change a diaper; this is unlikely to be true in even the most traditional real family. Men in commercials often seem to know nothing about housecleaning or cooking and have to be bailed out by their wives, who in the domestic sphere are portrayed as very knowledgeable experts.

In the late 1980s a fad emerged for TV shows and movies portraying the ineptness of men dealing with small children ("Full House," "My Two Dads," "Three Men and a Baby"). Although they always learned and grew as persons from the experience, their initial ineptitude would seem to suggest that child care is not a part of the normal male role.

In a similar vein, men are often portrayed as insensitive and rough interpersonally, for example, not knowing how to talk to their children about a sensitive personal issue. This is changing but is still a problem. Tony is extremely awkward trying to talk to his daughter about her needing a bra on "Who's the Boss?" and shoves the responsibility off onto his female employer. Cliff Huxtable turns his child's request for advice into a little joke to avoid having to deal with the serious issue.

Effects of Group Stereotyping

Even granted some stereotyping of gender role portrayals on television, the question of their effect remains unanswered. Negative video images become a serious concern if they are seen as reflective of real life. Although no single exposure to a sexist commercial or sitcom episode is likely to irreparably harm anyone, the huge number of multiple exposures to commercials (100,000 or more ads seen by one's high school graduation) is unlikely *not* to have some effect. The effects of repetition are often underestimated; if the same themes about how men and women are supposed to behave and think keep recurring on show after show, that is perceived as reality. For example, women may expect men to dominate them and be relatively insensitive, or men may expect women to be submissive to them and preoccupied with their appearance.

Not only may we take the television portrayals of the opposite sex as reality, but we may take the portrayals of our own gender as cues to the ways we ought to look and behave. When we fail to meet these standards, that "failure" sets us up for experiencing low self-esteem. For example, a woman feeling frazzled meeting the demands of career, family, and housekeeping may feel very inadequate comparing herself to the superwomen on TV who do all three so well. Similarly, a man losing his hair or a woman her girlish figure may feel like a loser when using video bodies as the standard.

Such concerns are especially important when considering children. Children who are heavy viewers of TV hold more traditional sex-role attitudes (Beuf, 1974; Freuh & McGhee, 1975; Lemar, 1977; O'Bryant & Corder-Bolz, 1978). Kimball (1986) found that sex-role attitudes of children were less strongly sex-typed than normal in a town with no access to television until 1974; however, their attitudes became more sex-typed after the introduction of television. Other studies have shown that advertising portraying women in more egalitarian fashion may be followed by more accepting attitudes in young viewers (Geis, Brown, Jennings, & Porter, 1984; Jennings, Geis, & Brown, 1980).

Obviously we cannot expect that any given type of portrayal of the sexes to have a uniform effect on the public. For example, McIntyre, Hosch, Harris, and Norvell (1986) found that more nontraditional males and females were more sensitive to and more critical of stereotypic portrayals of women in TV commercials, in contrast to more traditional subjects. Men more prone to use violence often are affected much more by violent media (see Chapters 9 and 10). The perceived reality is going to differ across individuals.

Now that we have looked at TV's view of the sexes, let's turn to minorities, starting with a developmental model of the portrayals of minorities in media.

THE FOUR STAGES OF MINORITY PORTRAYALS

Some years ago, Cedric Clark (1969) identified four chronological stages of the portrayals of minorities on television. The first stage is *nonrecognition,* in which the minority group is simply excluded from television. It is not ridiculed, it is not caricatured, it is simply not there. Someone from an alien culture watching the programming would never know that such people even existed in that society. For example, until quite recently this was the position of homosexuals on American television. To a large extent Asian-Americans are still absent.

The second stage of minority portrayals is *ridicule.* Here the dominant group bolsters its own self-image by putting down and stereotyping the minority, presenting them as incompetent, unintelligent buffoons. Very early television programs like "Amos 'n' Andy" and characters like Stepan Fetchit or Jack Benny's Rochester reflect this stage in terms of portrayals of Blacks. On the current scene, Arabs are a good example of a group at the stage of ridicule; we practically never see positive or likeable Arab or Arab-American characters on American TV.

A third stage is *regulation,* where minority group members appear as protectors of the existing order (e.g., police officers, detectives, spies). Such roles were typical of the first positive roles open to Blacks in the 1960s; one sees some of the same on U.S. TV in regard to Hispanics today.

The final stage is *respect,* where the minority group appears in the same full range of roles, both good and bad, that the majority does. This is not to say there is never a stereotyped character or that the characters are all sympathetic, but just that there is a wide variety, good and intelligent characters as well as evil and stupid ones.

Now let's turn to looking specifically at the portrayal of Blacks on television; they are the minority which has received the most study for the longest time.

BLACK AMERICANS

How Are They Portrayed?

The most studied group portrayal on U.S. television has been Black Americans. Up until the 1960s, there were almost no Blacks on American commercials (Colfax & Steinberg, 1972; Kassarjian, 1969; Stempel, 1971), and the only Blacks in prime-time programming were limited to a few stereotyped and demeaning roles, such as Jack Benny's servant Rochester or, most notoriously, "Amos 'n' Andy," the early 1950s sitcom about affable but dim-witted black friends. (At least the TV series employed black actors; the earlier radio version had used white actors using Black dialect).

Television was not the first medium to be criticized for stereotypical portrayals of Blacks. In the United States, media reflected this prejudiced viewpoint before radio or television were ever conceived. One of the earliest movies was *Uncle Tom's Cabin* in 1903, a film which highly stereotyped Blacks. This trend persisted in films for many years (Bogle, 1973). In 1942 the NAACP convinced the Hollywood studio bosses to abandon the characteristic negative roles for Blacks and try to integrate them into a variety of roles; this agreement did not produce overnight change, but advances did come eventually.

With the civil rights movement of the 1960s came changes on the tube as well (Berry, 1980). Black models were used in commercials, with none of the feared offense taken by Whites (Block, 1972; Schlinger & Plummer, 1972; Soley, 1983). Blacks also appeared for the first time in some lead roles in prime-time as well, such as "I Spy" (1965–68), with Bill Cosby, and "Julia," the first all-Black drama. In addition, there were Blacks as part of the starring ensemble on 1960s programs like "Mission: Impossible," "Peyton Place," and "Mod Squad." In the 1970s and 1980s there were usually some Black characters on TV, though they tended to be heavily concentrated in sitcoms and largely absent in daytime soap operas and children's programming. Some more recent characters are more rounded than early TV Blacks but still retain some stereotypic characteristics (J. J. on "Good Times," Sherman Hemsley's characters on "The Jeffersons" and "Amen"). The current situation is vastly improved from "Amos 'n' Andy" days, though some argue that there are still subtle indicators of racism on television (Gray, 1986; Greenberg, 1986; Pierce, 1980; Poindexter & Stroman, 1981; Waters & Huck, 1988). Blacks are still underrepresented in most TV genres except sitcoms (See Box 3.2) and are largely absent in high-level creative and network administrative positions.

Research done in the 1970s showed about 8% of prime-time TV characters to be Black (Gerbner & Signiorelli, 1979; Seggar, Hafen, & Hannon-Gladden, 1981; Weigel, Loomis, & Soja, 1980), with less than 3% in daytime soaps (Greenberg, Neuendorf, Buerkel-Rothfuss, & Henderson, 1982). Comparisons of Black and White characters in the same show reveal many similarities and some differences, specifics depending on the study and programs sampled (Reid, 1979; Weigel, Loomis, & Soja, 1980). Barcus (1983) found cartoons to be the most ethnically stereotyped of all television genres.

Blacks as Viewers

American Blacks of all ages watch more TV than Whites, even when controlling for socioeconomic status. They especially watch more sports, action–adventure shows, and news. They watch the so-called "Black" shows ("The Jeffersons," "The Cosby Show," "227," "Frank's Place") in relatively greater numbers than Whites do, but there is no evidence that Whites avoid such shows because of the Black characters (Comstock, Chaffee, Katzman, McCombs, & Roberts, 1978; Graves, 1980). Children of both races tend to identify more with characters of their own race (Eastman & Liss, 1980; Greenberg & Atkin, 1982). Black children preferred sitcoms, while White children preferred action–adventure shows.

Effect of Black Portrayals

One focus of some research has been on the effects of Black portrayals on TV on both Whites and Blacks (see Graves, 1980, and Greenberg, 1986, for reviews). Like anyone else, Blacks are more likely to identify with and emulate TV characters who exhibit personal warmth and high status and power. Often these models have been White characters, yet Blacks will identify with media Blacks as role models, especially with the more positive ones (Ball & Bogatz, 1970, 1973; Bogatz & Ball, 1971). This can have important positive effects on Black children's self-esteem, especially with regular viewing and accompanied by appropriate parental communication (Atkin, Greenberg, & McDermott, 1983; McDermott & Greenberg, 1985).

Two of the most successful American sitcoms of all time have been shows about Black families, "The Jeffersons" (1975–1985) and "The Cosby Show" (1984–   ). In one sense, both are stereotyped and atypical of American Blacks; both families are quite well off economically, though not among the super-rich of "Dallas" or "Dynasty." However, some Blacks have argued that The Jeffersons retained some earlier racial stereotyping in a more subtle way. The Black characters were mostly rather loud and brassy, not very bright, and often acted rather foolish. Still, George Jefferson is a vast improvement from Amos and Andy (Gray, 1986).

Cliff Huxatble and his family, on the other hand, are the epitome of upper middle-class gentility. In fact, some Black critics argue that their wealth and high status are so atypical of Black Americans that it is inaccurate and even offensive to consider "The Cosby Show" a black show at all. Some argue that the show is a sort of neo-tokenism in that it is a show at heart about Whites with black faces. Bill Cosby, while stressing his show is primarily a show about families, not a show about Blacks, disputes that claim. At one point a year after the start of his show, a consistent ratings topper, he threatened to leave the show if the network adhered to its intent to remove an anti-apartheid poster from the wall of teenage son Theo's room. Although the producers were afraid the poster might offend some viewers and not be realistic on the wall of a teenager's room, Cosby replied that it would be very realistic for a Black teen's room, even an affluent Black teen. The poster stayed, and so did Cosby. The next season, in one of the series' most moving episodes, the Huxtable parents and grandparents teach Theo about the work of Martin Luther King Jr.; the episode closes with the family watching a documentary of King's "I have a dream" speech, themselves epitomizing the fulfillment of that dream.

Sympathetic characters like Webster, the Huxtable children, Lydia Grant, or Mary Jenkins thus become potentially very important models for young Blacks.

Studies on White children have shown that prolonged exposure to television comedies or "Sesame Street" with regular Black and Hispanic cast members influences the attitudes of these White kids in a more accepting, less racist direction (Bogatz & Ball, 1971; Gorn, Goldberg, & Kanungo, 1976). Similar results have been shown for White adults' exposure to certain aspects of television, e.g., there is no evidence that white consumers react negatively to Black actors in ads (Soley, 1983).

In contrast to this picture, however, there is some tendency for TV to reinforce existing stereotypes. For example, more bigoted White viewers tended to identify with Archie Bunker of *"All in the Family"* and accept his racist views, while less prejudiced people decried these views and found Archie's attitudes offensive or laughable (Surlin, 1974; Tate & Surlin, 1976; Vidmar & Rokeach, 1974; Wilhoit & de Bock, 1976).

In contrast to this picture of some progress in TV's portrayal of Blacks, let's now turn to its far less benign portrayal of an American minority almost as large.

HISPANIC IMAGES IN THE MEDIA

The second largest, soon to be the largest, minority in the United States are the Hispanics, a diverse group of Americans with ethnic origins in Cuba, Puerto Rico, Dominican Republic, Mexico, Central America, South America, or Spain. They are racially diverse. Although many Puerto Ricans or Dominicans are black or part Black, most Mexican–Americans are mestizos (mixed White–Indian) but seldom Black. Many New Mexicans are pure White of Spanish descent, while some recent Guatemalan refugees are pure native Americans who speak Spanish only as a second language.

Their history is very different. Although some White ethnic Spaniards have lived in New Mexico since before the Pilgrims settled Massachusetts, many Mexicans and Central Americans are very recent immigrants. They are economically diverse, from wealthy Cuban–Americans of South Florida or the "Spanish" New Mexicans of Albuquerque and Santa Fe to the poor illegal immigrant underclass of southern California and Texas. Ironically, the economically poorest Hispanic group, the Puerto Ricans, are almost entirely urban and are all American citizens. Hispanics are politically diverse, from the staunchly Republican and conservative anti-Castro Cuban–Americans in Florida to the politically liberal Mexican–Americans starting to flex their voting muscles in south Texas.

With such a large and important set of groups in the United States, what is the image of Hispanics on American television (Greenberg, Heeter, Graef, Doctor, Burgoon, Burgoon, & Korzenny, 1983; Zoglin, May 30, 1988)? The answer seems to be largely nonexistent, with perhaps a few signs of coming change. According to one study (see Greenberg, 1980, 1986), only 1.5% of all characters in TV programs during a sample period were Hispanic, compared to 9% of the population at the time. When they did appear, they were usually crooks, cops, or comics and tended to be concentrated on a few shows, primarily unsuccessful series that did not last long ("Chico and the Man," "a.k.a. Pablo," "I Married Dora," "Trial and Error"). Five-sixths of the Hispanic characters were male. Almost no Hispanic characters appears on Saturday morning television (a total of two characters in the three years of the study). Mention of Hispanics in the news tended to focus on the group as a social problem, especially the illegal immigration issue (Greenberg, et al., 1983). In a 1987 discussion of television with Hispanic leaders in New York, Rivera (1987) reported people identifying only Victor Sifuentes on "L. A. Law," Lt. Castillo and Det. Calabrese on "Miami Vice," and Lt. Calletano on "Hill Street Blues" as prime-time Hispanic characters. All are involved in law enforcement or the legal system (Clark's regulation stage), none are leading characters, and only Sifuentes and Castillo are even strong supporting characters.

Historically, the current stereotyping of Hispanics follows an older tradition in films of the greasy Mexican bandit of the silent film era and the sensual and musical, but slightly laughable, "Latin lover" of the 1930s and 1940s (Amador, 1988). Although extremely blatant stereotypes like the Frito bandito are seldom seen on U.S. TV today, they do exist elsewhere. For example, the stupidity of the servant Manuel on Britain's "Fawlty Towers" sitcom (also seen on PBS in the United States) is usually explained by the throwaway line, "Oh, he's from Barcelona."

In the late 1980s a few signs were evident that Hollywood and the TV networks were beginning to discover the largely untapped Hispanic market. Spanish cable channels offered popular options to Latino populations. The unexpectedly great commercial success of the 1987 films *La Bamba* and *Born in East L.A.* inside and outside Latino communities allowed several new Hispanic films to be released in 1988 (Corliss, 1988). As of this writing, however, U.S. television has shown a different picture. Following the commercial failure of several very short-lived Hispanic-oriented sitcoms, the networks appear to be gun-shy about more such shows. When a TV show achieves the "crossover" success that *La Bamba* has in the theaters, we will no doubt see changes (Waters & Huck, 1988; Zoglin, July 11, 1988).

Overall then, in many ways Hispanics on television are at the point somewhat similar to that of Blacks 30 years earlier, that is, largely invisible and tending to be negative when they do occur. Greenberg attributes this at least in part to the low level of minority employment in the broadcast industry, not necessarily due to overt discrimination but often more to the low entry-level salaries that are not attractive enough to the relatively few qualified well-educated Hispanics, who typically have multiple job opportunities. Because the management level and decision makers are mostly Anglo, it is their world that tends to appear on television.

THE TV ARAB

Now let's turn to a much smaller American minority and look at a seldom-discussed stereotype, but one that is among the most unsympathetic and derogatory portrayals on U.S. television in the 1980s, that is, Arabs and Arab–Americans.

According to Shaheen (1984a; see also Shaheen, 1984b,c, 1987), there are several stereotypic ways that Arab men are portrayed, all very negative. One is the terrorist. Although only a minuscule fraction of real Arabs are terrorists, there are lots of them on television, especially among Arabs identified as Palestinians. Of course, continuing news events involving Arab terrorists do nothing to help ameliorate this stereotype.

A second stereotype of Arab men is the wealthy oil sheik, who is often greedy and morally dissolute. His wealth, often suggested to be undeserved, is spent on frivolities like marble palaces and fleets of Rolls-Royces. Sometimes he is portrayed as madly buying up land in America and erecting garishly kitsch homes in Beverly Hills.

A third stereotype is that of sexual pervert, often dealing in selling Europeans or Americans into slavery. This is an older stereotype, perhaps originally arising from medieval Christian Europe's enmity against the Moslem "infidels," who were, incidently, primarily non-Arab Turks. Though probably less prevalent than the terrorist or oil sheik portrayal today, this image does appear occasionally.

A fourth stereotype is the Bedouin "desert rat," the unkempt ascetic wanderer far overrepresented on TV in relation to the approximately 5% of Arabs who are Bedouins. Jokes about camels, sand, and tents are frequent in connection with American media Arabs.

Finally, Arab men are seen as villains generally, a stereotype especially rampant in children's cartoons, for example, Daffy Duck being chased by a crazed sword-wielding Arab sheik. These barbaric and uncultured villains are not usually balanced by Arab heroes or "good guys." One of the few exceptions is probably Corporal Max Klinger of "MASH"?. He is a sympathetic and rounded character, yet (especially in early episodes) he still comments about his relatives in unnatural relations with camels and other such stereotyped images.

How about Arab women? They are seen far less than Arab men on American TV, but, when they are seen at all, it is usually in an oppressed situation and often in highly stereotyped roles such as belly dancer or member of a harem. The reality about harems, as Shaheen (1984) points out, is that they were never common and today are nonexistent in Arab countries. The public veiling of women is presented as the Arab norm, rather than a characteristic of some Islamic traditions.

Arab children are practically nonexistent on American television, even though the negative adult Arab stereotypes are perhaps more prevalent in children's cartoons than on any other type of programming. Even as we routinely see Black, Hispanic, and Asian faces on programs like "Sesame Street," no Arabs appear.

Islam as a religion is often portrayed as cruel and vicious. Because most Americans know very little if anything about Islam except what they find in the media, this may easily become their perceived reality about one of the world's major faiths. Although many Americans have adequate knowledge to recognize a Christian extremist on TV as very atypical of Christians, we may not have the necessary knowledge to so critically evaluate a TV presentation of a Muslim fanatic, whom we may take to be typical of Muslims.

Historically, Arabs may be the latest villain in a long list of many groups who have been maligned by the U.S. media. The vicious Arabs of the 1980s have been preceded by the wealthy but cruel Jews of the 1920s, the sinister Asian villains of the 1930s, or the Italian gangsters of the 1950s. Each of these stereotypes has been tempered and balanced as a result of protests from the offended groups and other concerned citizens. Such media portrayals can provide unwitting social support for racist and discriminatory policies and legislation, such as the network of Jim Crow laws and racist practices against Blacks in the century following the American Civil War.

Recent historical events have probably encouraged unflattering media portrayals of Arabs, the OPEC oil embargoes of the 1970s, continuing Palestinian terrorist incidents, and the ongoing Lebanese and Arab–Israeli conflicts being primary among them. Ironically enough, the media Arab may have suffered the most from the action of their fellow Muslims, the non-Arab Iranians, in their actions following the 1979 revolution, especially the holding of the American hostages from 1979 to 1981. This protracted tragedy produced a wealth of bad feeling about the Islamic faith in the United States, even though the Ayatollah Khomeini may be in no way a typical Muslim.

The concern is not that there are some negative portrayals of Arabs and Arab–Americans. The concern is that such portrayals are not balanced by positive portrayals to feed into the perceived reality constructed by TV viewers in their minds. There is very little on Arab culture or society. The Arab world was more intellectually and technically advanced than Europe in the Middle Ages and gave us many of the basics of modern science, mathematics, and music, but how may Americans know that? Nor do the close family values and other positive features of the Islamic faith and Arab culture receive much press in the United States.

Let's turn our attention away from racial and ethnic groups to another large area of group stereotyping on television, namely, various occupational groups. Presence of positive media models can greatly increase the numbers of those entering that profession. For example, the number of journalism students (and unemployed journalists) mushroomed after the Watergate scandal of the early 1970s, where investigative reporters became the heroes. The number of medical school applicants surged sharply in 1962 to 1963, apparently due to the debuts of the popular medical TV dramas "Dr. Kildare" and "Ben Casey" (Goldberg, 1988). Events of media portrayals of occupational groups are not always so dramatic, however. We will examine a few especially interesting groups and see how television presents these professions.

POLICE OFFICERS AND THE LAW

An important group to study in regard to stereotyping are police officers. This group is especially interesting because (a) they are greatly overrepresented on television relative to their numbers in the population, and (b) most of us have relatively little intense contact with police in our daily lives. Thus a high percentage of our knowledge about cops is likely to come from television. Indeed, some research by George Gerbner showed that heavy TV viewers greatly overestimated the percentage of the population working in law enforcement. Real police officers and trainees see the TV police shows as unrealistic portrayals of their profession (Simon & Fejes, 1987).

Clearly some police shows are a lot more realistic than others. Law professor and author Alan Dershowitz (1985) concluded that, of the 1984–85 crop of shows on American television, "Hill Street Blues" portrayed the daily life of police officers most realistically, while "Miami Vice" offered the most realistic portrayal of the law as an abstract system. Such shows that are clearly realistic in so many ways may be perceived as being realistic in all respects; this could lead to some severe distortions of reality.

TV Myths about the Law

Dershowitz (1985) pointed out two myths about the law which he believes are very prevalent even on the best cop shows like "Hill Street Blues," "Cagney and Lacey," and "Miami Vice." The first myth is that the law is unambiguous, unforgiving, and controlling, though the people who administer it may be complex, forgiving, or ambiguous. However, Dershowitz argues that, in fact, real-life law is much more subjective and ambiguous than the police shows portray. For example, plea bargaining and decisions about bail and sentencing are seldom spelled out precisely in the law but leave considerable latitude to magistrates and attorneys. TV cop shows often present a judge or attorney's hand in such issues as being completely tied by the law.

A second "myth" pointed out by Dershowitz is that the Bill of Rights and Supreme Court decisions like the Miranda rule are to blame for freeing lots of criminals. Cop shows would have us believe that "silly" legal technicalities are undoing the valuable work of the police every day, such as critical evidence obtained illegally causing a conviction to be thrown out or overturned, allowing an obviously guilty person to go free. It sometimes may appear as if the Bill of Rights and the Miranda rule are inconsistent with adequate law enforcement. A study done by the General Accounting Office showed that, during the period of the study, only .5% of all serious Federal criminal prosecutions were thrown out by exclusionary rule violations (inadmissibly gathered evidence). If this figure had been represented accurately on the TV crime shows, it would come out to one episode on one show every two years!

The Reality of "Real-Life" Law Shows

Some controversy has arisen around the "realistic' courtroom TV shows like "Divorce Court," "Superior Court," and, especially "The People's Court." All of these shows present legal proceedings either dramatization of real cases (e.g., "Divorce Court") or actual court proceedings (e.g., "The People's Court"). In "The People's Court" retired judge Joseph Wapner actually presides over small claims court cases where both parties have agreed to have their case settled on "The People's Court" in lieu of a more traditional setting. The cases are real, as are all parties in those cases.

On the other hand, such shows have been praised for making the court system more available to the public, who now can better understand how this phase of our judicial system functions. In fact, the number of small claims cases has risen considerably since the advent of "The People's Court" (though not necessarily because of that show). Speaking to this point, however, critics argue that many such cases are frivolous, now that the public realizes that redress is so "easy" via the small claims route. Further, some judges report that litigants have become more contentious, dramatic, and emotional in court, apparently following the model of the parties on "The People's Court," Is the public well served by such shows? Do we have a more accurate perception of how courts function, or is our reality colored by some "Hollywoodizing" of the courtroom by the producers of these "real life" judicial programs?

Most viewers probably do not know if the way that police, the courts, and the law are presented on TV is realistic or not. Since the general tenor of some shows like "Hill Street Blues" or "Cagney and Lacey" appears so generally realistic, we probably accept many portrayals as truth without even realizing that we do.

FARMERS

A very different group from police officers are farmers, members of a profession (agriculture) very inaccurately portrayed on television. As a group, farmers are not highly visible on television, but the few rural shows that have existed have been among the most extremely stereotyped and unrealistic of the airwaves. In earlier days it was "The Beverly Hillbillies" and "Green Acres," then later "Hee Haw" and "The Dukes of Hazzard." All of these portrayed rural people as uneducated and stupid rubes totally lacking in worldly experience and common sense. True, there was also "The Waltons," perhaps the most popular rural show of all time, but its historical setting detracted from its use as a model of modern rural life. Many, if not most, of the farm shows have been set in rural Appalachia, one of the poorest and most atypical of rural regions nationwide. There is an occasional other extreme of the rural refuge of the very wealthy, through "Dallas" and "Falcon Crest" are as equally unrepresentative of rural America as "Hee Haw," though for entirely different reasons.

Nor is this stereotype limited to television. Use of Grant Wood-type figures in advertising to reach a rural audience reflect an archaic (if ever accurate) stereotype. The popular comic "Garfield" occasionally features Jon Arbuckle's farmer parents who come to visit and don't know how to use indoor plumbing and other modern conveniences.

Problems facing the profession of agriculture typically have been underreported in the news, probably because complex issues like the farm debt crisis of the 1980s are difficult to briefly encapsulize into a brief TV or newspaper story. Also, the people involved with producing media are virtually 100% urban, usually from New York City or Los Angeles, with few roots in the farm community.

As final instances of group stereotyping, let's examine the media portrayal of a couple of prevalent and growing demographic groups in our society, the elderly and the single adult.

THE ELDERLY

One of the most underrepresented demographic groups on American television throughout most of its history has been the older adult (Davis & Davis, 1985). According to 1982 census data, 15.7% of the U.S. population was age 60 or over, yet content analyses of the characters on American television have showed only 3% of over 3500 characters in prime-time series were over 65, with an even lower percentage of older adults in commercials (Greenberg, Korzenny, & Atkin, 1979). Other studies examining different types of programming have yielded similar figures (Aronoff, 1974; Harris & Feinberg, 1977; Northcott, 1975). Only daytime soap operas had a higher percentage of older people, 15.9% judged to be over 55 (Cassata, Anderson, & Skill, 1980).

Even that relatively small number of elderly people who did appear on TV were not particularly representative of the population. For example, two-thirds of the TV elderly were men, as compared with only 43% in that age population. A disproportionate number of the TV elderly were in sitcoms, with very few in action–adventure dramas.

Often the older adult who is portrayed is more a stereotype than a fully rounded character. These stereotypes are of several forms:

Physical and mental weakness and poor health.   Overall, older people on TV are often seen as quite healthy, perhaps even unrealistically so (Cassata, Anderson, & Skill, 1980; Davis, 1983; Kubey, 1980). Those who are sick, however, are ailing very badly, often seen as infirm, feeble, and sometimes senile. Moreover, they are usually sexless. The major exception to this is the other extreme, the so-called "dirty old man" (or woman), the older person who is preoccupied with sex and usually is a highly ludicrous character, for example, Mona on "Who's the Boss?". The very active and healthy senior citizen may be an object of ridicule (e.g., the grandmother who rides a motorcycle or cruises bars to meet men).

Crotchety and bitchy insensitivity.   This is the narrow-minded older person who is constantly complaining, criticizing, and generally making a pain of themselves for everyone else. Such characters as Mama on "Mama's Family" are examples. As with the physically weak stereotype, the crochety bitch is usually at best a laughable buffoon and at worst an object of scorn and derision.

Stereotyped positions and activities. Older people tend to be seen doing relatively trivial things like playing bingo and sitting in rockers on the front porch. Such identifying "tags" of an older person are especially common in advertising. The woman in a magazine ad for cookies is placed in a rocker to make sure we recognize that she is a grand-mother.

Physically unattractive. Unlike most of the unusually attractive young adults on TV, TV's elderly are often stoop-shouldered, mousy-haired, badly wrinkled, and usually wearing long out-of-style dowdy clothing. Such marks may be given to them so that we do not mistake them for younger people. Intentionally or not, it also contributes to their being perceived as buffoons. Seefeldt (1977) found that elementary children viewed physical signs of aging as horrifying and saw the elderly as infirm and incapable of doing much.

An interesting class of exceptions to these generalizations can be seen in commercials. Although the elderly are as underrepresented here as in the programs, the characterization is a bit different. The elderly in ads often appear as the "young–old," with a few of the stereotypic signs of aging, except the gray hair, which is almost always there. Although they suffer more health problems than young people in ads, they retain their vigor. It is as if the producers give the character gray hair so we all realize he or she is supposed to be older but allow that person to show very few other signs of age that our society finds so distasteful. Baldness, wrinkles, and otherwise general dowdiness is unseemly (Davis & Davis, 1985; Harris & Feinberg, 1977).

Even in cases where the elderly are portrayed very positively, they tend to be in rather a restricted and stereotyped range of roles. They are almost always in relation to family, very often a grandparent but also often as the antagonist in a relationship with their adult child. We seldom see an older executive or professional.

What was in one sense a truly new type of sitcom debuted to top ratings in Fall 1985. NBC's "The Golden Girls" featured four single women (3 widowed, 1 divorced), aged about 50 to 80, sharing a house in Florida together. What was new was the age of the stars. Never before had a sitcom, or perhaps any American TV show, had its regular cast consisting entirely of older adults. There were no preco-cious children, no squirrely teenagers, no "hunks" or bathing beauties, and no yuppie couple, yet the show had consistently high ratings. Nor were the characters the stereotyped TV old ladies. Three of the four were working professionals, and all showed depth of character beyond the typical TV grandmas. As the U.S. population ages sharply over the next few decades, a greater variety of portrayals of older adults is practically assured.

SINGLE ADULTS

Finally, let's turn to the single adult of the world of television. He or she is stereotyped in several ways. Some of them are love- and/or sex-starved (e.g., Jack Tripper on "Three's Company," Sonny Crockett on "Miami Vice," Blanche Devereaux on "The Golden Girls," Sandra Clark on "227," Dan Fielding on "Night Court," Victor Izbecki on "Cagney and Lacey"), either having an active life of love and romance or desperately trying to find it. Others are social misfits no one would care to marry (e.g., Les Nessman and Johnny Fever of "WKRP in Cincinnati," George Utley on "Newhart," Balki Bartoukomous of "Perfect Strangers," Cliff Claven of "Cheers").

Unlike some other groups, single adults are not really underrepresented on television. In fact, they may actually be overrepresented, especially on ensemble shows centering on the workplace. Shows like "The Mary Tyler Moore Show," "WKRP in Cincinnati," "L.A. Law," "St. Elsewhere," "Barney Miller," "Cheers," "Night Court," and "Hill Street Blues" are very heavy on the single characters, probably because the producers are reluctant to have spouses in the background who cannot be developed extensively. There is also the prevailing TV industry wisdom that single characters allow more options of story lines, especially romantic singles and occupations that take them away from home for extended periods.

Lead characters in police and detective shows are usually unmarried (e.g., "Simon & Simon," "The Equalizer," "Murder, She Wrote," "Hooperman," "MacGyver," "Miami Vice," and even "Perry Mason"). Single life often appears to be one of considerable glamour and excitement, judging from watching such shows. In fact, many such single characters who are tremendously wrapped up in their careers (e.g., Christine Cagney, Hawkeye Pierce, Thomas Magnum, Trapper John McIntyre, Sonny Crockett) and probably would have no time for families if they had them.

Many other groups are only beginning to be portrayed on American TV with anything even approaching a balanced and realistic treatment. See Box 3.3 and 3.4 for two such examples.

BOX 3.3 HOMOSEXUALS IN MEDIA

Although by the mid-1980s it had become acceptable to mention homosexuality on American television and even have an occasional gay or lesbian character, networks are still very cautious about introducing regular homosexual characters. With the partial exception of "Dynasty" and bisexual Steven Carrington, only an occasional guest character on dramatic shows is gay. Like all television programming decisions, this reluctance is basically economic, not moralistic.

In the early 1980s a sitcom called "Love, Sidney" starred Tony Randall as a middle-aged bachelor living with a young single mother and her daughter. Based on a stage play where Sidney was clearly gay, the TV show hedged a bit, suggesting Sidney's homosexuality but never unequivocally so. To the show's credit, it dealt with realistic situations and only occasionally took laughs on sexual preference jokes. However, it did not survive its first season.

Another short-lived sitcom "Sara" (1985), featured an ensemble of young lawyers in a San Francisco legal clinic. One of the group was openly gay, and every line addressed to him seemed to comment on that fact in one way or another. Although not a stereotyped limpwristed character himself, he was consistently responded to by others in a highly stereotyped fashion.

There have been several TV movies dealing with homosexuality and/or AIDS. Some of these have been at least moderate commercial successes. TV and studio films have encountered an unusual difficulty in casting such films, however. Actors are reluctant to accept gay parts, because they perceive such roles preclude their being considered for straight roles later. Actor Harry Hamlin feels that his gay role in *Making Love* (1982) sent his career into a nose dive that only recovered with the success of "L.A. Law" in 1986. Actors playing gay roles frequently report greater difficulty landing subsequent jobs, while producers report difficulty casting gay parts. One recent film was unable to cast a gay leading role, in spite of the producer taking out full-page ads targeted at actors listing 92 "big names" who had played gay or lesbian roles (Clarke, 1988).

CONCLUSION: WHAT DO YOU KNOW ABOUT HOOKERS?

For most of the groups described in this chapter, television is a very large, perhaps the predominant, source of information for most of us. However, it is usually not the *only* source; there is almost always at least *some* reality to temper the television picture. Thus, the perceived reality that our minds construct will not be totally taken from the media, though it may be very heavily influenced by it. Occasionally, however, media may be the *only* source of information. Consider the example of prostitutes.

Another group that is very concerned about media stereotyping are the physically disabled. Although largely absent from TV shows through most of the medium's history, they have occasionally appeared in the "bitter crip" or "supercrip" stereotypes. In the former, the disabled person is depressed and bitter due to their disability and people's failure to accept them as full persons. Often such story lines revolve around a character challenging the disabled person to accept themselves. Often, miraculously, they find this leads to a physical cure, perhaps subtly suggesting that happiness comes only from being physically whole. The "supercrip" image, on the other hand, is the superhuman and selfless paraplegic who wheels hundreds of miles to raise money for cancer research or the blind girl who solves the baffling crime by remembering a crucial sound or smell that sighted people had missed (Kalter, May 11, 1986).

One of the fullest media portrayals of a physically disabled person was in the 1986 movie *Children of a Lesser God,* for which actress Marlee Matlin won the best actress Oscar award for her role as a young deaf woman in love with a teacher at a school for the deaf. Such portrayals can have substantial impact. When a popular Brazilian soap opera introduced a character who was ruggedly handsome and very sexually active but also deaf, interest in learning sign language soared in the country.

Practically all adults know what prostitutes are and could give some information about them. Few readers of this book, however, have probably ever known a real prostitute or knowingly had any contact with a person with any first-hand experience. Where does our perceived reality about prostitutes come from? It most cases it comes not mostly, or partly, but *entirely* from television and movies. the overdressed TV hooker standing on the street corner in the short short skirt, high heels, and too much makeup is probably the reality of prostitutes, as far as most of us know. We might describe someone we see dressed this way as "looking like a hooker." But is this what hookers really dress like, or is it just the way TV portrays them? Even as the author of this book, I honestly don't know if it is or not. All I know is what I see on TV.

If I were to meet a woman tomorrow who was identified as a hooker, my TV-stereotype would come into my mind to process information about this woman. It wouldn't matter if that image was accurate or not. It would be the perceived reality for me. This is what is happening with children growing up learning about groups of people from television. Many children have had no more personal contact with Arabs, Blacks, lawyers, homosexuals, or even single adults than their exposure to the media. This is why stereotypes matter.

Advertising

Thinking back to my childhood in the fifties, I remember TV friends like Mighty Mouse, Lucy Ricardo, Sky King and Penny, and Burns and Allen, but also Ipana's toothpaste's Bucky Beaver, Colgate's Happy Tooth and Old Mr. Tooth Decay, the proto-Rambo Mr. Clean, and Speedy Alka-Seltzer. They were all part of the TV experience.

By any count, media advertising is a multimillion-dollar business. With the exception of public television like the Public Broadcasting Corporation or the BBC in Britain, commercial non-cable television is virtually 100% dependent on ad revenues for financial support. Everything else except commercials costs money for networks and stations, while commercials bring in all the money. Even for print media, newspapers, for example, typically derive around 70% of their revenue from advertising.

In spite of the tremendous costs paid for network TV spots (up to $600,000 for a 30-second spot on the 1987 Super Bowl), such ads are still a remarkably efficient way to reach the buying public. Because of the huge size of the audience for highly-rated shows, the cost per viewer is often in the neighborhood of a quarter to a half a cent per ad. These, of course, only include the purchase of air time; production costs are extra. On a smaller scale, local newspaper and radio ads are far more reasonable in cost but quite effectively reach the target area of interst to the advertiser.

This chapter will examine aspects of the perceived reality from advertising but is by no means a thorough examination of the effects of advertising. After some initial historical and introductory material, we will consider some psychological appeals in advertising, followed by a more specifically cognitive examination of ads, focusing especially on the issue of deceptive advertising, where the perceived reality is at particular odds with objective reality. Next we shall examine how children understand ads and finally how sexual appeals are used to build a reality of positive feelings and associations about a product.

HISTORICAL BACKGROUND

The earliest known written advertisement was a classified ad from around 1000 BC and was discovered by archaeologists at Thebes, Greece; it offered a "whole gold coin" for the return of a runaway slave. Advertisements in the true sense of mass communication did not really exist before Gutenberg's invention of movable type in the mid-15th century, however. This discovery was essentially the beginning of cheap printing. Newspapers started carrying ads regularly in the mid-1600s. The rapid commercial growth associated with the Industrial Revolution in the 19th century gave great impetus to advertising, as did the rise of magazines during this same period, when transportation infrastructure, especially railroads, allowed distribution of national publications for the first time in a large country. The rise of radio after 1920 and television after 1945 provided tremendous new outlets for advertising dollars and creativity.

Although there were early experiments with radio by Marconi in Italy in the 1890s and DeForest in the United States in 1906, the first experimental radio station was set up in 1919 in a Pittsburgh garage by some Westinghouse engineers. Station KDKA broadcast the 1920 Presidential election results. There were 30 stations on the air by the end of 1920 and 400 by two years later. Ensuing concerns and debate about how to finance this new medium culminated in the Radio Act of 1927 for licensing and control of radio stations. This piece of legislation endorsed the free enterprise model to pay for radio, that is, complete subsidy from the sale of advertising time with no government subsidy. About the same time, Great Britain made a very different decision in establishing the government-supported British Broadcasting Corporation (BBC). Both of these economic models were naturally carried over from radio to television in the late 1940s and still provide the modal form of broadcasting in their respective societies, although the United States now has some public broadcasting and Britain some commercial TV.

TYPES OF ADS

Although we tend to think of ads as trying to persuade us to buy particular brands of products, product ads are only one of several kinds. In addition, ads may be for services, such as banks, plumbers, or electricians. They may also be primarily image-building or good-will rather than directly selling. For example, when a multinational corporation spends 30 seconds on TV telling us how they provide fellowships for foreign study, they are trying to encourage us to think of that company as a fine, upstanding corporation citizen. This is done by associating the company with very positive images and dissociating it from negative ones. Image-building advertising is especially prevalent following a time when a corporation or industry has received a public relations black eye, such as chemical companies being associated with manufacturing napalm or Agent Orange during the Vietnam War or oil companies charged with price gouging during one the petroleum crises. It also is common when a corporation tries to get involved in consciousness-raising on some issue of importance and public interest, such as when a distillery runs an ad encouraging people not to drive drunk. They clearly seem to believe that the goodwill they achieve by being perceived as taking such a responsible public position will more than offset any decline in sales arising from people buying less of their product due to concern about driving under the influence.

A different kind of ads are public-service announcements (PSAs), usually sponsored by some government agency or the Advertising Council. Ads for agencies like the American Cancer Society or the United Way are examples of PSAs. Historically, the Federal Communications Commission (FCC) has usually mandated that stations must offer a certain amount of time free for PSAs but does not usually specify when that time must be; thus, PSAs frequently air heavily at off-peak hours like late night or weekdays. With the deregulation and weakening of regulatory agencies in the 1980s, PSAs have suffered even more.

A final kind of advertising is political advertising, usually designed to persuade the viewers to support some candidate, party, or issue. In many ways political advertising is very similar to commercial advertising, although there are some important differences. Political advertising will be considered in more detail in Chapter 8.

Whatever the type of ad, it is trying to affect the reality perceived by the consumer, that is, give us a new image of a product, candidate, or company or make us feel we have a need or desire for some product we were not particularly wanting before. The establishment of this perceived reality about a product and our need and desire for it involved attempts to change our attitudes. Our *attitudes* about products (or anything else for that matter) actually have three components. The *belief* or *cognition* is the informational content of the attitude. For example Jim prefers Toyota cars because of features a,b,c, and d. The *affective* (emotional) content of the attitude is the *feeling* toward that product. Jim prefer Toyotas because he trusts them, he likes them, he feels safer with them. Finally, the *intention to act* is the attitude's potential translation into behavior. In the case of ads, the advertiser typically intends the final step in the chain to be a purchase. Some ads are designed primarily to influence our beliefs and others our affect. See McGuire (1985) for a massive review of psychological research on attitude change and persuasion. Now let's turn now to see how advertising shapes our attitudes and constructs a reality for us.

PSYCHOLOGICAL APPEALS IN ADVERTISING

Any type of media advertising, whether print or broadcast, uses a variety of psychological appeals to reach the viewer. It attempts to tie the product or service to our deepest and most basic psychological needs. Implicitly, then, buying the product will do more than give us something useful or pleasant; it can help us be better people as well.

Informational Appeals

Although not the most common type, some ads primarily provide information, in an attempt to influence the belief component of our attitudes. A good example of this type would be an ad for a new product; such an ad may explain what that product does and what its features are.

Some of the most common appeals to our belief are exhortations to save money or receive a superior product or service. The feeling that we are getting a good bargain is a powerful motivator in deciding to purchase something. It is so powerful that often official list prices are set artificially high so that products may be advertised as costing considerably less, when in fact they may have never been intended to sell at the full list price. Some classes of products (e.g., stereos) are notoriously often "discounted" in such ways.

Emotional Appeals

Very often ads appeal to the affective component of our attitudes. Influencing emotions is often the best first step to influencing beliefs and ultimately behavior. For example, there are many ads that appeals to our love of friends, family, and good times and the good feelings that these bring us. We are asked to call people long distance to affirm our love, buy diamonds and flowers for them to show we care, and drink beer or soft drinks with friends as part of a good time. Such slogans as "Reach out and touch someone" or "The good times go better with ——" illustrate such appeals. Products are shown to be an integral part of showing our love and caring for others. The more closely the advertiser can link the product with those natural and positive emotions, the more successful the ad.

Closely related is the linking of the product with fun. This is especially clearly seen in ads for soft drinks and beer. Photography and copy intertwining good times at the beach, in the ski lodge, or just relaxing at home with friends using the product enourages people to think about that product whenever they have or anticipate such good times. After awhile it may just not seem as much fun without Coke (or whatever the product may be). The product has become an integral part of that activity, and, more importantly, the feelings associated with that activity.

Certain cultural symbols have come to evoke warm feelings in viewers, which advertisers hope will transfer to warm feelings about the product. A boy and his dog, Grandma baking an apple pie, the flag, or a family homecoming are examples. Such symbols appear frequently in advertising for all sorts of products and services. Connecting one's product with the positive feelings people have for such symbols can associate a lot of positive affect with that product.

Frequently the major selling pitch focuses on how the product will affect your psychological well-being and deep-seated personal needs. For example, a camera ad may say, "Look how good you can be" with their product, not simply "Look what good pictures you can take." The product goes beyond providing you with a good product; it actually makes you a better person. A baby food company once advertised that it helps babies learn to chew. Such an appeal links the product with a very basic developmental event in the baby's life, thus giving it a much more central role in the child's growth than any mere product, even an excellent product, would have.

Often an appeal is made centered around the uniqueness of the product or consumer. Interestingly enough, this type of appeal is especially common from the largest corporations, trying to fight an image of large, impersonal, and uncaring corporate institutions. For example, McDonald's "we do it all for you" campaign and Wendy's ads against "assembly-line burgers" illustrate this approach, as does General Motors' "Can we build one for you?" campaign. Personal attention and showing interest in the individual is almost always appealing.

Patriotic appeals.   Appeals to consumers' national pride are frequent in ads. They are most abundant during the quadrennial Olympic game season and other events like the U.S. Bicentennial in 1976 and the Statue of Liberty centennial in 1986. The nationality of the manufacturer is of minor importance. Toyota is probably just as likely as General Motors to use a American patriotic appeal to sell cars in the United States. Volkswagen saluted the U.S. Olympic hockey victory in America in 1980 and McDonald's helped raise money for the Irish Olympic team in Dublin. In terms of advertising themes, patriotism is where the market is, not the home office!

Sometimes particular international events have their repercussions in advertising. Shortly after the Soviet invasion of Afghanistan in late 1979, a strong wave of anti-Soviet sentiment swelled up in the United States. One Turkish vodka manufacturer began a campaign of "Revolutionary vodka without the revolution," that is, "buy our vodka and still get imported quality without supporting those dirty commies." Still, when nationalism crosses the line to tasteless jingoism, it may become commercially counterproductive, as when a small-town American restaurant in 1980 published an "Iranian coupon—good for nothing," or a bar in 1986 advertising a "Gadaffi-bashing" night. Public outcry against excessively mean-spirited patriotic appeals backfires on the advertiser in ways that tend to discourage such campaigns, at least in the most blatant form.

Fear appeals.   These involve some kind of threat of what may happen if one does not buy the product. A scenario of a child trying unsuccessfully to phone parents when in danger because the parents don't have Call Waiting to interrupt their social call is an example. Selling home computers by asking parents "You don't want your child to be left behind in math because you wouldn't buy him a computer, do you?" is a subtle but powerful emotional appeal to guilt and fear. Such appeals to parents, playing on their love and responsibility toward their children, are common and probably highly effective (see Sutton, 1982, for a review of research on fear-arousing communications).

Psychological research on persuasion shows that fear appeals have varying effects. The conventional wisdom in both social psychology and advertising for many years has been that there is an optimal level of fear for persuasion to be the strongest. A weaker appeal will be less effective, but, if the fear induced becomes too strong, the ad may turn people off and make them defensive, in which case they tune out the message. As Rotfeld (1988) points out in a careful review paper on fear appeals and persuasion, however, there is no consistency in the research on this point. It is hard to draw firm conclusions because what each researcher has used for a strong, moderate, and low fear appeal has varied widely, and there typically has been little assurance that the subjects in the studies have viewed the appeals similarly to the researchers. Fear appeals in ads are effective, but exactly which ones are most effective is not yet entirely clear.

Achievement, Success, and Power Appeals

Another popular theme in ads is striving to win, whether the prize may be money, status, power, or simply having something before the Joneses do. A candy ad may blatantly say "Winning is everything," picturing a chocolate Olympic-style medal, or it may more subtly suggest that only the people who use the particular product have "really arrived." The idea that using some product enables us to "be a winner" is a powerful appeal, whatever the prize.

Humorous Appeals

Humor is often used as an effective selling tool in ads. The audiovisual possibilities of television offer a particularly rich set of possibilities for humor, although there is much humor in print and radio advertising as well. Indeed, some humorous ad campaigns have become classics of popular culture—for example, Alka-Seltzer's "I can't believe I ate the whole thing" campaign in the 1960s or Wendy's "Where's the beef?" of the 1980s. Radio's "see it on the radio" campaign drew on people's ability to use visual imagery to imagine a humorous situation described only through sound (Cantor & Venus, 1980; Madden & Weinberger, 1982, 1984; Sternthal & Craig, 1973).

One caution regarding the use of humor concerns its distractibility potential. Some humor clearly attracts attention and increases motivation and general positive feeling about the product or service. A very funny spot, however, may be so entertaining that it detracts from the advertiser's message. Viewers may remember the gimmick but forget what product it was selling (Gelb & Zinkhan, 1985).

A related concern in regard to humorous ads is the wearout factor. Any ad depends on repeated presentations to reinforce its message. If an ad appears too often in too short a time, its effect may wear out and even become counterproductive by turning people off due to overexposure. Humorous ads have a shorter wearout time. They seem older, more tired, and more obnoxious faster than other ads.

Testimonials

In the *testimonial* type of ad, some individual and identified person, typically a well-known personality, offers a personal pitch for some product or service. They may clearly be an expert in the particular field, such as Lee Iacocca selling Chryslers, or they may be no more informed than the average person, such as Joe Namath selling panty hose or Bob Hope selling gasoline. Social psychological research on persuasion shows that we are more likely to be persuaded by a prestigious and respected figure, even if that person has no particular expertise in the area of the product being sold (Hass, 1981). We tend to trust that person more, and the positive associations and feelings we have about them may be transferred in part to the product.

Thus far we have primarily focused on the psychological appeals in the ads. Now let us turn more directly to the cognitive perspective introduced in Chapter 1 and examine its application to advertising.

ADS AS INFORMATION TO BE PROCESSED

The cognitive approach to advertising considers an ad as information to be processed. A broadcast commercial or print ad is a very complex stimulus, involving language (presented orally or in writing) and, for print and TV, pictorial stimuli as well. Television is a particularly complex medium because it contains both the visual and auditory modalities (Shanteau, 1988). Typically there is a close relationship between the audio and video portion of a TV commercial, but this is not always the case, for example, when a disclaimer is presented only in writing across the bottom of the screen. The issue of how the consumer processes and integrates information from the verbal and visual components of TV commercials is a complex and important issue in itself (Alesandrini, 1983; Gardner & Houston, 1986; Percy & Rossiter, 1983; Shanteau, 1988).

Stages of Processing

When we perceive and comprehend an ad on TV, there are eight stages of processing involved in understanding it and acting upon it (Shimp & Gresham, 1983). First of all, we must be *exposed* to the ad. Secondly, we choose to *attend* to it, perhaps selectively perceiving some parts more than others. Third, we *comprehend* the message. Fourth, we *evaluate* the message in some way, for example, agree or disagree with it. Fifth, we try to *encode* the information into our long-term memory for future use. Sixth, some time later we try to *retrieve* that information. Seventh, we try to *decide* among available options, such as which brand of cereal to buy. Finally, we *take action* based on that decision (e.g., buying the product).

These eight stages are involved in our processing of every aspect of the ad. Even something as simple as the choice of name or slogan for a product can have important ramifications for processing, depending on the nature of that name or slogan. For example, the memorability of a name may vary depending on various characteristics. A name which lends itself to an interactive logo or mental image may be remembered due to its amenability to organizational working memory strategies called chunking, which lead to a greater number of possible avenues of retrieval from long-term memory (Alesandrini, 1983). For example, a basement waterproofing sealant named "Water Seal" once used a logo of a seal (animal) splashing in water in the middle of a seal (emblem). This choice of a name allowed information about the product name (Water Seal), its use (sealing), and its sound (/sil/) to be unified into one mental image that is easy to remember.

Schemas in Understanding Advertising

The cognitive principle known as construction (See Chapter 2) argues that people do not literally store and retrieve information they read or hear but rather modify it in accordance with their beliefs and the environment in which it is perceived. What guides the encoding and later retrieval of information about the product are knowledge structures called schemas, and a major theoretical development of the last decade has been the growth of schema theory (Brewer & Nakamura, 1984; Rumelhart, 1980; Thorndyke, 1984).

A schema is a knowledge structure or framework which organizes an individual's memory of information about people and events (see Chapter 2). A schema accepts all forms of information, irrespective of the mode—visual or auditory, linguistic or nonlinguistic. The individual is likely to go beyond the information available to draw inferences about people or events that are congruent with previously formed schemas (Harris, 1981; Harris, Sturm, Klassen, & Bechtold, 1986; Singer, 1984).

The organizing effect of schemas for information processing of ads is seen in the use of advertisement slogans. For example, a commercial for Lucky Soda might depict a group of dripping, smiling youth running up on a beach and opening a cooler filled with soda. In bold letters at the bottom of the screen are the words, "Get Lucky." Emotional appeals of the sort discussed earlier try to place the idea in readers' minds that, if they drink Lucky, then they, like those in the picture, will experience happiness, friendship, and good times. The slogan, along with the picture, evokes a schema from memory, a schema containing information about such events, based on the viewer's experience. This schema helps the viewer draw inferences to fill in information about the scene, as well as ascribe meaning to it, meaning that is not specified directly in the ad. In this example, the readers' "beach party schema" lends a sense of coherence and meaning to a scene that is otherwise incomplete in letting them know exactly what is happening, has happened, or is about to happen. The viewer used the schema to infer a number of things that are not specifically provided by the ad, such as (a) the people have been swimming, (b) the temperature is hot, (c) the people are thirsty, and (d) drinking Lucky makes the people happy and playful.

DECEPTIVE ADVERTISING

One of the issues in advertising of greatest concern to the general public is the issue of deceptive advertising. This relates directly to the theme of perceived reality of media and is at heart a question of information processing. How one comprehends an ad may be tested to determine whether or not the consumer is led away from the truth, that is, "deceived" (Burke, DeSarbo, Oliver, & Robertson, 1988; Harris, Dubitsky, & Bruno, 1983). Ads may deceive either by increasing a false belief held by a consumer or by exploiting a true belief in ways designed to sell the product (Russo, Metcalf, & Stevens, 1981). This issue will be examined in some depth as an example of an advertising issue eminently amenable to a cognitive analysis.

Miscomprehension Versus Deceptiveness

Preston and Richards (1986) made a helpful distinction between *miscomprehension* and *deceptiveness*. Miscomprehension occurs when the meaning conveyed to the hearer (perceived reality) is different from the literal content of the message. Deceptiveness, on the other hand, occurs if the conveyed meaning is inconsistent with the facts about the product, regardless of what the ad stated. From an information processing perspective, the question is much more complex than merely determining the truth or falsity of the ad itself. Studies examining comprehension and miscomprehension of ads and other information from media have shown high rates of miscomprehension, typically 20–30% of the material misunderstood in some way (Jacoby & Hoyer, 1987; Jacoby, Hoyer, & Zimmer, 1983; Morris, Brinberg, Klimberg, Rivera, & Millstein, 1986).

If both the literal and conveyed message are true, there is neither miscomprehension nor deceptiveness. If the literal message is false and is conveyed the same way, there is deceptiveness but no miscomprehension. That is, the hearer constructed a meaning not consistent with reality, but not because he or she misunderstood the ad. For example, if an ad states an incorrect price for a product and we believe it, we have been deceived but have not miscomprehended the ad. Such advertising is clearly both illegal and bad business and is thus fairly unusual. One type that does seem to occur fairly frequently are ads like (1) for weight-loss products and diets, perhaps banking on the gamble that dissatisfied customers will be too embarrassed or ashamed to want to admit being duped by such a claim.

1. You can lose 30 pounds of ugly cellulite in a week.

It is also possible to miscomprehend without being deceived. An ad may state a claim which is literally false, but we comprehend it in some nonliteral way which is consistent with reality and thus are not deceived. For example, claims like statements 2, 3, and 4 are unlikely to be comprehended literally; thus a "miscomprehension" will lead to *not* being deceived. Generally the U.S. Federal Trade Commission (FTC) and the courts have allowed advertisers to assume some degree of intelligence in the consumer (See Box 4.1). Although it is an interesting psychological, and occasionally legal, question of how much intelligence may reasonably be assumed (according to a 1983 policy statement, interpreting earlier legislation, advertisers may assume the consumer is "acting reasonably"—see Ford & Calfee, 1986), the general notion of such an assumption seems eminently appropriate.

See Box 4.2 for a discussion of another type of clearly false but not so clearly deceptive advertising convention.

2. Our cookies are made by elves in a tree.
3. The secret of our taste is magic.
4. We sent little green leprechauns to work in your lawn.

Sometimes the distinction is made between factual and evaluative advertising. *Factual* advertising involves objective claims that are clearly verifiable by reference to the external world, for example, statements about price, research findings, or physical attributes of a product. In contrast to this is *evaluative* advertising, which involves subjective judgments of an unverifiable and unfalsifiable nature. One particularly common type of evaluative advertising is puffery, the superlative "puffing up" of one's product, for example, "the best," "the greatest" (Preston, 1975).

Assuming an ad does contain factual, rather than evaluative, information, determining whether or not an ad is either deceptive or miscomprehended is not the same as assessing its truth value. Truth may be considered a legal or linguistic question, which may be resolved by examining external reality. Miscomprehension, however, is a function of the understanding of the consumer and is thus basically a question of information processing. As such, it is covert and unobservable and must be inferred from an assessment of someone's understanding of an ad. One may be deceived by an ad that is either true or false in some objective sense; the deception may or may not result from miscomprehension.

True-but-Deceptive Ads: Induced Miscomprehension

The type of advertising claim which is potentially the most damaging is the statement which is literally true, but miscomprehended, thus deceiving consumers by inducing them to construct a meaning of the ad that is inconsistent with reality. Such statements may be either evaluative or factual statements which imply something beyond themselves. This class of claims is the one on which we focus. We have long recognized the inferential nature of information processing, and studies on inference strongly suggest that, in order to derive the meaning of a statement, subjects typically interpret beyond what is explicitly stated in the ad. When applied to advertising, the consumer may be led to believe things about a product that were never explicitly stated, for example, an ad states that a mouthwash fights germs and the reader infers that it destroys germs.

There are several different types of linguistic constructions that may deceive the consumer without actually lying. Such claims may invite the consumer to infer beyond the information stated and thus construct a stronger interpretation. This inference-drawing tendency draws on our knowledge in the form of mental schemas discussed earlier and is a natural component of our information-processing system.

Hedges.   One common class of true-but-potentially-deceptive claims are the hedge words or expressions (e.g., *may, could help*), which considerably weaken the force of a claim without totally denying it:

5. Scrubble Shampoo *may help* get rid of dandruff *symptoms*.
6. Rainbow Toothpaste *fights* plaque.
7. *Although I can't promise to make you a millionaire* by tomorrow, order my kit and you too *may* become rich.

Elliptical comparatives.   Another common type of linguistic construction that may imply false information is the elliptical comparative (see statements 8 through 10). Comparative adjectives or adverbs necessarily involve some sort of standard that something is being compared to. When a product merely says it gives *more*, the statement is largely vacuous without knowing the basis of comparison ("more than what?"). As long as anything true could be used to complete the comparative, the statement cannot clearly be considered false. However, our minds tend to construct the most plausible basis of comparison, not necessarily the most accurate.

8. The Neptune Hatchback gives you *more*.

9. Fibermunchies have *more* vitamin C.

10. Powderpower cleanser cleans *better*.

Implied causation. Often a causative relationship may be implied when no more than a correlational one in fact exists. This invitation to make a further inference beyond what is stated directly is one way that active cognitive processing by the consumer may be increased, which in turn may improve memory. One particular technique that does so is the juxtaposition of two imperatives.

11. Help your child excel in school. Buy an Apricot home computer.

12. Shed those extra pounds. Buy the Blubberbuster massage belt.

In neither statement 11 or 12 does the ad state that buying the product *will* have the stated effect, but the causative inference is very easy to draw.

Such a cause-and-effect relationship may also be implied in a more general sense. For example, consider a radio commercial for diet soda where a young woman talks about using and liking this product. Then at the end of the ad we hear a male voice saying, "And I like the way it looks on her too." Listeners may infer that drinking that product will *cause* female listeners to be more attractive to men, though the ad never states that directly.

An implicit conditional logical argument may be drawn upon in a similar fashion. For example, statement 13 may be interpreted as statement 14, a conditional statement. Conditional reasoning research (Evans, 1982; Wason & Johnson-Laird, 1972) has shown that people often fallaciously infer a biconditional (if and only if) relationship from statements like 14, so consumers may infer statement 15 as well as 14 from 13.

13. Euphoria Capsules make you healthy.
14. If you take Euphoria Capsules, you will be healthy.
15. If you don't take Euphoria Capsules, you won't be healthy.

Implied slur on competition. Something unfavorable may be implied about a competitor's products or services. While direct false statements about the competition are usually not tolerated, false implications are less clearly proscribed. For example, consumers may infer from statements 16 or 17 that competing companies do not provide the same service, while most in fact do so.

16. If you are audited by the IRS, we will accompany you to the audit.
17. Our company gives refunds quickly if your traveler's checks are lost or stolen.

Pseudo-science. Reporting of scientific evidence in incomplete fashion may also imply considerably more than what is stated. In reporting results of surveys, for example, mentioning a per cent or absolute number responding without the sample size (statement 19) or the number sampled without the number responding (statement 20) is seriously incomplete and potentially misleading. For example, statement 18 would not be false if only four people were questioned.

18. Three out of four doctors recommended Snayer Aspirin.
19. 2000 dentists recommended brushing with Laser Fluoride.
20. In a survey of 10,000 car owners, most preferred Zip.

Comparative advertising may employ very selective attribute comparisons to imply a much more global impression. For example, statement 21 may imply that the car has a more spacious interior on most or all dimensions than any of the competitors, which is not necessarily true from the statement.

21. The Egret Pistol has more front-seat legroom than a Ford Taurus, more rear-seat headroom than a Nissan Stanza, and a larger trunk than a Toyota Camry.

Studying Deception Scientifically

Using materials like the ads illustrated above, Harris (1977) demonstrated experimentally that subjects do in fact make the invited inferences described and remember that inferred information as having been stated in the ad (e.g., remembering that a toothpaste prevents cavities when the ad only said it "fights" cavities). This is a stable finding that occurs with a variety of dependent measures (Burke, DeSarbo, Oliver, & Robertson, 1988; Harris, Dubitsky, & Bruno, 1983; Harris, McCoy, Foster, Krenke, & Bechtold, 1988; Harris, Trusty, Bechtold, & Wasinger, in press; Russo, Metcalf, & Stevens, 1981). Burke, et al. (1988) have even developed a computer-based measurement technique for assessing the deceptive effects of advertising claims.

Training subjects *not* to make such inferences is very difficult, because the tendency to infer beyond the given information is so strong. However, a training session that had subjects individually analyze ads, identify unwarranted inferences that may be drawn, and rewrite ads to imply something more or less strongly does have some significant effect in teaching them to put a brake on this natural inference-drawing activity (Bruno & Harris, 1980). Such research has direct application to the preparation of consumer-education materials. See Harris, Dubitsky, and Bruno (1983) for a review of this research.

For the rest of the chapter, let's turn to looking at two specific types of advertising that raise especially important and controversial psychological issues in regard to the perceived reality about advertised products. First we will examine advertising targeted at children and

next we will turn to sex in advertising, including the issue of subliminal advertising.

CHILDREN'S ADVERTISING

An important special concern in advertising are TV commercials
aimed specifically at children, primarily on programs aired on Saturday morning and, to a lesser extent, after school. We must keep in
mind, however, that children's programming, the so-called "kidvid
ghetto," constitutes only a minority of the hours of TV that children
watch. Kidvid represented only 24% of the viewing time for 6-year-
olds and a mere 5% for 11-year-olds. The rest of the many thousands
of ads a child sees each year are seen on general programming—that
is, prime time and daytime offerings such as game shows, soap operas, and syndicated sitcom reruns.

Turning now to kidvid ads specifically, over 90% of them advertise
products in a mere four categories: toys, cereal, candy and snacks,
and fast-food restaurants. One study showed 82% of all children's ads
were for some type of food, usually heavily sugared (Barcus, 1980).
The toy ads are many but primarily occur during the Christmas
season, their numbers being much lower during the rest of the year.

Children's ads are technical marvels, full of lots of color, movement, and animation, all emphasizing how much fun you can have
with the product. Special visual and sound effects are common and
captivating. The pace is fast. There is less "hard information" presented than in adult ads and more of a global association of the
product and fun times. There is lots of alliteration (Crazy Cow, Kit
Kat, Bubble Yum, Alpha Bits) and wordplays ("fruitiful," a character
yodelling "Cheerio-ios"). Commercials are made to be fun, far more
so than adult ads. Behind all the fun, however, lie some serious
concerns about the effects of these ads; let us turn to those now.

Issues of Concern

Differentiating ads and programs.   One major concern about children
and commercials is that very young children do not discriminate
between commercials and program content and do not understand
the persuasive intent of ads or the economics of television. Studies
show that kindergarten children have almost no understanding that
commercials are meant to sell products. Depending on how much
understanding is tested, elementary-school children show various
stages of development of the understanding of the purpose of ads

(Bever, Smith, Bengen, & Johnson, 1975; Dorr, 1980, Robertson & Rossiter, 1974; Sheikh, Prasad, & Rao, 1974; Ward, Wackman, & Wartella, 1977). Discriminating ads and programs is especially difficult if a primary character in the show is also the spokesperson in the ad, such as one of the Smurfs (Kunkel, 1988).

Children show increasing distrust of ads as they grow older. Most 5- to 7-year-olds say that ads "tell the truth," whereas older children are less likely to be so trusting (Blatt, Spencer, & Ward, 1972; Robertson & Rossiter, 1974; Ward et al., 1977). Typical explanations of middle-elementary children center around the truth (or lack thereof) of the material, however; not until late elementary school is the distrust based on perceived intent and an understanding of the advertiser's motivation to sell the product. Among demographic groups, Blacks and lower socioeconomic class children tend to be the most trusting and least critical of ads (Wartella, 1980).

Disclaimers. A particularly interesting issue in children's advertising is the question of disclaimers, those little qualifying statements like "partial assembly required," "batteries not included," "action figures sold separately," or "part of a nutritious breakfast" (Geis, 1982). For obvious reasons these are hardly the central focus of the commercial. In fact, the disclaimers often occur in vocabulary far beyond the age of the target viewer and often occur only in writing superimposed at the bottom of the screen. This is completely lost on a pre-reading child and probably on an older child as well, because the colorful activity in the background is so much more enticing and interesting. In a content analysis of 1000 children's ads, Stern and Harmon (1984) found that 36% had some sort of disclaimers, most of these appearing only at the end of the ad and most in audio-only (60%) or visual-only (30%) format. Unlike the rest of the ad, almost all of the disclaimers used adult terminology.

Drug advertising. A particularly emotional issue in regard to children and advertising concerns their reactions to ads for drugs. The criticism argues that advertising implicitly assumes a chemical cure for every physical, psychological, or social ill, and that children grow up learning from television that the answers to all of their problems may be found in the medicine cabinet. Although this is a difficult question to carefully study scientifically, the research has generally failed to show a relationship between the amount of TV viewing and use of either OTC or illicit drugs or the instances of accidental child poisoning from ingesting overdoses of household drugs (Robertson, Rossiter, & Gleason, 1979).

Programs as commercials.   Although not the first such instance, in 1983 Mattel's popular He-Man toy made the move to television ("He-Man and the Masters of the Universe") and within a year became the second best-selling toy in the country (Diamond, 1987). This successful marketing approach has been massively copied since then and has raised a new issue in regard to children's TV ads, namely, the commercial-as-show phenomenon. As of 1987, over 40 television shows are linked to toys in some way. Some of the most popular are "The Transformers," "She-Ra: Princess of Power," "G.I. Joe," "The Real Ghostbusters," "He-Man and the Masters of the Universe," "ThunderCats," "Smurfs," "The Care Bear Family," and "All New Pound Puppies." Toy companies routinely seek TV shows to promote their toys, as when Hasbro, Inc. subsidized the production of "G.I. Joe," "Jem," and "The Transformers" from their $217 million marketing budget. Thus have the toy industry and television been wedded almost as significantly and profoundly as have sports and TV.

This marriage raises several concerns. Critics argue that children's programming is driven too much by the marketability of associated toys rather than by the quality of the shows. Toy and broadcasting executives defend the policy by arguing that creative animated shows are preferable to tired syndicated reruns of "Gilligan's Island" or "Leave It to Beaver," often the alternative for after school or Saturday morning. Still, producers of non-toy-related children's programming report difficulty funding and selling their products. Programming is increasingly initiated around an existing (or soon to be marketed) toy. Although toys from successful shows have always been around ("Mickey Mouse Club," "Sesame Street"), until recently, the show has come first, not the toy. That is no longer the case.

Violence.   Another concern is violence. Many, though by no means all, of the toy-related shows are highly violent in nature. Children's cartoons have always been the most violent shows on TV, in terms of numbers of violent incidents (see Chapter 9). A particular concern with the newer shows, however, is that the availability of toys (weapons, dolls—or as they are called when marketed to boys—"action figures") makes it easier to act out the violence modelled by the cartoon characters. As yet, there is little definitive empirical evidence to confirm or question this concern.

Interactive television.   Very recently a new phenomenon has begun with interactive television. Some programs had either high-frequency tones or infrared lights to signal viewers to turn on their interactive toys. For example, "Captain Power and the Soldiers of the Future" invites young viewers to score points by firing a $30 Mattel Power Jet at the screen. An electronic signal keeps track of the "hits" and reports the player's score. Unlike earlier shows, purchasing the toys will not only be encouraged by the program/commercial, but it will be *necessary* to do so to have full enjoyment of the program (Diamond, 1987).

Now let's turn to a very common type of ad we have not yet considered—the sexy ad.

SEX IN ADVERTISING

Obviously one of the most common types of appeals in advertising is the use of sex. Although some products such as perfume and cologne are sold almost exclusively through sexual appeals, practically any product can be pushed through associating it with a beautiful woman or man. The sexual association and allure then becomes a part of the perceived reality of that product for many consumers.

Classical Conditioning

A psychological process called classical conditioning sheds some light on how sex in advertising can affect us. Classical conditioning is the process discovered by Ivan Pavlov studying the physiology of hunger in dogs in the early years of the 20th century. In his studies he noticed a curious fact; his dogs would often start to salivate merely to the sight of an empty food dish. There is no natural connection between plastic dishes and drooling. Why did they do it? Pavlov eventually decided that they had been *classically conditioned*. This process is equally important for consumers of commercials as it was for Pavlov's dogs.

An *unconditioned stimulus* (UCS) naturally without learning produces an *unconditioned response* (UCR). For example, meat (UCS) naturally produces salivation (UCR) in a dog. Similarly, the sight of a gorgeous woman (UCS) naturally elicits mild sexual arousal or at least some positive feelings (UCR) in most heterosexual males. So far, there is no conditioning. The conditioning occurs when the UCS is *paired (associated)* with the *conditioned stimulus* (CS), which does not normally elicit the UCR. For example, Pavlov's dog dish (CS) was associated with meat (UCS), just as the beautiful woman (UCS) is associated with a product (CS) in a commercial. There may be some natural and obvious connection of the woman and the product, such as a cologne ad that suggests a man will attract sexy women if he wears that product, or there may be no intrinsic connection at all, such as the beautiful woman next to the steel-belted radials.

After enough association of the UCS and the CS, the CS by itself comes to elicited the *conditioned response,* (CR) which is very similar to the UCR. Just as Pavlov's dogs eventually began to salivate (CR) to the empty food dish (CS), so may we have positive feelings (CR) about the tire (CS) when we see it without the gorgeous model. This basic classical conditioning paradigm is the psychological process being employed by most ads using sexual stimuli.

Subliminal Advertising

Whenever people discuss the effects of advertising on society, particularly if they focus on negative effects, it is not long before someone mentions subliminal effects—those subtle attempts to "manipulate" us into buying something by use of devious techniques that we are not even aware of. "Subliminal" means below the threshold of conscious perception; we are not normally aware of something that is subliminal. Such stimuli may be a subaudible sound message in a store ("Don't shoplift"), a very brief message in a movie or TV show ("buy popcorn"), or a visual sexual stimulus airbrushed into an ad photograph ("S-E-X spelled in the crackers or sex organs in the ice cubes). What are the alleged effects of such stimuli? Do they in fact work to sell products?

An important distinction to bear in mind in considering this problem is the difference between demonstrating the *existence* of some subliminal stimulus and demonstrating that such a stimulus has some *effect.* Books like Wilson Bryan Key's *Subliminal Seduction* (1974), *The Clam-plate Orgy* (1981), and *Media Sexploitation* (1976) focus on demonstrating the existence of subliminal messages, sexual implants, and so forth, but give few arguments to demonstrate any effects that such stimuli have. Implicitly such critics often seem to be assuming that showing its existence also shows it has an effect. Such is not the case at all, however. Although there is some apparent evidence (Cuperfain & Clarke, 1985; Kilbourne, Painton, & Ridley, 1985) of an effect, much of the so-called evidence is anecdotal or open to other interpretations. In fact, however, there is little evidence that it affects people very much (see Merikle & Cheesman, 1987; Moore, 1982; and Saegert, 1987, for reviews of this topic).

Timothy Moore wrote an excellent article in 1982 examining this problem very carefully. He identified three possible problem areas: subliminal visual perception, subaudible speech, and embedded sexual stimuli, and carefully examined research evidence on possible effects in all three areas. Moore concluded that there is only a little evidence, though it is far from compelling and not directly related to advertising, that subliminal stimuli may in some cases have a weak positive effect of a general affective nature, that is, they make us feel a little better about the product. However, there is virtually no evidence for any effects of subliminal stimuli on *behavior*. Saegert (1987) looks at the very few studies that seem to suggest effects and argues that other interpretations are possible. The conclusion at this point seems to be that subliminal stimuli *may* exist on occasion but that their *effects* are minimal, if not totally nonexistent. Subliminal advertising seems to be a perceived reality in the mind of much of the public, but not an actual reality that stands up to scientific scrutiny.

Similar issues are involved in a heated controversy over allegedly "satanic" messages recorded backwards into certain rock music recordings. See Box 4.3 for details of a careful research program designed to test for effects of such stimuli.

Having associations to sex is not always a positive association for an advertiser. Mainstream advertisers clearly do not want their ads to appear in extreme pornographic magazines. Sometimes it is not even the publication itself but rather its readers that scare away the advertising dollar. See Box 4.4.

CONCLUSION

This chapter has in no way been a comprehensive review of the psychological effects of advertising or even of all issues relevant to the perceived reality of advertising. Rather, the emphasis has been on looking at a few areas where advertising attempts to create a reality within our minds, which is conducive to purchasing a product. We are "taught" positive emotional associations about the product through classical conditioning or association of the product with positive experiences in our past. Natural information-processing tendencies like drawing inferences and invoking knowledge schemas to interpret ads around are used by advertisers to encourage us to draw certain inferences and interpretations. Knowledge of the way that the mind processes information allows the advertiser to construct ads designed to encourage the mind to construct a meaning favorable to the advertiser's ends. On the other hand, knowledge of such processes also allows consumers to take steps to be less "manipulated." Activist consumer response will be explored in the concluding chapter of the book.

BOX 4.3. SATANIC MESSAGES IN ROCK MUSIC?

Periodically one hears the claim that some rock music contains embedded messages recorded backwards. Although no one claims they can be consciously perceived easily when the record is played forward, concern has been expressed that there may be some unconscious effect unknown to the listener. Further, some conservative Christians have been concerned that such messages may be satanic and have caused legislation to be introduced in several states that would call for warning labels about such messages to appear on album jackets.

Psychologists John Vokey and Don Read of the University of Lethbridge were contacted by a radio announcer for information about this phenomenon. Their subsequent research program on the subject appeared in Vokey and Read (1985). They first make the point that the *presence* of such embedded messages does not presuppose any *effect* of such messages on the listener. The evidence presented by concerned members of the public is highly anecdotal and often debatable but nearly always speaks to the presence issue, not the effects issue. Too often a simple anecdotal demonstration of a message's existence is assumed to demonstrate its effectiveness as well, a connection that Vokey and Read point out as completely unwarranted.

These psychologists conducted a careful series of studies designed to test the effects of such messages, even assuming for the moment that they exist (an assumption not at all established, but we'll leave that for now). When verbal messages on tape were played backwards for subjects, they showed almost no understanding of the meaning; identifying the sex or voice of the speaker was about all they could perceive. Next, they tested for *unconscious* effects by giving subjects a spelling test where some of the words were homophones *(read, reed)*. A biasing context sentence *(A saxophone is a reed instrument)* was played backwards but subjects were no more likely than a control group to write *reed* instead of *read*. When backward messages were played and subjects merely asked to assign the statement to the category Christian, satanic, pornographic, or advertising, based on its content, they could not do so at greater than chance level. The only time that subjects ever perceived and reported anything at greater than chance level was in one study where the experimenter picked out words in advance and asked the subject to listen for them. Only under conditions of such strong suggestibility could subjects perceive anything from the backward messages.

Vokey and Read's studies clearly demonstrate that, even if backward messages do exist in albums, it is highly unlikely they could be having any effect on the hearers. This conclusion is all the more striking considering that, in their studies there was no competing forward message like the music in rock albums. In at least a couple of cases, proposed record-labelling legislation was withdrawn based on the results of Vokey and Read's research.

BOX 4.4. ADVERTISING TO HOMOSEXUALS

In spite of the overriding principle of economic reality driving the advertising dollar, one sizable market has been largely ignored by national advertisers. The prospect of increasing sales to readers of gay publications seems to be more than offset by the fear of losing heterosexual buyers as a result of having one's product associated with the gay audience. Although gay magazines and newspapers successfully recruited some major advertisers in the late 1970s and early 1980s, the AIDS scare of the late 1980s apparently scared away most of those advertisers. Gay publications have been struggling financially, with most mainstream national companies (with the exception of liquor companies and movie studios) pulling out in recent years. Even condom manufacturers fear association of their product with gays. Ironically, this drying up of ad money has caused many publications to rely increasingly on ads for sexual videos and paraphernalia and sexually explicit personal classifieds, exactly the sort of material that national advertisers shudder to be associated with. Whether advertisers' homophobic fears of guilt by association are justified remain untested. In the meantime, a sizable minority market, which probably has significantly more than the average disposable income, remains largely ignored (Alsop, 1988).

Media and Values

In the movie *Ordinary People* the lead character is faced with a question of the right way to handle his feelings in a difficult situation. In searching for the answer, he wonders how John-Boy on the Waltons would handle it. He feels John-Boy always knows how to deal with situations and turns to him for guidance.

One of the major concerns of mass media in society is its role as a teacher of values, "passing the social heritage from one generation to the next" (Tuchman, 1987, p. 195). What the content of this social heritage is continues to be debated, however. Although relatively few print media stories or radio or TV broadcasts have the explicit purpose of teaching values, values are being taught implicitly, particularly by television. In this chapter we will consider values as being very broadly defined as attitudes dealing with any subject where there is a perceived "right" and "wrong" position. If we can readily speak in terms of right and wrong, it's probably a value issue.

On the one hand, the media may be seen as mirroring the values of the society in which they occur. If sexual values are promiscuous in a society, this will be reflected in its media, if certain religious values predominate in a society, they will also prevail in its media. On the other hand, in line with the overall theme of this book, the media may be seen as a catalyst for value change in a society. Values in the media may not exactly reflect those prevailing in society but may serve, probably not intentionally so, as a catalyst for moving society's values in the new direction. This is, of course, exactly the concern of media critics who argue that television most strongly reflects the values of the New York and Los Angeles communities where most programming originates, but that it tends to cultivate those values in the rest of the otherwise more conservative country.

Because most of the concern and study has focused on the medium of television, this will basically be the focus of the chapter. We will begin by first looking at some changes in values in the 40-plus years of television. Then we will spend most of the chapter looking at specific value issues and how television is involved in teaching or reinforcing those values. These areas are offered as examples and are not meant to be considered an exhaustive list of values with which television is involved. Most of the comments are reflective of television in the United States and may not necessarily be similar elsewhere.

Although most of our attention will be devoted to television, print media and radio are by no means uninvolved in value issues. See Box 5.1 for two challenging value issues faced by newspapers and Box 5.2 for some value issues in regard to rock music.

CHANGES IN MEDIA VALUES

We often hear laments that television is so much more permissive today than it used to be ("Oh, if we could just have back the good old days of "Ozzie and Harriet" and "Leave It to Beaver" when family values were solid"). Clearly, in many respects TV is more permissive today than it used to be, though it is far from "anything goes." However, this is not the whole picture; there are also ways in which TV is *less* permissive and more strict today than it was 30 years ago. We'll examine that in a little while, but let's begin with some ways TV is more permissive.

What Is More Permissive

Sex. This is probably the area most people think of first in connection with changing standards on TV. Much more explicit sex is seen today on television than we used to see, but there are still firm standards that no network TV shows dares cross, such as frontal nudity or explicit sexual intercourse.

We clearly have come a long way from the days where Lucy and Ricky Ricardo slept in two twin beds and referred to her state as

BOX 5.1. HOW MUCH DO WE NEED TO KNOW?

How explicit should the media be in reporting certain unsavory events? When is the public's right to know overshadowed by its right to standards of good taste? A couple of cases in point:

1. A small Midwestern U.S. city is the scene of a child sexual abuse case involving a prominent businessman and two 13-year-old boys. Each day's court proceedings are reported in great detail in front-page stories, always identifying the accused but not the boys. Sexually oriented entertainment involving pornography and alcohol in the man's home was described in detail, along with extensive direct quotes from the testimony: "He rubbed our butts in the showers," "He called me to where he was sitting and told me to play with his penis," "He also made me [and the other boy] lay on the floor and have oral sex with each other while he watched." Other episodes such as the man asking the boys to reach inside his underwear and squeeze his penis hard were also explicitly described.

   Predictably, this coverage provoked considerable community comment, though even the most outraged somehow always managed to read the articles. Although few defended the events that had occurred, some argued that children should not be exposed to such stories in the paper. Their values might be distorted. Others countered, however, by saying that such events are horrible and need to be reported in detail to show everyone how horrible they are and increase commitment to insure they do not happen again. Each side took a strong value-oriented position about publication of this information.

2. In January 1987 Pennsylvania treasurer C. Budd Dwyer killed himself at a news conference by putting a pistol in his mouth and pulling the trigger. Stunned photographers recording the news conference had the whole episode on videotape. Network news, TV stations, and newspapers were then faced with the decision of whether to run the entire sequence. Most TV stations did not show the tape or showed it only to the point of Dwyer placing the gun in his mouth. A few TV stations and newspapers carried pictures of what happened after that, saying it was an important historical event and ought to be covered.

   Much news is quite unpleasant. How does one decide how explicitly to cover highly violent, sexually explicit, or distasteful happenings?

"having a baby" but never as "pregnant." Issues like premarital sex and homosexuality are openly discussed today, at least superficially, even on family sitcoms. Even in such cases, however, it is often the traditional values that are affirmed in the end. For example, Mallory

BOX 5.2. MUSIC LYRICS AND CENSORSHIP

The lyrics of popular songs have long been a concern of censors and the public, as nicely illustrated in a TV documentary "America Censored." Back in 1933 the song "Reefer Man" was cut from versions of the Cab Calloway film "International House" because of its reference to marijuana. Many years later the Beatles "Lucy in the Sky with Diamonds" and the Byrds' "Eight Miles High" were also controversial for the same reasons. Even the innocent "Rocky Mountain High" by John Denver was the target of some censors who did not realize that the song referred to invigoration from mountains, not chemicals.

When Mick Jagger and the Rolling Stones appeared on "The Ed Sullivan Show" in the 1960s, they had to change the line "Let's spend the night together" to "Let's spend some time together." When Jagger performed this line, he did so with exaggerated gesture and body language to communicate his feeling about the censoring.

When John Lennon said offhandedly in 1966 that the Beatles were more popular than Jesus, many were highly offended. Even subsequent "clarifications" or apologies of a sort failed to mollify everyone.

When Charley Daniels recorded "The Devil Went Down to Georgia," he recorded two versions, which were identical, except for one line which was "son of a bitch" in one and "son of a gun" in the other; radio stations could take their choice.

Keaton openly considered having sex with one boy friend on "Family Ties" and discussed it openly with family and friends. In the end, however, she decided she was not ready and chose not to.

Very often, however, such issues are avoided altogether. Mallory Keaton and her long-term boyfriend Nick have seldom if ever discussed the issue of premarital sex; the scripts are silent on this point, with no indication of where Nick and Mallory stand on either attitudes or behavior. Perhaps this is by intention; the viewers can then project their own values on the couple and assume they are consistent with their own.

Language.   We hear certain words on TV today that were not considered acceptable for the medium 30 years ago, for example, "damn," "hell," and expressions like "oh, my God!." Still, there are limits, and prime-time network TV is much more conservative than much print media, cable TV, and movies. Even in the late 1980s, we seldom hear "shit," "fuck," or any expletive with religious language stronger than "my God." These words are even edited out of movie clips shown on movie review shows on public TV.

Models of family. We see many more diverse models of families on TV today than in the 1950s and '60s, although this has only been the case since about the mid-1970s, in the case of sitcoms. The debut of "One Day at a Time" in 1975, featuring a divorced mother and her two teenage daughers, was the first sitcom to show a fully rounded and realistic divorced adult as a featured character. Not all TV children today are in nuclear families with mother, father, and 2.3 children. In recent years American sitcoms have featured children living with two divorced mothers ("Kate and Allie"), two single men ("My Two Dads"), widowed mother and widowed grandfather ("Our House"), widowed father and divorced aunt ("The Hogan Family"), widowed father and single uncle and single male friend ("Full House"), widowed father and divorced female employer and employer's child and mother ("Who's the Boss?"), adoptive single father ("Different Strokes"), older brother, sister-in-law, and uncle ("One Big Family"), as well as a few traditional nuclear families ("The Cosby Show", "The Wonder Years," "227," "Family Ties," "Growing Pains," "Mr. Belvedere").

Even the traditional nuclear families show some changes, though. Most often both parents have careers outside the home ("Family Ties"), or one parent brings their career into the home ("Growing Pains" where the psychiatrist dad has his office in the home). Indeed, one of the major concerns today is that modern TV families appear to be managing career and family so successfully that the difficulties inherent in modern 2-career families are glossed over, if not totally ignored (Maynard, 1987). The presentation of family values on TV and the socializing role of TV *vis-a-vis* societal values is a continuing object of concern (Gumpert, 1987; Gunter and Svennevig, 1987; Morley, 1986).

Even in the context of traditional families some of the patterns of interaction are greatly changed from the more authoritarian days of "Father Knows Best" and "Leave It to Beaver." Psychiatrist Alvin Poussaint, a consultant to "The Cosby Show," says that today's TV parents seem to have no needs apart from their children and "are more like pals . . . overly permissive, always understanding . . . never angry . . . no boundaries or limits set" (Kalter, July 23, 1988, p. 10). See Box 5.3 for an example from a popular sitcom, illustrating just how much family values have changed.

BOX 5.3.   CASE STUDY OF FAMILY SINS OF THE EIGHTIES

A episode of "Family Ties" in the mid-1980s presented a story whereby high-school-senior Alex Keaton anticipated his 18th birthday by withdrawing from family responsibilities and interaction. The final blow was his going off with his friends in defiance of parents and family plans of a birthday dinner together. His mother Elyse drives some distance to retrieve an embarrassed Alex from this peer gathering. After they arrive home, both are seething with anger. After Alex sarcastically yells at his mother about his right to do as he likes now that he is an "adult," she responds in only slightly more controlled fashion, "you have complained to me, grunted at me, lectured to me, and presented me with ultimatums" but never "even come close to talking with me." She accuses him of cancelling out on family dinner plans "without a moment's thought to *my* concern." Growing contrite, Alex acknowledges "I'm sorry I wasn't more sensitive," and both acknowledge that they have made mistakes in dealing with each other. When Alex asks "How do we figure out who's right and who's wrong?" Elyse responds that there is no absolute right or wrong and then offers a startling statement about parent–child relations in the eighties: "It's my job as a parent to set boundaries and it's your job to negotiate the changes."

In this scene, fairly typical of contemporary family shows, the morally serious transgression of the child is not disobedience but *insensitivity*. If there are troubles in the family, the parents have probably made mistakes as well as the children. Parent–child interactions are to be negotiations, not decrees and obedience. Even though traditional family solidarity and family values are in many ways affirmed today as they have always been on TV, the specific nature has changed somewhat.

Emotional expression.   Men and women are permitted a wider range of emotional expression today than was the case 20 years ago. Women can get angry without losing their femininity or appearing hysterical, and men can express tenderness and occasionally even shed a tear without appearing emasculated. In the early 1980s a "One Day at a Time" episode featured brothers-in-law Max and Mark in a tender moment crying together at the kitchen table. Max has just accepted the fact that his wife, whom he still loves very much, has left him and their infant daughter. Mark is empathizing greatly, though there is nothing concrete that he can do. The scene, however, expressed a range of emotion for men not often seen on prime time.

It is not the case that everything is loosening up, however; in some ways standards on U.S. television are much more restrictive than they used to be.

What is More Restrictive

Racism and sexism. Perhaps most prominent among the restrictive trends is any content or language that could be considered racist or sexist. The early TV hit sitcom "Amos 'n Andy" was considered too racist even to show in reruns in the mid-1950s; today it would be extremely offensive and inappropriate, if not downright grotesque. Racist jokes simply are not acceptable, except possibly from a very bad character in a drama. Different cultures, of course, vary in their sensitivity to such issues. Until recently, a brand of toothpaste called "Darkie," with an Al Jolson-like minstrel character on the tube, was marketed in Hong Kong.

Any real or implied violence against women, unless taken very seriously such as being the subject of a TV movie, is a very touchy area. Ralph Kramden's gag line in "The Honeymooners" of shaking his fist in his wife's face and angrily saying, "One of these days, Alice, pow! Right in the kisser!" was hilarious in 1955. Today it strikes many as offensive and inappropriate, perhaps as Ozzie Nelson having a homosexual experience would have seemed in 1955.

Drug abuse. Some very deeply held values center around substance use and abuse. Perhaps the greatest change of this type since the early days of TV is in the attitudes and behavior about smoking. Like many early TV characters, Lucy and Ricky Ricardo smoked cigarettes regularly in the old "I Love Lucy" show, sometimes at the specific request of the tobacco company sponsor. With very few exceptions, however, regular characters on TV series have not smoked since the 1960s, clearly out of health concern over a possible negative effect on youth from seeing admired TV characters smoking. Although this certainly reflects the great decline in the percentage of adult smokers since 1960, it may have in part contributed to that decline. Even among teens, smoking is much "less cool" than it used to be, and television may be part of the reason for that.

In regard to alcohol, the most widely abused drug, the United States has seen decreasing acceptance of alcohol abuse during the decade of the eighties. Although social drinking remains at high, though modestly reduced, levels and alcoholism as a disease and social problem is still rampant, attitudes against excessive drinking are much less tolerant. The drunk is not so much an object of humor as of pity or disgust. Portrayals of drinking on TV have had to, at least implicitly, take note of this. Whether TV has been a factor in producing this societal change in values or merely reflecting what has been caused by other social forces is unclear at this point.

Finally, TV shows today are careful not to model illicit drug use by respected characters. Adults or teens may occasionally be shown using drugs, but it is nearly always presented as a "mistake." This mindset even carries over into news: When conservative U.S. Supreme Court nominee Douglas Ginsburg admitted in 1987 to past marijuana use, the media treated this as a very serious issue, ultimately culminating in his withdrawal, even though polls showed most Americans thought marijuana use should not disqualify one from the Supreme Court. Once in a while producers even feel a responsibility to turn an entire show into an explicit value lesson. See Box 5.4 for an example.

The question of whether television could or should teach values often revolves around such controversial issues as violence or sex. Less often examined are the more subtle values regularly promulgated by TV series. Let us turn now to some of these issues.

WEALTH AND MATERIALISM

Affluence as the TV Norm

A concern is often heard that TV encourages excessive consumption and a desire to acquire money and the trappings of wealth (e.g., Greenfield, 1985; Hardaway, 1979). According to this criticism, television's fascination with affluence, even opulence, is sending subtle messages to middle-class and poor viewers. Continually seeing the glitz and glamor of daytime soap operas and primetime shows like "Dynasty," "Dallas," "Moonlighting," or "Magnum, P.I." may lead viewers to accept such lifestyles as commonplace and appropriate aspirations for themselves. Even sitcom families, though certainly not super-rich, typically live in very large well-decorated homes in surprising splendor given the great amount of time that the wage-earners spend at home.

Another target of criticism about money values concerns the fact that wealthy people are disproportionately represented among series characters. The most obvious examples are the super-rich of the night-time soaps like "Dallas," "Dynasty," and "Falcon Crest." Many police and adventure shows also revel in the glitz and glamour of the moneyed set ("Miami Vice," "Magnum P.I.," and "Moonlighting"). There are exceptions, however, such as the gritty settings of "Hill Street Blues" and "Cagney and Lacey." Some (e.g., Stein, 1987) argue that American television disproportionately reflects the values and lifestyles of the largely upper-middle-class Los Angeles base of most of the writers and producers.

BOX 5.4. SITCOMS AS SOAPBOXES

Producers and actors are well aware of the potential of television to teach values. How to mesh these goals with priorities of entertainment is not always clear. An interesting example occurred with an episode of the ABC sitcom "Growing Pains" in early 1987, during a time of considerable concern about the use of cocaine among young people. Sixteen-year-old actor Kirk Cameron, playing wise guy Mike Seaver, attends a party of college students where cocaine was being snorted. Mike and his two friends experience considerable peer pressure to participate. This causes them anxiety, and Mike finally leaves the party to avoid the situation, although his friends stay. He later discovers they left shortly thereafter also. At the end of the show actor Cameron, who strongly holds such views himself, steps out of character and gives a mini-sermon on the evils of drugs. An earlier version of the script called for character Mike Seaver to deliver an anti-drug lecture to the cocaine users at the party. This was rejected as being too unrealistic for a high-school student. The less preachy approach, coupled with the actor's epilogue, was chosen instead as being more effective in communicating the antidrug message.

Even the popular sitcoms of the more-or-less typical families are relatively affluent. The top-rated "Cosby Show" presents a very affluent family, though clearly financial gain is not their dominant value. Other popular sitcoms like "The Golden Girls," "Growing Pains," "Who's the Boss?," and "Kate and Allie" are less affluent but still living in very fine surroundings considering the occupations of the wage-earners. One family with a dad sports writer and mom law student even has money to hire a full-time English butler ("Mr Belvedere")! Although a content analysis of U.S. family shows between 1978 and 1980 found that the primary value disseminated was that money doesn't buy happiness, and that the poorest families were the happiest (Thomas & Callahan, 1982), by the mid-1980s there were no popular prime-time family shows of people struggling financially, like "The Honeymooners," "Taxi," "The Waltons," "All in the Family," "Sanford and Son," or "I Love Lucy" of earlier days.

Why are affluent people so interesting to watch and poor people apparently so uninteresting? There is some evidence that hard economic times bring on more escapist stories of the perils of great wealth, as seen in the many movies of wealthy people that were popular in the Depression, in contrast to the "poor" movies and TV shows popular in the affluent 1950s. People like to watch rich people and their fine trappings like sports cars and fancy clothes but also like to be reminded that these people have serious problems too, often even more serious than the viewers'. Somehow this seems reassuring.

Still another factor is that the producers of television and films tend to be rather affluent, mostly from southern California. Impressive arguments can be made that the media grossly overrepresent the world of those who produce the programming and tacitly present this world as far more typical of overall American life than is in fact the case (Stein, 1979). A similar argument was considered in Chapter 3 as a reason for the underrepresentation of women and minorities on television.

The Glitz Travels Overseas

One disturbing aspect of international telemarketing is that the most popular American TV shows exported are very often the shows with the most affluent characters and settings, most notably the nighttime soaps like "Dallas" and "Dynasty". For many, especially in Third World countries, such programs become the reality of what U.S. is like. International visitors to the U.S. frequently express surprise that most people are not as wealthy as the Ewings on "Dallas." Some research has suggested that exported programs like "Dynasty" and "Dallas" may be cultivating negative images of Americans in viewers elsewhere (Massing, 1987; Tan, Li, & Simpson, 1986). Popular TV programs dwelling on the rich are by no means a uniquely North American phenomenon, however; many Third World countries' domestic shows also present such affluent lifestyles.

Sometimes the affluence in the context of one particular culture may be highly inappropriate, if not downright grotesque, when seen elsewhere. For example, the Bolivian government distributed 5000 television sets in a poor tin-mining community in 1974. One Indian woman in that community described her child's reaction to the (largely imported) programming:

> My son watched a program on our neighbor's television that showed him a marvelous world full of beautiful castles and parks and mice that spoke. He came home and said to me, "Mommy I'm going to be a good boy. Why don't you send me to Disneyland? I want to play with the little bear and the little mouse and the little train!" For weeks he didn't want to go out in the street or play with his toys anymore—his sardine cans and milk cans. He dreamed about Disneyland. (Will, 1987, p. 44)

This dream was sharply in contrast to the reality of living with his parents and six brothers in a 2-room house with no running water, bathroom, or kitchen.

Probably the most controversial international media campaign in Third World countries has centered around the selling of infant formula as an alternative to breast milk. Although it is sold as being healthier than mother's milk, the fact that it was often mixed with unsafe water and/or in dirty containers actually led to greater danger of disease, to say nothing of the added expense to many already desperately poor families. Concern over the alleged social irresponsibility of such media campaigns led to a worldwide boycott of Nestlé products in the 1970s.

The nearly ubiquitous presence of television around the world has led to numerous advertising campaigns that have come under fire on grounds of social responsibility. Poor children often spend what little money they have on expensive junk food and soft drinks rather than wholesome school lunches, thanks to the influence of advertising. How the commercial demands of television and other media confront the real world of desperate poverty leads to many questions of media transmission of values.

PATRIOTISM

Political Values

Values of patriotism change with current events. In the 1950s, patriotic values in the United States were assumed and almost universally accepted and applauded. In the Vietnam era, patriotism and even its symbols like the flag became co-opted by the political right; for some years it was difficult to express both patriotism and opposition to the Vietnam War. Remember Archie Bunker's patriotic expressions to his son-in-law Mike Stivic in "All in the Family." In the 1980s, patriotic values again became very fashionable and somewhat less politicized.

Patriotism expressed on television is determined more by the audience than the producer. For example, foreign car companies routinely use patriotic American themes in U.S. ads, whereas McDonald's in various countries run promotions to raise money for the national Olympic team of that country.

Television is a part of the overall political socialization of a society, whether it be in the heavy-handed propaganda of Soviet television or the more subtle values in American sitcoms. American TV children and real American kids are taught that political freedoms, as exemplified in the Bill of Rights, are of the highest priority. Children in other places (e.g., Cuba, East Germany, U.S.S.R.) may learn that economic freedoms (e.g., freedom to have a job and livable lodging) are higher priorities.

Although patriotism is a popular and powerful appeal, it has the danger of backfiring if perceived to be tacky or in poor taste. This is a particular concern in regard to advertising. As columnist Roger Simon (1985) once wrote, using the Statue of Liberty as a symbol to *sell* Budweiser beer is probably perceived as okay, but having an animated Statue of Liberty *drink* a Budweiser may well be considered exploitive and disrespectful.

Patriotic values are generally cheered, but they can draw criticism if presented too stridently or chauvinistically. See Box 5.5 for a case study of a drama that may have crossed that line, a drama many people feared would be damaging to superpower relations.

SOLIDARITY

One of the most pervasive values in TV series programming is what might be called solidarity; that is, loyalty, support, and love for one's fellow group members, most typically family or office coworkers.

Family Solidarity

One area of TV solidarity is the family, most clearly seen in the family sitcom. The basic message here, as true for "Family Ties" and "Growing Pains" this week as it was for "Leave It to Beaver" or "Father Knows Best" 30 years ago, is that one's family is more important than money, power, greed, status, or professional advancement. For example, on one "Family Ties" episode Alex is having a very important college interview with a very stuffy dean. Although always eager to impress such a person, Alex in his interview is disrupted by the anguished protestations of his sister Mallory, who has just been jilted by her boy friend. After she breaks in on Alex's interview and destroys his chances of acceptance at that prestigious institution, Alex's pique is later tempered with the good feeling that, after all, his sister is more important than any college anyway. Thus Alex' natural pomposity and self-importance are brought down by the even stronger "family ties." Box 5.3 illustrates another example of family solidarity being affirmed, though in a new way.

BOX 5.5. THE "AMERIKA" CASE

In March 1987 ABC television broadcast a $35 million, 14.5-hour miniseries set in the American Midwest in 1997, after a fictitious Soviet takeover of the United States. Even during production the series elicited strong protests from the Soviet Union, which predictably argued that it vilified the U.S.S.R. and its international intentions. The largest sponsor, Chrysler Corporation, became so jittery that they withdrew their ads a few weeks before airing, forcing ABC to discount their $175,000 per 30-second spot rate to fill up all the commercial breaks.

Just how the Soviets took over in their bloodless conquest was never well specified in the script, though Reagan administration cries about the communist menace expanding from Nicaragua were probably subtly reinforced. Most critics argued that the series was inflammatory and misleading, grossly exaggerating the possibility of any such event occurring and subtly suggesting that dissent is unpatriotic and even dangerous, rather than being a constitutional right of all citizens. In a dangerous world greatly in need of more, not less, trust and communication between the superpowers, such an epic seemed less than helpful, perhaps even irresponsible. There is enough paranoia without inducing more of it through television. On the other side of the political spectrum, some right-wing critics argued that "Amerika" was too soft on the Soviets, portraying their occupation as more benevolent than it really would be.

All of the cries about the show reduced to whimpers afterward. In spite of all predictions and considerable hype, "Amerika" drew only modest ratings, which deteriorated as the eight days wore on. It may be remembered primarily for being a major influence away from long expensive miniseries in the tradition of the more successful "Roots," "Shogun," "The Thorn Birds," and "North and South," expensive gargantuan epics that were only commercially viable since they received blockbuster ratings.

One may ask if such family solidarity is a realistic reflection of our society. It clearly is so with many families and just as clearly is not for many others, whose troubled family dynamics would more typically be characterized by vicious backstabbing, betrayal, and generally putting self above other members. Still, even those families might agree that the sitcom characterization is a worthy ideal to hold up as a model, even if it not totally realistic. Maybe this is a socially helpful model to portray. See Gunter and Svennevig (1987) for a thorough review of television's portrayal of the family and its effect on family life.

Solidarity in the Workplace

A second major area of TV solidarity is in the workplace. This is most characteristic of ensemble shows of characters who work together, such as "The Mary Tyler Moore Show," "Taxi," "WKRP in Cincinnati," "L.A. Law," "Cheers," "Night Court," "Trapper John M.D.," "St. Elsewhere," or "Hill St. Blues." The strong message here is "always love your coworker" (even if you don't) and "put his or her needs above your own." This, even more than family solidarity, is very questionably tied to reality. Let's examine aspects of workplace solidarity.

One area of workplace solidarity is probably a direct consequence of the TV series format. This is the way that coworkers are so intimately involved in the personal lives of fellow workers, employers, and employees. Although real-life coworkers may sometimes be close friends, this is typically not the case, and it is almost unheard-of in the real world for *all* of the workers in a unit to be close personal friends. Yet this is the typical case in television land. For example, when WKRP station manager Arthur Carlson's wife delivered her baby, the entire staff of the radio station was at the hospital. In real life this would not only be unlikely but most probably obtrusively inappropriate and unappreciated, even if for some reason it did occur.

Perhaps even more of a deviation from reality is the way that this workplace solidarity is extended to the clients of a professional. For example, Dr. Gonzo Gates on ""Trapper John M.D." regularly went running off hundreds of miles to find a lost family member of a patient or smooth out a domestic quarrel he felt was interfering with the recovery of his patient. In real life no surgeons would do this sort of thing and would doubtlessly be derelict of their duty back at the hospital if they did. Still, such an image of a professional is appealing because that is what we want to think our doctor would be like. Even if we have never been a patient in a hospital, it comforts us to feel that our doctor would be as caring as Gonzo.

Another area where workplace solidarity seriously distorts reality comes in coworker response to one employee receiving a job offer elsewhere. With the exception of an actor's death or leaving a series, a prime-time employee cannot truly resign. Still, as in the real world, TV workers do receive other opportunities for employment. Unlike in the real world, however, the employee's coworkers will go to unbelievable (literally) lengths to keep the lucky coworker from leaving, even to the point of trickery and other underhanded practices sure to engender furor if tried in the real world. For example, the whole

WKRP staff resorted to an elaborate ruse to coerce Johnny Fever to turn down a clear professional advancement. Even more incredibly, people offer great sacrifices to keep a clearly obnoxious and incompetent employee like Ted Baxter on "The Mary Tyler Moore Show," Dan Fielding on "Night Court," or Herb Tarlek on "WKRP" from leaving. In the real marketplace, the graceful departure of an incompetent or obnoxious coworker is greeted with discreet relief, not elaborate self-sacrificial ruses to prevent its occurrence. When one makes real job-changing decisions, they tend to be based on one's own personal considerations and professional advancement, not the reactions of coworkers.

All of this is understandable, however, with the realization that such shows really portray the workplace members as family. The characters on "Night Court" or "Cheers" or "L.A. Law" are essentially a family, not a court or a bar or a law firm. It is not accidental that an unusually high proportion of the characters on such shows are single, childless, in troubled marriages, or in other situations where they might be more likely to turn to the workplace for family-type support.

Soap Operas: A Counterexample?

Before leaving the subject of solidarity, we should consider one important class of apparent exceptions to television's solidarity theme, namely the nighttime family soaps like "Dallas," "Dynasty," "Knots Landing," or "Falcon Crest." The Ewing family clearly differs from the Keatons or the Cleavers in not showing much obvious solidarity. Indeed, the meanspirited and self-serving backstabbing and other conniving on "Dallas" would seem to be the opposite extreme. In this light, it is interesting to note the great popularity of such shows which arose very fast as a genre with the onset and subsequent success of "Dallas" in the early 1980s. Perhaps the prime-time audience was wearying of solidarity.

Although night-time soaps may provide a useful balance to the solidarity shows, it is interesting and somewhat troubling to note that it is "Dallas" and "Dynasty," more often than "Family Ties" or "Growing Pains," that are most typically exported around the world as representatives of America. Even in the United States it is worth considering whether or not television is presenting realistic portrayals of families and the workplace and what the effects of these portrayals is. One set of values of the most concern in regard to soap operas involves sexual values.

SEXUAL VALUES

One of the most value-laden and emotional aspects of human life is sexuality, yet it is one of the most frequent themes on television, advertising, and many magazines. Although Chapter 10 later will deal with effects of sex in the media, let us turn now to some value-oriented issues in this area.

Media Portrayal of Adultery

In television and movies adultery is a frequent topic (The 9200 scenes of suggested sexual intercourse shown each year on TV occur six times as often outside of marriage as inside). Depending on the situation, it may be treated farcically or seriously. If treated seriously, it may carry the implicit message that adultery is okay, or at least doesn't have terribly serious consequences, or it may convey the message that adultery has serious repercussions for all concerned.

The first shows that come to mind are the soap operas, both daytime and nighttime variety. Adultery is a frequent theme, even an accepted way of life for many of the characters (Hardaway, 1979). In terms of values, both approval and condemnation come through at different times. A sympathetic character like Sue Ellen Ewing "trapped" in an unhappy marriage uses an affair for a relatively healthy outlet for her needs. On the other hand, sometimes the resulting pain and hurt of adultery are dealt with in the plot line as well.

What is the perceived reality from viewing such shows? In a study of cultivation effects of soap-opera viewing by college students, Buerkel-Rothfuss and Mayes (1981) found that heavy viewing of soap operas was positively correlated with higher estimates of the percentages of people having affairs, divorces, abortions, and illegitimate children, although it was unrelated to their perception of how many people were happily married. Later research using a uses and gratifications approach noted that the motives and purposes of viewing must also be considered (Carveth & Alexander, 1985; Greenberg, et al., 1982; Perse, 1986). The perceived reality constructed from such shows apparently depends not only on the program content but also on the viewer's motives and uses.

AIDS Education and Birth-Control Advertising

Although we accept great amounts of implied or semi-explicit sex on TV, at least until the AIDS scare of the late 1980s, birth control ads were still seen as too controversial for most U.S. network television, though such ads appeared regularly in print media (Kalter, 1985). It is as if the action of having sex is acceptable if done in a passionate moment, but that planning for it is somehow unseemly; this is a potentially dangerous reality that may be perceived. Kalter points out that the teen pregnancy rate is far higher in the United States than in any other industrialized country, and that such rates elsewhere have fallen dramatically after media campaigns, which included birth control announcements on TV. It is an interesting paradox that all sorts of nonmarital sex, much of which would clearly be against the personal values of most Americans, was not seen as inappropriate for story content, but that birth control, which is consistent in value and practice with most Americans, was seen to be unacceptable in advertising.

The spread of the deadly disease AIDS brought changes, however. As AIDS spread beyond the gay and drug cultures in the mid-1980s, the general population in many countries became concerned and even alarmed. The introduction of AIDS education in the schools suggests that fear of AIDS (and death) was gradually becoming stronger than fear of exposing children to sexual information. In terms of media, the advertising of condoms became a hot issue. Although long advertised in magazines in the United States and broadcast media in many European countries, networks and TV stations, at least until 1987, seldom aired condom ads on television, for fear the public would not accept them as appropriate. In spite of occasional earlier calls for birth control ads to be run on shows that seem to feature particularly active libidos (Kalter, 1985), it took the AIDS scare to give some the courage to plug condoms.

RELIGION

Perhaps no topic is so intimately tied up with values as is religion. Gallup polls show the United States to be the most religious industrialized country in the world (90% of Americans believe in God; 41% attend religious services weekly), yet religion has often a more taboo topic than sex, in regard to media. Religion often becomes invisible on television, or rather invisible except for the overtly religious programming, which is most typically viewed by those already of that faith.

Religion in TV Series

Religion apparently plays no part at all in the lives of sitcom and series characters. Even very traditional familes like the Huxtables or the Keatons hardly ever mention going to church or believing in God.

They also, however, do not mention that they *don't* go to church or *don't* believe in God. It appears that producers are reluctant to offend anyone by identifying their favorite TV family with a particular faith or with saying that they have none. At least one prominent theologian has suggested that religious themes could be integrated into sitcoms in tasteful and non-offensive ways (Marty, 1983). Action–Adventure shows have no mention of religion, with an occasional exception of having a crazed religious fanatic character as a villain. This absence of religious themes probably reflects (a) TV producers' relative lack of involvement with religion themselves, compared to most Americans, and, (b) an implicit recognition that it is a very touchy subject and one in which people are easily offended. Perhaps they fear that Protestants and Jews will stop watching "Family Ties" if the Keatons are identified as Catholic or that atheists and agnostics will lose interest in "Murder, She Wrote" if Jessica Fletcher were a Presbyterian.

Adherents to religions other than Christianity are as a whole seldom seen but are often stereotyped when they are present. Jews may be stereotyped by name, occupation, and perhaps a particularly grating New York dialect. In the news they seem to appear especially in stories about the Holocaust, particularly as protesting against something they view as disrespectful to Holocaust victims, such as President Reagan's visit to a Nazi cemetery or Austrian President Waldheim's audience with the Pope. Muslims appear as bomb-throwing terrorists or arrogant oil sheiks, with limousines and harems in tow. Members of some Eastern religions appear as airhead airport panhandlers or ascetic navel-gazers.

Religious Professionals

Except for the explicitly religious programming like Billy Graham crusades or programs on the Christian Broadcasting Network, religious professionals are greatly underrepresented on American television. When they do occur, they are often at best rather saintly but very shallow, even insipid, characters, and at worst vicious hypocrites hiding behind their clerical collars. Perhaps the most rounded and developed religious character of long-running American prime-time TV history is *MASH*'s Father Mulcahy. Compared to the cardboard clergy who make occasional cameo appearances on other shows, Mulcahy is interesting and complex, yet compared to practically every other character on *MASH*, he is rather shallow.

A more insidious religious type is the fanatical cult preacher, a religious fanatic of the James Jones mold. These characters are very extreme and very evil. Such characters have to be very perverted so as not to evoke any sympathy or any criticisms about the program saying negative things about a real "Man of God."

Religious News

Although overall religious news has traditionally been under-reported, relative to its importance, in what *is* reported, however, there are some interesting trends.

Religious news that is centered around an individual person receives relatively heavy coverage, following the "star" model of political news coverage. Travels and pronouncements of the pope, for example, are rather easy and predictable to cover, much more so than comparably important Protestant or Jewish happenings that are less focused on a particular person. One exception to this is a flamboyant TV preacher, particularly one with extreme views. Fundamentalist sects and bizarre cults receive more coverage than mainstream religion, because they are more often focused in a charismatic individual with controversial views.

When religious events are covered by TV news, they tend most often to focus either on Roman Catholicism, whose colorful pageantry and identifiable newsmakers (especially the pope) make good photographable copy, or on Protestant fundamentalism, whose dogmatic theology and contentious political activism make good controversy-ridden stories, especially when centered around a colorful individual like Jerry Falwell. Groups of mainline Protestants politely discussing multiple points of view on social welfare or Jews examining different degrees of support for Israel may be just as important but less telegenically newsworthy.

Some changes in religious news reporting occurred starting in 1987 with several key events. Early that year Oral Roberts announced that God had told him He would "call Oral home" if several million dollars were not donated to his Tulsa ministry and hospital before a certain date. The subsequent revelation that popular TV evangelist Jim Bakker had had a sexual liaison with a secretary was sharply at odds with the pious image he and other televangelists sought to portray. This was followed by discoveries of financial mishandling of Bakker's PTL Ministries funds and extravagant lifestyles by Bakker and his wife Tammy. Such items as an air-conditioned doghouse were auctioned at a public sale to raise money to pay off PTL debts. Subsequent public name-calling among evangelists Jim Bakker, Jerry Falwell, Jimmy Swaggart, and others had more the character of the family feuds on "Dallas" or "Dynasty" than what people had come to expect from the electronic pulpits. Unlike many earlier religious stories, these were widely reported in the media and widely ridiculed by comedians. Johnny Carson, "Saturday Night Live," and most other comics for months spewed forth Jim Bakker sex jokes and Tammy Bakker mascara jokes.

The media apparently decided in this case that comedy about religion, even scathing and derisive comedy, was acceptable to the public. Such public criticism of religious leaders was almost unprecedented, however. When evangelist Jimmy Swaggart's sexual escapades were revealed in 1988, he too came in for heavy, even smug, criticism from the press. The classic theme of the fall of the sanctimonious and mighty was an appealing one, so appealing that even very unsympathetic critics of the TV evangelists raised concerns they were being treated unfairly by the media (e.g., Greeley, 1988).

Religious Television

In the United States, although not many other places, religious programming is a multimillion dollar business. It is, however, produced and distributed separately from other television. This is consistent with the separation of religion from other aspects of American life. Religious books are sold in separate bookstores from secular books, religious music is typically recorded by different artists and marketed separately from other music, and religious television is produced by religious networks. There is some evidence of international growth of TV evangelism, especially in Latin America (Assman, 1987a,b). The TV evangelism scandals of 1987–88 became watershed events in the history of religious broadcasting. It seemed to confirm what critics of televangelism had been saying for some time but now allowed them to say much more publicly. Fundraising for all TV ministries, even those uninvolved in scandal, became more difficult. The media reality of the tainted preacher, long suspected by many skeptics, became the perceived reality for many.

Effects of TV on Religion

It may be that the mere presence of television as a medium has altered all religion in subtle but profound ways, so much that the perceived reality about religion will never be the same again. In a provocative 1985 book, *Amusing Ourselves to Death,* Neil Postman argued that television has radically reshaped practically everything about our

lives. One domain that has been greatly changed is religion, in ways
that go far beyond the Sunday broadcasts and the TV evangelists.
Postman argues that, because TV is entertainment, then the preacher
is the star performer, and "God comes out as second banana."
Although Christianity has always been a "demanding and serious
religion," its TV version can acquire its needed share of the audience
"only by offering people something they want." This is hardly historical Christianity. Further, Postman argues, TV is such a pre-
dominately secular medium that religious TV uses many of the same
symbols and formats (e.g., "700 Club" modelled after "Entertainment
Tonight").

Thus TV preachers are "stars" who are attractive and affluent just
like movie stars. Worship on TV is not participatory, as the audience
can sit at home and absorb but cannot have the corporate worship
experience of group singing, praying, or liturgy. Although a church
may be considered "holy ground" where people act with more rever-
ence, there is nothing comparable when one is sitting at home watching church on TV. Finally, Postman argues, as more and more
religious services are broadcast on TV and pastors are more ac-
quainted with the television medium, the "danger is not that religion
has become the content of television shows but that television shows
may become the content of religion" (p. 124).

Pastors become concerned about providing the kind of worship
conducive to television, even if the service is not being televised.
Congregations subtly expect to be "entertained," even "amused."
Places of worship have no particular sacred character, because one
can worship through TV while at home. One church worships regularly in a former roller rink, whereas another rents space Sunday
mornings in a large university classroom. There is no sense of the
sacred as was found in the magnificent Gothic and Renaissance
cathedrals of Europe.

CONCLUSION

In this chapter we have examined several issues in regard to values
and the media. Questions of what is right and what is wrong provide
different answers over time, but those questions are always there. As
influential as television is in our lives, it becomes an obvious source to
turn to for guidance on moral and ethical issues. How do our role
models act? Is what we are taught "right?" What are possible consequences of moral positions taken? How can television socialize values?

Returning to the question addressed early in the chapter, do media merely reflect the values of society, or do they serve as a catalyst for changing those values? Clearly, they do in some sense mirror somebody's values, but that somebody may hardly be a typically media consumer. More importantly, they can and do serve as a catalyst for change. How this change occurs is of great importance but is far more difficult to study. The same processes discussed in earlier chapters, by which we respond to media and construct a world based on its teachings also apply to values.

The cultivation theory approach of Gerbner and his colleagues may be particularly relevant here (e.g., Gerbner et al., 1986). TV and other media cultivate a system of values through the interaction of the viewer and the content presented. The social reality presented in media gradually becomes the reality for the public (see Chapter 9 for a more thorough discussion of cultivation theory).

Mechanisms of reinforcement, modelling, disinhibition, and classical conditioning are also at work. For example, some values held by the viewer are reinforced more than others. Certain values and those holding them are associated with very positive or negative stimuli and thus may be classically conditioned. Watching a trusted model hold certain values and act on them may disinhibit contradictory values held by the viewer. More and better research on the ways that media teach values is desperately needed to further elucidate these issues.

Sports

The 1960 World Series was a formative epic event in the life of every child growing up in Pittsburgh at that time. The Pirates had not won a pennant in over 30 years, and they faced the mighty and powerful New York Yankees. After six games of the best-of-seven series, it was 3–3. We had won three close ones and lost three lopsided contests (10–0, 16–3, and 12–0). The schools gave up on classes the afternoon of that last game and broadcast the radio play-by-play over the P.A. system. My parents were given a pair of tickets, and my model-student sister decided she was so sick she had to stay home alone to watch the game on T.V. The Pirates won in the final minutes, but not before Mom truly feared Dad was having a heart attack from excitement. That night the city went wild with celebration until highways had to be blocked to limit the number of revelers. On the NBC evening news, the result was reported as a final footnote, with Chet Huntley giving only the score and a misprounciation of hero Bill Mazeroski's name. Maybe the whole world really didn't care.

Media sports are a part of the consciousness of everyone today, even if they have no interest in sports themselves. Events like the Super Bowl and the Olympics become cultural phenomena that touch the lives of people far beyond those regular TV sports fans. The media, particularly television, are the way we learn about sports. Our perceived reality about particular sports is heavily a media creation. In the case of sports not played locally, media may be the only source of information. The marriage of sports and television is so commonplace and taken for granted today that it is easy to overlook the enormous influence that television and other media have had on the games themselves.

This chapter will begin with a bit of historical perspective of media and sports. Next we will look at the influence of media, especially television, on the games themselves. Finally, we will examine several psychological issues related to sport (e.g., competition, hero worship) and see how media have become formative influences in our perceived reality about sport and playing sports.

HISTORY OF SPORTS IN MEDIA

To fully understand the perceived reality of sports and the role media play in the construction of that reality, some familiarity with the history of sports and media is essential. This relationship is not a new one, and it is one that has evolved in often strange and unexpected ways.

Sports in Print

In spite of the recent profound effect of television on sports, the marriage of athletics and the media is not a new relationship. The first sports story in an American newspaper appeared in 1733, when the *Boston Gazette* reprinted a British press story on a boxing match in England. The first British sports publication appeared in 1801, followed by the first U.S. sports periodical in 1819. Oddly titled *The American Farmer,* it included primarily results of hunting, fishing, shooting, and bicycling matches, plus some essays on the philosophy of sport. *The Spirit of the Times* began publishing in 1831 and featured a sort of classified ad program, whereby one sportsman could contact others to issue public challenges for boxing or racing. American newspapers began regular reporting of sporting events in the 1850s, especially cricket and horse racing, followed by baseball in the 1860s, when Henry Chadwick invented the box score and the batting average, thus allowing fans to compare present and past performance much more easily (Rader, 1984). Reports of early horse and yacht races were sent over the telegraph.

By 1890 most major daily newspapers had established sports departments. The first play-by-play reporting appeared in 1889, when the *New York Sun* devoted three columns to coverage of the Harvard-Princeton football game (Loy, McPherson, & Kenyon, 1978). In the 1920s large dailies began to sponsor sports promotions like the Chicago *Tribune's* Golden Gloves boxing program. There was even a poetic period in the early twentieth century, particularly exemplified by Grantland Rice, who wrote of Notre Dame's 1924 defeat of Army, "Outlined against a blue-grey October sky, the Four Horsemen rode again . . ." (Rader, 1984, p. 21). Other sportswriters of the period were busy inventing colorful nicknames of heroes like "The Sultan of Swat" for Babe Ruth. Sports myths were even being developed, such as the baseball origin myth (see Box 6.1). Sports journalism has continued to occupy a strategic place in print media. The sports pages are, at least by males, the most widely read sections of newspapers.

Sports Illustrated, with circulation in the millions, has been a top-circulation magazine for decades since its 1954 inception. Many newer and more specialized magazines fulfill interest in particular sports. On the whole, readership of sports magazines tends to be heavily male (87% for *Sports Illustrated*, according to Guttman, 1986) and disproportionately middle-class and well-educated, although this varies greatly according to the sport.

Sports on Radio and TV

With the advent of broadcasting new horizons were opened to sports reporting. Baseball games were broadcast on radio almost from its inception. The Dempsey-Carpentier fight was broadcast from Jersey City in July 1921. A month later pioneer Pittsburgh radio station KDKA broadcast a Pirates–Phillies game live. The first regular play-by-play season programming of baseball and football was in place by 1925, although for some years it was primarily the World Series that was carried play by play. Some apparently live play-by-play broadcast as late as the 1950s were in fact "re-creations" by a local sportscaster reading Morse code transcriptions over the telegraph and ad-libbing a commentary about the far-off game, such as Des Moines station

WHO's Ronald "Dutch" Reagan's re-creations of the Chicago Cubs' games.

The first sporting event to be telecast were the Berlin Olympics of 1936, which were broadcast to 150,000 people around Berlin. The first TV sports in the United States came in 1939, with the broadcast in the New York area of a Columbia–Princeton baseball game and the Lou Nova–Max Baer boxing match, sent live to the approximately 200 TV sets in greater New York (Guttman, 1986). Widespread TV ownership had to wait, however, until after World War II. Early television technology was such that only sports with a small and fixed arena of action worked well on television. Boxing and wrestling thrived on 1940s and 1950s TV, while baseball and football became far more popular with the advent of technology allowing multiple cameras, zooming, panning, and instant replays.

Regular television broadcast of sports has grown steadily since the 1950s, until sports in the mid-1980s occupied around 15% of the total programming on commercial television. Audiences for major sporting events are huge, and television has become an integral part of the financing of most professional sports as well as amateur sports such as the Olympics, regularly seen by over a billion people, 20–25% of the population of the entire planet! Although such American classics as the World Series and the Super Bowl are seen by millions, even these events are eclipsed by the billion or so people that see the quadrennial World Cup soccer championships.

Although sports have been on television almost since its inception, TV was relatively uninportant to sports before the late 1950s, when professional teams began to see television as a potentially lucrative source of revenue. This revenue source was considerably more stable with greater potential for increase than ticket sales and other more traditional sources. Traditionally broadcast on weekend afternoons, TV sports offered a chance to greatly increase the audience at traditionally low-viewing times. However, the great popularity of sports has led to prime-time broadcasting of games as well, most notably ABC's "Monday Night Football," the many evening baseball games, and the Olympics. Over the years the television audience has become considerably more important than the stadium spectators, and sports have been changed much more to adapt to the needs and desires of TV and its viewers than to the fans in the stadium. For economic reasons the perceived reality of the TV audience has come to be more important than the reality perceived by the fans in the stadium (Powers, 1984).

In spite of the rampant growth of sports and television, there does seem to be a saturation point. This is perhaps most dramatically illustrated by the spectacular failure of the United States Football League in the early 1980s, formed in part in response to the apparently limitless reservoir of fans for the NFL. There are also signs of tedium and lower-than-expected ratings as division playoffs and tournaments seem to extend the season of different sports longer and longer. People often tire of baseball by late October or basketball and hockey still going on in summer.

Social Changes Affecting Sports and Media

Exodus to the suburbs.   Although television profoundly affected sports in its early years, there were other profound social changes occurring during that time as well. In the post-World-War II years, unparalleled economic prosperity fueled a building boom and a mass migration from the inner cities to the new suburban areas. The suburbs were far more dependent on the automobile, and the shift from public transportation to cars was on. Before long this led to construction of better highways and freeways and decline and loss of public transportation. With all of this change came a privatization of leisure. As more people owned their own homes, with more space inside and lovely yards outside, their recreation and leisure time was increasingly centered around the home, or at most the neighborhood. One major activity of this home-based leisure was watching television. No longer did one have to ride the trolley to the theater to watch a movie; similar entertainment was available for free and more conveniently from television. The same was true for watching sports. The fact that most of the ballparks were ancient edifices in decaying and dangerous parts of town with little parking and few modern conveniences did nothing to stem this tide of change. The rise of auto racing as a local spectator sport and softball as a participant sport also competed with baseball.

Class differences.   There are noticeable class differences in the popularity of TV sports. Certain sports like wrestling or boxing are notoriously low-class, while others like bowling may be low-class to watch but not necessarily to play. More subtle differences include football fans being slightly higher class overall than baseball fans. Such differences take on great importance when it comes to marketing the products in the commercials. A higher-income audience allows the producer to command higher ad fees than a comparable-size audience of lower income. Professional football telecasts offer the highest percentage of middle- to upper-middle-class males in the audience. This has obvious and significant advertising ramifications.

Now let's look at how media, primarily television, have changed the nature of the games themselves. They will never be the same again.

HOW TV HAS CHANGED SPORTS

Probably the biggest change in sports thanks to TV is simply the fact that many more people participate in many more sports than they used to, following exposure to these sports on TV. Team owners' early fears that radio (and later TV) would keep people from attending games in person proved temporary at worst. The potential financial bonanza from selling TV rights was only gradually appreciated.

The New Look of Games

Television has changed sports in myriad of ways. There is much more color in sports than there used to be. Before TV, tennis balls were always white; the so-called "optic yellow" really should be called "TV yellow." For centuries a sport of the elite, tennis was brought to the masses by television coverage of major tournaments. Before TV, football stadiums less often had colorful sections in the end zones. Female cheerleaders, even chorus lines of precision marchers, replaced the pre-World War II male "yell captains" at college football games. The increasing number of domed stadiums has lessened the number of boring rain delays that interfere with TV programming. Computer technology has allowed for lively and colorful scoreboards that play well on television. Hockey changed the center line from a solid to a broken line to show up better on television.

In several cases there have been rule and practice changes to accommodate television. Golf changed from match to medal or stroke play to help insure big-name golfers in the final stages (i.e., most televised and watched time) of PGA tournaments. Tennis introduced the sudden-death tiebreaker in the early 1970s to avoid long, nontelegenic deuce games. The National Football League reduced its halftime on some games to allow a better fit into a 2.5-hour slot.

The technical advances in broadcasting have affected sports. One of the most dramatic is the instant replay, the first of which occurred in 1963. The same play can be seen over and over at different speeds, from different camera angles. In the mid-1980s some pro leagues were experimenting with allowing instant replays to possibly change referees' decisions. Advances in editing allow the editing and delayed broadcast of long events with interpretation added and uninteresting sections deleted; such techniques have been used especially effectively with TV coverage of the Olympics. The growth of cable and satellite technology have greatly increased the available hours of sports programming, most notably, though not exclusively, through the founding of the USA network in 1975 and ESPN in 1979, although both networks later expanded to include some nonsports programming.

Some sports are much better suited to commercial television than others. Baseball with its many half-inning divisions is a natural for commercial breaks. Football and basketball have fewer structured breaks, but the frequent time-outs and foul calls help some. The continuous action and low scoring of hockey and especially soccer make them relatively poor TV sports. Some have suggested this to be why soccer, by far the most popular spectator sport worldwide, has never caught on in a large way in the United States. Soccer lacks a focus of attention like the pitcher to home plate area in baseball or the opposing lines in football. The ball often flies off in unexpected fashion, making TV closeups worthless. Still, however, this lack of "TV-friendliness" is not an entirely satisfactory explanation, since soccer (often called football) is seen on TV daily in dozens of countries. The quadrennial World Cup series is the most-watched professional sporting event worldwide. Sometimes a bit of the action is not broadcast due to commercial breaks, but there are also increasing experiments with alternatives like windowing, where, for example, we see the game in the middle of the screen and ad around the edges or across the bottom.

Very minor aspects of games may have telegenic importance. Even the size of the ball makes a difference. In this sense, basketball is excellent for TV, whereas golf balls, hockey's tiny puck, and even the baseball are relatively hard to see. Other kinds of "props" like baseball bats, basketball nets, and hockey sticks also add to the visual interest. Certain nonplaying characters like the Dallas Cowboy Cheerleaders or the San Diego Chicken add further to telegenic interest.

In spite of what one might think, some of our most popular sports in terms of attendance are not that popular on television. Two of the top American sports in gate receipts are auto racing and horse racing, yet they are seldom seen by large audiences on TV, except for the very top contests like the Indianapolis 500 and the Big 3 of thoroughbred racing (Kentucky Derby, Preakness, and Belmont Stakes). There are also considerable regional differences in sports interest (See Box 6.2)

BOX 6.2. GEOGRAPHICAL DIFFERENCES IN SPORT

There are huge international differences in what sports are popular, both in terms of participation and TV viewing. The two most popular TV sports in the United States do not command much worldwide interest. Baseball is popular in Japan, the Caribbean, and northern Latin America (about as far south as Venezuela), but it is largely unknown in Europe, Asia, Africa, and most of South America. There are a few occasional exceptions, most notably the professional Italian league, and there are some indications interest in baseball is spreading into Europe and southwest from Japan into east Asia. Football is popular in the United States and Canada but practically nowhere else, though its name "football" is often used for soccer ("American football" for the U.S. variety). Some recent efforts to export it to Western Europe are having mixed success. Bicycling as a major sport is immensely popular in France and Italy; the fact that an American won the Tour de France in 1986 was completely unprecedented, and in some quarters unappreciated. In Britain and some Commonwealth countries (but nowhere else) cricket is popular. Bullfighting is popular on the Iberian peninsula and northern Latin America but nonexistent elsewhere.

Even within the United States and Canada there are considerable regional differences in sports preferences. Throughout Canada and the extreme northern United States hockey is often the major sport, far eclipsing football and basketball in quality and popularity at schools like the University of Maine and the University of North Dakota. Though college football is popular all over the United States, it is even more so in the Midwest and mid-South. Similarly, basketball is most popular on the mid-Atlantic coast generally and especially in the state of Indiana, which begins interscholastic competition in elementary school and draws college recruiters from all over the country. Women's field hockey is popular in the Northeast, as is jai alai in south Florida. Obviously, winter sports like ice skating and snow skiing are more popular in colder climates

Institutional Changes

There have been some structural changes in the institution of sport. One of the most dramatic examples is baseball. The 59 minor leagues of several different classes after World War II were down to about 15 thirty years later. The chance to see major league baseball on television all over the country has largely destroyed the appeal (and thus financial viability) of the minor leagues. A parallel development occurred with the soccer leagues in Great Britain after the onset of TV. Even the attendance at American pro football and major league baseball was at first cut by regular TV ("blacking out" in home areas moderated this trend somewhat), but the huge financial bonanza of selling TV rights ultimately far more than compensated, eventually even increasing stadium attendance through the interest generated from seeing the games on television. The old American Football League (AFL) was saved from bankruptcy in 1964 by NBC's offer of $42 million for a 5-year TV contract (Guttman, 1986).

Now let's look at several specific sports to further examine the effects of television coverage on the sport itself.

College Football

In college football, the NCAA severely restricted the TV broadcast of games in the 1950s, in spite of occasional disgruntled schools and legal challenges on antitrust grounds. With the advent of very "big bucks" contracts in the early 1960s, far more games appeared on television, though this primarily enriched the few very strong teams and conferences and weakened many others. This trend was accentuated by the post-season Bowl games, which sold TV rights for multi-million contracts back as far as the early 1960s. By 1983 the Rose Bowl sold TV rights for $7 million, while even "minor" bowls like Gator, Bluebonnet, and Liberty earned half a million or so each (Rader, 1984). Power conferences like the Big Ten, Big Eight, Southeastern, and Pacific Ten increasingly depended on Bowl appearances to recruit strong talent and Bowl receipts to finance their programs.

The style of play also changed. A new, more wide-open offense and an increasing number of plays per game (more passes, scoring, rushing, and receiving in the 1960s than any time previously) made the game more exciting to watch on TV. More complicated strategies like the "I" and triple-option formations or Oklahoma's famed wishbone added to the fan appeal, especially as technical advances allowed the camera to follow them adequately. Although TV has brought big-time college football into the lives of many who never would have attended a game, it has been at the cost of heavily, even crassly, commercializing the football programs of the major schools, effectively leaving them amateurs in name only. It has also drawn a large TV audience in part at the expense of small college and high school football, whose supporters often prefer to watch Oklahoma vs. Nebraska on TV instead of attend a local game in person.

Pro Football

Although college football had been around and popular since the 19th century, pro football was only an athletic footnote on the American sports scene before the age of television. The National Football

League was formed in 1920 by a group of mostly Ohio teams meeting in a Hupmobile auto showroom in Canton, Ohio. When Pete Rozelle became NFL commissioner in 1960, the entire staff consisted of "two guys and an 80-year-old Kelly girl" (Rader, 1984, p. 83); by 1984 the same headquarters occupied five entire floors of a Park Avenue skyscraper. Pro football learned how to deal with television more adeptly and in a more unified fashion than did baseball. NFL commissioners Bert Bell and later Pete Rozelle negotiated craftily and with the support of the owners, using local blackouts often enough to preserve stadium audiences but not so often as to engender fan resentment. The closeup focus of television, coupled with interpretation by the sportscaster, served to make a previously opaque and uninteresting game fascinating to large numbers of new fans, who now were able to follow what was happening with the ball.

One of the most brilliantly marketed ongoing media events has been the Super Bowl, beginning in January 1967 after the merger of the NFL and AFL the year before. By the early 1970s the Super Bowl overtook the World Series and the Kentucky Derby in audience size. Unlike these other events, the Super Bowl was a creation of television, not a pre-existent institution adapted to the new medium. "Super Bowl Sunday" practically became an annual holiday, complete with ebullient media hoopla weeks in advance. The games themselves were frequently watched in over half the households of the United States, in spite of a string of very uneven and unexciting games for many of those years. The broadcast in itself became the event; what happened in the game was almost irrelevant. By the 1980s major advertisers paying top dollar for ad time launched new ad campaigns with commercials presented for the first time during the game; this "new advertising season" became a significant media event in itself. Networks alternated the privilege of broadcasting the game. A whole serious of satellite events sprang up, from numerous televised parties and pre- and post-game specials to a truly atrocious (but nonetheless popular) music video made by the Chicago Bears in 1986.

The Olympics

Two immensely important sporting events, in terms of their TV impact, are the quadrennial Summer and Winter Olympics. Although these games have occurred in modern times since 1896, the interest in them has soared exponentially since their broadcast on television worldwide. Although the initial World Cup TV rights were given away in Bern, Switzerland in order to get free publicity, Olympic committees have been selling broadcast rights ever since the 1960 Rome games, with ABC paying a record $309 million for the rights to televise the Winter Olympics from Calgary in 1988 (up from $92 million for Sarajevo in 1984). This was an overextension, however, as ABC lost $65 million on the project. The 1992 Winter Olympics TV rights went to CBS for a mere $243 million, without even an opposing bid from ABC (*Time*, 1988)! The Olympics have become totally dependent on television financially, a status which gives them a "professional" character they never had before (Seifart, 1984).

Due to the traditionally amateur status of the Olympics, however, TV has popularized sports that have not traditionally been high-revenue sports. Most notable here have been all women's sports, which have received a tremendous boost from Olympic coverage. Certain sports which have little audience elsewhere are very popular in the Olympics (e.g., gymnastics and ice skating). In such "minor sports" television serves an important education function; people learn about new sports from watching the Olympics. Sometimes this translates into their own participation in these activites. As sports does so predictably, the Olympics have produced many heroes and heroines, including Mark Spitz, Olga Korbut, Nadia Comaneci, Carl Lewis, Greg Louganis, Jackie Joyner-Kersee, Eric Heiden, Brian Boitano, Bruce Jenner, and Mary Lou Retton. Olympic stars, through the catalyst of TV, can be catapulted to athletic or show business stardom, to say nothing of economic well-being.

Sometimes the commercial pressure to pay back the enormous cost of the broadcasting rights may lead to less than quality television. For instance, according one count the 1988 Winter Olympics ran about 20 minutes per hour of commercials (Stewart, 1988). Not only was the total ad time unusually high but the placement was often poor. Hockey goals were scored during commercials. The announcement of the scores for medal-winning figure skaters Gordeeva and Grinkov occurred during an ad aired immediately after their performance. Rights to televise the Olympics are a valued plum for a network but one that viewers expect to be done in a high-quality fashion.

Synthetic Sports

Another product of the marriage of television and sports was what has come to be called "synthetic sports" or "trashsports." One type, frequently broadcast on ABC's "Wide World of Sports," runs the gamut from cliff diving at Acapulco or national logrolling championships to a rattlesnake hunt in Keane, Oklahoma or national wrist-wrestling championships in Petaluma, California. Audiences enjoyed the "World Buffalo Chip-Tossing Contest" and the "Joe Garagiola/Bazooka Big League Gum Blowing Championships." These unusual, even bizarre, activities were not necessarily invented for television and were easily and cheaply photographed in advance for use whenever the network needed them. Of course, they varied widely in their audience appeal.

A second kind of trashsports were celebrity contests, usually created entirely as television events. Such programs featured famous athletes or show business personalities participating in some competition outside their own area of expertise, from billiards or golf tournaments to track and field events featuring teams of present or former cast members of different TV shows ("The Brady Bunch" versus "Days of Our Lives"). Because of the parasocial interaction we have with our TV "friends," we will watch them participate in events we would find totally uninteresting in most other circumstances. It is not unlike watching one's own child in a ball game; we are there because of our relationship with one of the participants, not necessarily because of intrinsic interest in the sport itself.

Now we have looked at how the media have affected and changed various sports themselves and the reality about them that we perceive. Next let us turn to examining several psychological factors which are directly affected by the perceived reality of media sport.

PSYCHOLOGICAL ISSUES IN SPORTS AND MEDIA

Sports Media Consumption as a Social Event

More often than other TV viewing, part of the reality of the experience of sports media consumption involves the presence of others. Friends gather at someone's home or patrons congregate in a bar to watch a big game. Often the game seems more enjoyable in a group than it would be watching alone, with the presence of others somehow seeming more important than it would watching a movie, a sitcom, or the news. The expression of emotion, discussed below, may be part of the reason. Also, a group watching with you in some sense partially recreates the stadium situation of watching the event in a crowd.

Food and drink. One interesting aspect of this social reality of sports TV viewing is the eating and drinking that accompany the viewing.

People eat and drink more watching sports than watching other events on TV, especially when viewing in groups, but the range of what they consume is fairly narrow. The food is most often junk food, snacks, or perhaps hot dogs, whereas the drink is typically "junk drink," especially soft drinks or beer. In short, we eat and drink the same sort of substances at home that we might consume if we were in attendance at the stadium. It seems somehow odd to have coffee and croissants while watching the Chicago Bears and Green Bay Packers or to savor a fine red wine while watching the heavyweight championship fight.

Competitiveness and Achievement

Obviously one of the major psychological components of sports is the competition and the achievement of victory. Part of the perceived reality of TV sports also involves this desire to win, which is learned early by the fans consuming through the media. Part of the natural socialization process of child development often involves an identification and support for certain sports teams and individuals. Who this will be is often, though not necessarily, determined by geographical considerations. We most often root for the local team, the team of our school, or the team our family has rooted for, perhaps for generations. Still, major teams have fans all over. The hapless Chicago Cubs have supporters who have never been near Wrigley Field, while Roman Catholics throughout North America cheer for Notre Dame's football team.

Patriotism comes into play in international competition. The U.S. hockey upset victory over the Soviet Union in the 1980 Winter Olympics was especially savored in a nation annoyed and frustrated by the Soviet invasion of Afghanistan a few weeks before. The World Cup, with one team per nation, becomes a national competition, during which the business life of certain soccer-happy countries in Western Europe and South America takes a *de facto* holiday. When the Toronto Blue Jays made the American League baseball playoffs in 1985, all Canada celebrated the victory in the U.S.-dominated league. When Jamaican-Canadian Ben Johnson lost his gold medal for failing a drug test at the 1988 Seoul Summer Olympics, Jamaicans and West Indian Canadians cried foul.

There is some evidence of negative behavioral effects of watching aggressive sports. In research studies, fans leaving an Army-Navy football game (Goldstein & Arms, 1971) or wrestling or hockey events

(Arms, Russell, & Sandilands, 1970) scored higher in hostility and aggressiveness than control subjects who had watched a swimming meet. It did not matter if one's team won or lost or if the aggression was stylized (wrestling) rather than spontaneous (hockey). Though these studies have not been replicated with fans who are television spectators, the results are provocative and suggest the presence of aggressiveness may be more important than merely the element of competition.

Sometimes sports competition carries all out of proportion. In 1969 Honduras and El Salvador fought the so-called "soccer war," precipitated by a particularly bitter soccer game. In 1985, 39 people in Brussels died and 450 were injured in a deadly brawl among fans watching a championship soccer game between Liverpool, England, and an Italian team. Such incidents have caused fans to be screened with metal detectors, nations to exchange information on the most violent fans, and heavily armed soldiers to stand guard between the seating for fans of the opposing teams. These security measures have come to be part of the reality of sport.

The reward in sports is generally for winning, with very few kudos or dollars for coming in second, much less third or tenth. With its carrying of so many more sports into so many more lives than knew them before, television has certainly at least indirectly encouraged competitiveness. With the star mindset that focuses on individuals, television lavishes attention and acclaim on the winner, while often virtually ignoring everyone else. This helps construct a reality in viewers that coming in first is what is important. Athletes are not interviewed after the game for "doing their best" or being good sports. Sports metaphors carry over into our speech and thinking in many other areas of life, such as relationships. A fellow goes on a date and "scores" or "strikes out." A woman complains that men see women as "conquests" or "trophies." Someone feels like a "loser" as a parent if their child is not accepted to a prestigious college.

A very different, and subtler, way that competitiveness can manifest itself in the sports viewer is in the accumulation and exhibiting of copious, seemingly endless, sports trivia and statistics. Sportscasters encourage this through their endless recitation of such information during radio and TV broadcasts, in part probably to fill the time where there is no play or commercial to fill what would otherwise be dead air. The computer has only made it even easier to amass and retrieve such figures. Such statistics have become part of the reality of media sports. Even young children seemingly unable to remember much in school may recite voluminous facts about RBI's, passes completed, and shooting percentages.

Teamwork and Cooperation

Probably the major positive value cited for participation in sports is the learning of teamwork and cooperation. Parents most often give such reasons for encouraging their children to become involved in school and community sports. Team sports are indeed excellent ways to learn how to work with others as a team where each member must depend on fellow team members. How do televised sports teach teamwork?

The star versus the team. Some disturbing indications suggest that, in terms of television, less noble values may overshadow the loftier ones. Often the "star mentality" of television and the entertainment business in general affects the presentation of sports in the media. The superstars are exalted and glorified far more than the praising of fine teamwork on the field. Stories about sports tend to focus on the outstanding athlete, much as stories about religion tend to focus on the pope or Jerry Falwell or stories about government tend to focus on the President. This extolling of and emphasis on the individual may subtly undermine the importance of teamwork and cooperation for the viewer, especially the young viewer.

The thrill of the fight. Even more serious is the way that media, especially television, tend to heavily focus on, perhaps even glorify, the occasional brawl or fight on the field. In a sense this is an auxiliary competition to the primary one being played. Although no sportscaster celebrates or even condones a serious tragedy like the Belgian soccer fan deaths, the camera and media attention immediately shift routinely to any fight that breaks out in either the stands or the field. When results of that game are reported on the evening news later, it is more likely to be the brawl, not the play of the game, that is shown on the screen. Even if fighting is clearly condemned by the sportscaster, the mere fact of the heavy coverage of the fight shows it to be important. The perceived reality to the viewer, especially a young one, may be that the winner in the brawl is to be admired as much as the winner in the game itself.

Emotional Benefits

Although there are clear benefits from participating in sports, those benefits are somewhat less clear when it comes to consuming sports through media. Clearly physical health and fitness are not enhanced by watching ball games on TV and may even he hindered if watching prevents the viewers from exercising themselves. Emotionally, the picture is a little less clear. The tension reduction or emotional release called catharsis may result from physical exercise where we release stress through muscular and aerobic exercise. Some psychologists going back to Sigmund Freud argue that catharsis may also be achieved through substitute activities. Whether we achieve this emotional release through watching sports is somewhat debatable, however.

There clearly is often a lot of emotion felt while consuming media sports. Zillmann, Bryant, and Sapolsky (1979) propose a "disposition theory of sportsfanship" to describe such feelings. The enjoyment we experience emotionally from witnessing the success or victory of a competing party (individual or team) increases with the degree of positive sentiments and decreases with the degree of negative sentiments we feel toward that party. The reverse is true for what we experience when we witness a failure or defeat. The more we care about a team's success, the more emotional satisfaction we feel when they do well and the worse we feel when they do badly. Thus it is much harder to get highly emotionally involved, or sometimes even interested at all, in watching a game between two teams we know or care little about.

Still, feelings about the competitors are not the only determinants of emotional response to sports. As with any drama, the degree of perceived conflict is crucial. A game which is close in score and hard-fought in character evokes more emotional reaction, regardless of team loyalty, than one where the final victor is never in doubt or one where the participants appear not to be trying very hard. As with other kinds of drama, the unpredictability and suspense are important (Zillmann, 1980). A close basketball game settled at the final buzzer carries the viewer along emotionally throughout its course. A game whose outcome is known is less likely of interest to watch in its entirety. How many ball games are ever rerun on television? How may people care to watch a videotaped ball game to which they already know the final score? However, a few people may actually prefer the predictable to the uncertain; see Box 6.3.

Sex Roles and Gender Bias

Men's and women's sports.   It is an undisputed fact that male sports are covered much more heavily in the media than female sports. It is also true that attendance at men's events is higher than at women's events.

BOX 6.3.

PERFECTIONISM, PROBABILISM, AND SPORTS FANATICISM

Why are some people rabid sports fans, while others couldn't care less? It doesn't seem to be particularly related to personality, because meek and nonassertive people can be extremely competitive watching sports. The author's personal theory, completely untested, offers a possibility.

Like statistics within mathematics, sports is a very probabilistic venture. One can make all kinds of odds on who will win the game or the race, but they are only that—*odds*. If team A is better on most relevant criteria than team B, it will probably win. Probably, but not necessarily. Once in awhile even the most invincible team is knocked off by a lowly challenger.

On the one hand, this uncertainty is part of what makes sports exciting to watch. On the other hand, uncertainty is handled very poorly by some people, particularly perfectionists. Perfectionists think in all-or-none terms; either they win (succeed) or they are a total failure. Perfectionists like predictability; if one side is objectively better on all relevant criteria, they should win—always. Unlike most people, perfectionists sports fans may prefer a 55–0 shellacking by their football team to a close victory.

More often, perhaps, perfectionists are not that drawn to watching sports at all. It's too unpredictable and it hurts too much when their side doesn't win. It may not be that they don't care. They may care too much.

The nature of the relationship between the two is interesting and complex, however. Is the heavier media coverage of men's sports merely reflecting the reality of greater fan interest in men's sports, for whatever reason, or is the the greater media coverage a cause of greater fan interest in men's sports?

Some major media sports, most notably football and baseball, are male only, without parallel female teams for the media to cover. In other sports, such as pro golf and tennis and college basketball, there are parallel women's teams and competition. Only in tennis and the Olympics does the media coverage of women's competition even approach the attention given the men, however, and both of these cases are fairly unusual in that competition for both sexes occurs in the same structured event (e.g., Wimbledon includes both men's and women's matches). Only in these cases is the perceived reality of sport gender-balanced.

The Olympics are an instructive and somewhat exceptional instance. Generally, the summer and winter games are completely covered by television, often with both live coverage and extended edited excerpts broadcast a few hours later, often at more convenient times. For example, the 1984 Winter Olympics at Sarajevo, Yugoslavia were seen by most North Americans as delayed summarized coverage, instead of live in the middle of the night at United States time. Because of the nature of this coverage, women's events received nearly, if not entirely, as much coverage as men's events. Interest in women's Olympic sports often has been very high, and many women superstars such as Mary Lou Retton, Nadia Comaneci, Jackie Joyner-Kersee, or Dorothy Hamill have become genuine heroes every bit as popular as the men.

Sportscasting and sports reporting is probably the last and most stubborn bastion of male supremacy in the journalism industry. Although female news anchors and reporters, meteorologists, and even editors are increasingly common and accepted, the female sportscaster or sports reporter (covering men's sports) is still highly exceptional. Whether this absence reflects the public's true dislike or distrust of females reporting men's sports or merely an industry fear that such a reaction would occur is unclear. Clearly the issue touches deeper chords than over-publicized superficial issues such as the problem of sending female sportscasters into men's locker rooms for post-game interviews.

Sex-role socialization.   Although not nearly as different as it used to be. boys are still encouraged to participate in sports of all kinds much more than girls are. Less obviously, the same asymmetry applies to media consumption of sports. Boys are encouraged by their parents (usually their fathers) to watch ball games on TV as well as play catch in the yard. Not only the playing of sports but also the watching of sports on TV has become a part of the socialization of being a man in our society. The boy who is not particularly interested in spending his time this way, but whose father is, often receives subtle or not-so-subtle messages that such lack of interest doesn't measure up and perhaps even undermines or calls into question his masculinity. Consuming media sports together has become a part of the reality of many father–son relationships.

One advantage of watching sports for men is that it is probably the one arena where they are most free to express emotion. Men watching a ball game together, somewhat like the players themselves, may relatively freely express feelings and even touch one another. In mainstream Anglo North American society this is practically the only time when most men feel comfortable embracing. Most heterosexual men probably never hug another man in their lives outside the context of playing or watching sports.

In the past, girls were often given messages, especially after reach-

ing puberty, that participation in sport was tomboyish and un-
feminine and could be a serious liability in attracting a man. With the
women's movement this has changed considerably, and girls and
women are now allowed to be both athletic and sexy at the same time.
It is less often considered surprising or inappropriate for women to
watch ball games or to know more about sports than their men,
though TV audiences for most sporting events are still a large majority male.

Hero Worship

Media coverage of sports has enhanced, or at least altered, the perceived reality of the hero. Sports stars have long been heroes emu-
lated by youth, but the age of television, and to a lesser extent other
media, has changed this role somewhat. On the one hand, Mary Lou
Retton or George Brett may be seen by many more people on television than was previously possible. On the other hand, the close scrutiny of television shows up the faults as well as the nobler aspects of a
potential hero.

Children emulate their TV-sports heroes in some very traditional
ways but also in some new ways. A child may imitate Reggie Jackson's
swing but also John McEnroe's temper tantrums. Nor is emulation of
athletes limited to children. Long-time golfers report that play on golf
courses slowed noticeably after the start of televising of major golf
tournaments. This occurred primarily because amateur golfers
started lining up their putts and other behaviors they saw the pros do
on TV, no matter that the amateur may not have understood what he
or she was doing or looking for when lining up that putt.

One particular area of concern in regard to hero worship has been
the use of drugs by sports stars and resulting effects on youth. The
widespread cocaine use in the 1980s by baseball and basketball stars
seemed somehow worse than such use by other citizens, even by other
public figures, since sports figures are heroes to youth. This has
caused persons and institutions like the Commissioner of Baseball,
the National Collegiate Athletic Association (NCAA), and the National Basketball Association (NBA) to be tougher on drug users among
their athletes than they might otherwise be. The hero status is often
used more directly to discourage drug use, as when "Magic" Johnson
is hired to do an antidrug testimonial PSA.

Another fringe benefit of hero status is lucrative product endorsement contracts for the major stars. For Olympic athletes this is often
the critical part of their financial support allowing them to pursue

their "amateur" career. For wealthy professional athletes it is more the icing on the already rich cake. These endorsement campaigns lead to an even greater media presence, as that person becomes familiar as a spokesperson in advertising for that product. Sometimes a single individual may endorse several different products in different classes. In the months following the 1984 Olympics comedians had a field day with jokes about the omnipresent smile of Mary Lou Retton endorsing a large number of products. Overexposure was a definite concern.

Another aspect of emulating athletic heroes is seen in the area of fashion. Thanks to the influence of television, we not only want to act like the stars but want to dress like them as well. Dress of different sports becomes chic at different times and places. Jogging clothes became high fashion, not only for nonjogging adults but even for infants who cannot even walk! Clothing manufacturers make large sums selling high-fashion clothes for tennis, skiing, or even bicycling to folks who have never played those sports and have no intention of ever doing so.

In spite of television's enhancement of sports heroes, some (e.g., Rader, 1984) argue that today's sports heroes are not on the pedestal of past stars like Willie Mays, Johnny Unitas, Jesse Owens, or Stan Musial. The huge salaries and high living seem to separate such persons from ourselves and stress their narcissistic and hedonistic tendencies rather than the righteous and humble characteristics we at least used to like to think our heroes possessed. The intrusive eye of television focuses on a ballplayer not only when he makes that glorious play but also when he is petulantly fuming on the sidelines or selfishly proclaiming he cannot make ends meet on half a million a year. No matter that all of us have our selfish and petulant moments; we like to think that true heroes do not, and the age of television makes it harder to maintain that fiction.

CONCLUSION

Media reporting ball games are doing more than reflecting the reality of that game. Television has changed the very sports themselves. Television has also changed the way that our minds consider these sports. TV sports is a world all its own, a world only imperfectly related to the world of real sports in the stadiums and the racetracks. Today when people think of sports, they are most likely to think first of watching television. The perceived reality of sports acquired through television is thus what sports are, for most people. Just as media are our knowledge source about groups of people, social values, or products for sale, so do they tell us about sports and what we should learn from sports.

News

Vivid childhood memories of mine are associated with news broadcasts. As our family watched the TV news report of Sputnik in 1957, Dad commented that this was as profound a development as the European discovery of America by Columbus . . . The high school informed us in 1962 that they would announce over the P.A.system if a war started during the Cuban missile crisis . . . Seven years later on a Sunday afternoon I sat in a roomful of people in a dormitory at the University of Oregon watching Neil Armstrong set foot on the moon . . . In that time of bitter national divisiveness over Vietnam, the whole room spontaneously cheered.

If there is one area of media whose job it is to reflect rather than create reality, it surely must be the news. We turn on the evening news or open the newspaper to find out what actually happened out there in the world that day. Even here, however, the perceived reality may not correspond to the "real world." Though they try to accurately and fairly represent the day's events, producers and editors must select which items to cover, how prominently to cover them, and in what manner to cover them. These choices necessarily involve some *agenda-setting*, that is, telling us what is important (Berelson, 1942; McCombs, 1981). Agenda-setting tells us *what* to think *about*, what is important. It does not necessarily tell us what to think *about* that topic. When the seemingly endless Presidential preference primaries receive massive media coverage, the public receives the implicit message that they are important. What a particular voter's opinion about candidates is or even whether or not he or she agrees that the primaries are so important is another issue. Likewise, when stories receive little cover-

131

age, that communicates a message that they are not important. In extreme authoritarian cases this is carried its farthest. For example, when the White South African government in the mid-1980s prohibited any coverage of unrest in Black townships, it was trying to create a reality where such activity was unimportant, or at least where that was the perceived reality.

Although there is much to be gained from a careful study of the *text* of the news messages themselves (see Van Dijk, 1985 a), a full understanding of the effects of media news requires an examination of the nature of the medium itself, as it transmits news. This is particularly important in regard to television.

News programming is put in an especially tricky position by the economic realities of the mass communications industry. Even though news divisions are separate from entertainment divisions at the U.S. television networks and news clearly has the primary function to inform rather than entertain, the "success" of news is determined by ratings, just as the success of a series is, and that increases the pressure to entertain. Similarly, a newspaper must try to maximize its advertising dollars, usually closely related to number of subscriptions. In deciding what news to include in a publication or broadcast, pressures clearly exist to tell people what they want to hear, in order to keep them coming back.

After some background on television news, this chapter will examine what news is, in a psychological sense, and how the perceived reality about world events is constructed from reading or watching the news reports. The rest of the chapter will examine effects of consuming news, including cognitive, attitudinal, and behavioral effects and even effects on foreign and domestic policy.

THE RISE OF TV NEWS

Although print news journalism has been with us for many years, television news as a medium has its roots in the movie newsreel of the early to mid-20th century. With such news shorts, shown before feature films, the audience experienced an immediacy with world events, even if delayed several weeks, that had never been possible before. This use of visuals to convey the news brought a new power to the media, that of *montage,* the juxtaposition of images for dramatic effect. To a large extent the reporter or editor must reassemble the pieces of the event's reality to best express what he or she perceives as the experienced reality. Montage allows the telling of a news story using many of the dramatic techniques from drama and fiction writing to make the event more compelling and entertaining. This of course opens the door for other elements of fiction to enter as well.

Although news has been on television from its early days, it really did not become a major source of news until the 1960s. The TV coverage of the JFK assassination and subsequent events in 1963 gave a tremendous impetus to TV news with its immediate live coverage. In the next five years, the TV news audience jumped 50%, the sharpest increase ever. By 1977, 62% of all adult Americans watched at least one newscast per weekday, making television the major source of news in the United States. This 62% broke down to 12% network only, 30% local only, and 20% both. These figures point to the great popularity of local news, including weather and sports. Local news shows are extremely crucial for local stations to establish their unique identity in the community, since the large majority of programming is either network-initiated or syndicated reruns, both of which are identical regardless of the station. See Box 7.1 for further discussion of weather reports and reporters.

TV news reporters, especially news anchors, become trusted "friends" in our lives. More than other types of TV, they are a part of our mealtimes, expecially the morning news shows at breakfast and the evening news at dinner. It is almost like Dan Rather or Tom Brokaw as a regular dinner guest. We invite them into our homes through our choice to turn on the TV to the particular channel. It is not unusual for people to audibly respond to a greeting, such as responding "Hi, Tom," back to Brokaw as he signs on with "Good evening." They become substitute friends in what some have called a "parasocial interaction" (Rubin, Perse, & Powell, 1985). There is a sense of solidarity with them. As one person explained, "I grew up watching Walter Cronkite. I guess I expect him to be there when I turn on the news. We've been through a lot together. Men on the moon and things like that" (Levy, 1982, p. 180). That feeling of "being through a lot together" captures very well why news anchors are far more important people in our lives than merely folks who read us the day's events.

Network anchors command high salaries but also high respect. When long-time CBS anchor Walter Cronkite was asked in 1980 if he would be available for a vice-presidential nomination, he made a joking reply. However, his teasing was seen as equivocation and he later had to issue a categorical denial of any political ambitions. Although it may have never occurred to him that any answer to such a question would be taken seriously, by many it was. A few years earlier Cronkite had been deemed the "most trusted man in America" by the polls, ahead of the President, the pope, and movie stars.

BOX 7.1. TV WEATHER FORECASTS: MORE THAN TELLING US IF IT WILL RAIN

Local news anchors, sportscasters, and weathercasters are extremely important to local TV stations in establishing their "signature" and identity in their market. Although a large majority of programming on commercial television is either network or syndication, local news is one of the few programs where a local station has control of all aspects of the programming. A popular team of local broadcasters can bring an extremely helpful ratings boost that greatly raises the visibility of that station in the target market.

A seemingly indispensable part of all local news shows, as well as some national ones, is the weather forecaster. There is even an entire cable channel devoted to weather. Though all U.S. weathercasters use essentially the same data, those gathered by the National Weather Service, clearly not all weathercasts are equal. Some weathercasters, though a minority, actually have training in meteorology, and are always very prominently so labelled. Some are more performers than reporters; NBC's Willard Scott has done the weather dressed in various costumes and always with more pizazz than most. Although Scott is very successful, too much gimmickry may backfire. A Chicago weatherman giving his Thanksgiving forecast to a turkey or the Milwaukee station whose sometime weathercaster years ago was a puppet named Albert the Alleycat would seen unlikely in the 1980s. Weather reports have come a long way from the early days of TV when "Today"'s Dave Garroway phoned the one-man media department at the National Weather Service and repeated to the audience what he was told. The high-quality computer graphics now allow even small local stations to give a weathercast of high technical quality, a far cry from 1950s weatherman Bill Carlsen who squirted his map with shaving cream to show snow! (Garelik, 1985).

Although weathercasts are often seen as the "frivolous" or "soft" side of the news (the first on-the-air newswomen were the "weathergirls" of the late 1950s and early 1960s), often the subject is deadly serious. Forecasts and warnings of tornadoes, hurricanes, and floods can mean the difference of life and death. Although the National Weather Service issues the watches, warnings, and advisories, often the local weathercaster does additional interpretation as to how strongly to advise precaution. A wrong judgment call in such a situation could have tragic consequences.

WHAT IS NEWS?

Jamieson and Campbell (1988, p. 20) defined "hard news" as any "report of an event that happened or was disclosed within the previous 24 hours and treats an issue of ongoing concern." The event itself need not be recent (though usually it is), but it must involve some new revelation or previously unknown connection. Revelations of Kurt Waldheim's Nazi past, a previously unknown Franklin Roosevelt affair, or even the discovery of the shroud allegedly used to wrap Christ's body when taken down from the cross have all been TV news in the mid-1980s.

In contrast to hard news are human interest stories, which touch universal concerns and are less tied to place and time. These features are most prevalent on so-called "slow-news days" and may include anything from a farmer in west Texas who plants 1959 Cadillacs vertically in his field, a bizarre feat celebrated in Bruce Springsteen's "Cadillac Ranch," to the poor Mississippi sharecropper whose nine children have all graduated from college, most with advanced degrees (a favorite Charles Kuralt "On the Road" story).

Qualities of a Newsworthy Event

Jamieson and Campbell (1988) identify five qualities of a newsworthy event. They may not all be present in every story, but no doubt several of them will be for each hard news story. The more of these characteristics a story has naturally, the more likely it is to be heavily covered in the news.

1. The story is personalized, about individuals. This allows audience identification with the person and may make a dauntingly complex event easier to comprehend. It lends itself well to the interview format (e.g., Heritage, 1985), which works well on TV, but it may be at the cost of oversimplifying (and possibly distorting) complex events and overemphasizing "stars" such as the President, other political leaders, the pope, or some extremist spokesperson.

2. A newsworthy event is dramatic and conflict-filled, even violent. We are used to entertainment TV as being dramatic (Zillmann, 1980). Shots of South African police beating demonstrators makes "better copy" for TV news than a debate on apartheid among politicians of different views. With its emphasis on conflict, this helps to insure coverage of opposing views but, on the negative side, may overemphasize the conflict and violent nature of the story. Very infrequent violent events may be assumed by viewers to be the norm. Nonviolent events may be neglected and very important issues not conducive to drama, conflict, or personalization may be grossly underreported. For example, complex economic stories like the Third World debt crisis or rising interest rates in the United States are often covered on TV news only through specific events that reflect those problems.

3. A newsworthy event contains action and some observable occurrence. This often becomes the "hook" on which to hang what is essentially a more abstract story. For example, trends in inflation may be covered by interviews with specific consumers shopping and expressing their views on rising prices. Important stories that do not have such a convenient "hook" or discrete encapsulating event receive less attention. For example, the dramatic shift in the Third World over the last 30 years from domestic-food-producing to export agriculture is a profound and important change, but it is seldom mentioned in the news because it is not easily symbolized by discrete events.

4. An event is more newsworthy if it is novel or deviant. Contrary to popular views, most news is not particularly surprising. For example, much political and economic news is covered by the normal beat reporters who know in advance that certain speeches will be made, votes taken, or meetings held. Events outside this predictable range of news will stand a better chance of being covered if they are novel, with chances of coverage increasing as the events get more strange and bizarre. A junkie being shot to death in New York City is not big news, but a Sunday school teacher killed in a Satanic ritual in rural North Dakota is. Once in a while, merely being bizarre is enough to insure news coverage (e.g., the Cadillac ranch), but in most cases it needs to be related to some prevailing theme, the last characteristic of newsworthy events.

5. Events are more likely to be covered in news if they are linked to issues of ongoing interest in the media. Some of these themes are deep-seated, almost archetypal, at least in the United States. For example, the theme of appearance vs. reality has always been a common theme in literature and drama. News stories about deception and hypocrisy make good copy; Watergate was one of the hottest news stories in U.S. history. The television evangelism scandals and "holy wars" of 1987–88 received heavy media coverage because their reality was revealed to not fit their appearance. Secondly, the "big guys vs. little guys" is a powerful theme, nicely captured by some of the crusading stories on "Sixty Minutes", the most popular prime-time TV news show of all time. Closely related is the good vs, evil theme. Finally, we have the themes of efficiency vs. inefficiency and the unique vs. the routine.

Besides the underlying, archetypal themes we also have cyclical themes such as the quadrennial Presidential elections in the United

States and seasonal, holiday, and weather themes. For example, we know we will see the pope saying midnight mass on Christmas, the report on the groundhog seeing his shadow on February 2, and local news reports of how to protect yourself from tornadoes in the spring. Such events appear in the news because they fit the cyclical themes, in spite of having few of the other characteristics of newsworthy events.

The surest way to obtain coverage of one's activities is to imbue them with these five characteristics. The more of these an event has, the more likely the media will show interest. Being heavy on these characteristics does not necessarily ensure that the event is important or unimportant, but it does ensure that the perceived reality will be as a newsworthy event.

A final consideration determining newsworthiness in the local "hook," the connection of the story to the community of readers, viewers, or listeners. At the local level, a newspaper or station will be much more likely to cover a national or international event if it has a local angle (e.g., local resident caught in uprising in Angola, Mexican economic policy may cause local plant to close). On a national level, the hook in the United States may be a current policy debate in Washington. For example, civil wars in Nicaragua or El Salvador receive attention primarily when there is an upcoming vote in Congress about aid to one of the governments or opposition movements. When U.S. troops invade (or are "invited" into) a country, that receives coverage.

Sometimes the need for a local or national hook can seriously distort reality. For example, any intermittent harassment, censoring, or closing of the independent newspaper *La Prensa* by the Sandinistas in Nicaragua generally received heavy media coverage in the mid-1980s in the United States, while the violent and permanent closing of *El Cronico del Pueblo* and *El Independiente* in U. S. ally El Salvador in 1980 and the 65 journalists killed in the next eight years went basically unreported in the United States. Was this due to a pro-Reagan administration bias in the press? Perhaps, but it also could have resulted naturally from a greater focus on Nicaragua, where U.S. policy on aid to the opposition contras was frequently, and controversially, up for votes in the U.S. Congress. Whatever the intent or the cause, the perceived reality for many was clearly that Sandinista Nicaragua was censoring the press. Although this was true at times to differing degrees, the failure to report worse conditions of the press in U.S. ally El Salvador allowed many to perceive the Reagan administration's painting of that country as a free democracy as reality.

NEWS MEDIA AS CREATING A PERCEIVED REALITY

The very term "media" suggests that mass communication "mediates" between the audience and some objective reality out there in the world. In Western culture, at least, we assumed that such a reality exists. More than with any other aspect of media, we tend to assume that news conveys that objective reality to us in clear and unbiased form. It may occur to us that news writers and producers communicate their interpretation of that world reality both through their choice of topics and amount of coverage (agenda-setting) and by what they actually say about the story in question. News is a "frame that delineates a world" (see Altheide, 1976; Schlesinger, 1978, 1987; Tuchman, 1978). Elie Abel (1981, p. 68) said it well:

> Reality does not come neatly package in 2- or 3-minute lengths; raw history is filled with perversities, contraditions, ragged edges . . . TV is a storytelling medium. It abhors ambiguities, ragged edges, and unresolved issues . . . The effect all too frequently is to impose upon an event or situation a preconceived form that alters reality, heightening one aspect at the expense of another for the sake of a more compelling story, blocking out complications that get in the way of the narrative.

Although choices of media coverage are usually motivated from a sincere desire to present news stories to the public in the most complete and accurate way possible, there are occasional instances when the construction of reality goes beyond the bounds of what most would consider acceptable (see Box 7.2).

Manipulation of News

Sometimes forces inside and outside the government also impinge on journalists in ways that affect the reality of news they create.

Censorship.   In countries with prior censorship, where material must be submitted to government censors for advance approval before being aired, or where the government owns and controls all news media, a very selective piece of reality may be offered, so much so that history may be substantially rewritten. For example, Soviet citizens' view of the United States is very heavily colored by news stories about crime, racism, homelessness, and imperialism that appear in their press. Perhaps very little there is actually false, but one's overall perception is grossly distorted if a true example of some crime is believed to the rule rather than the exception.

More subtle censorship is the rule in many countries. Some nations have official crimes of broadcasting material that is against the state.

In their desire to make, as Bogart (1980) calls it, "an invisible truth visible, dramatic, and entertaining," networks sometimes go too far. In 1966 CBS helped to finance an armed invasion of Haiti in exchange for exclusive TV rights of the event; the invasion was aborted by U.S. customs. The next year a U.S. soldier cut off the ear of a dead Vietcong; it later came out in his court martial that he did it after being offered a knife on a dare by a TV news cameraman (Lewy, 1978). There are numerous accounts of TV news crews arranging for demonstrations or drug parties to be staged again for the cameras if the "original" event did not happen to be timed right for the camera.

News journalists may become newsmakers in more positive ways. For example, Egyptian President Anwar Sadat's historic trip to Israel in 1977 was arranged not by the United Nations or U.S. State Department diplomats but by CBS news anchorman Walter Cronkite. It was Cronkite who persistently called Sadat and Israeli Prime Minister Menahem Begin to arrange their eventual meeting (Weymouth, 1981).

Such vague legislation is used according to the political vagaries of current rulers. Other times the government and large business interests are so close that politically suspect TV stations and newspapers cannot get the advertising they need to survive. Even in democratic countries, the government issues licenses for TV and radio stations. Sometimes these are withheld or delayed for political reasons. Some countries require journalists to be licensed, a practice consistently condemned by the International Press Institute as eroding freedom of the press. In other cases the supply and distribution of newsprint is controlled by the government and allotted according to political considerations.

Manipulation of news in a democracy.   Even in a thriving democracy, with constitutional guarantees of free speech, there are limits on news. Release of classified information damaging to national security is not permitted, though just how broad this doctrine should be has been the subject of many court challenges. In many ways the government manipulates, but does not control, the press. For example, U.S. President Richard Nixon's firing of Watergate special prosecutor Archibald Cox in October 1973 was announced on Saturday evening; the next year his successor Gerald Ford's pardon of Nixon for any Watergate-related crimes was announced on a Sunday morning, both unpopular policies announced at times sure to receive the least possible coverage of any time during the week. Often government sources strategically leak stories about upcoming policy to guage public reaction ("trial balloon"). If that reaction is negative, the policy need never be officially announced and the government will not be blamed for proposing it.

Media self-censorship. Sometimes censorship is self imposed by the media. Diamond and Noglows (1987) argued that the three American commercial networks gave very short attention to major corporate changes involving themselves (e.g., General Electric's takeover of NBC). Often newspapers or the TV networks are in possession of information that they choose not to reveal for some reason. For example, the networks knew about the transfer of some American hostages in Teheran in 1980 but said nothing to avoid jeopardizing the hostages' safety.

Other times the press concludes (rightly or wrongly) that the public just does not care to hear certain highly negative news about their country or government. For example, when the Soviet Union shot down a Korean commercial airliner (KAL 007) in September, 1983, the Kremlin made the predictable charge that it was an American spy plane. This claim was widely reported in the United States but practically never taken seriously. In a careful analysis of the coverage of this issue by *Time, Newsweek,* and *U.S. News & World Report,* Corcoran (1986) concluded that all three publications, with an estimated combined readership of around 50 million (Gans, 1979), followed a virtually identical Reagan administration party line of anti-Soviet diatribe and paranoia. Outside the United States, for example in reputable British publications like the *Guardian,* examination of evidence supporting the theory that KAL 007 was on a spy mission were fully examined and seen to be credible explanations. Why was this perspective not heard in the United States? It was not due to government censorship, but perhaps it was due to the press sensing that the American public did not want to seriously consider such a claim.

In the Watergate scandal of the early 1970s, the press chose to call President Nixon and other high government officials liars but only after a considerable period of time and after compelling evidence had been presented. In the mid-1980s, however, the press was very hesitiant to directly expose the very popular President Reagan's apparent misinformation about Soviet involvement in Nicaragua. Only after the revelation in late 1986 that the Reagan administration had been sending arms to Iran with the profits being diverted to the Nicaraguan contra rebels did the press seem to give itself permission to seriously criticize the President. Finally, the Washington press corps long knew of the Reagan administration's disinformation campaign in attributing the Berlin disco bombing on 1985 to Libya's Muammar Gaddafi but said nothing.

Now that we have looked at what news is and how it creates and reflects the reality perceived by the public, let us turn to examining the impact and effects of news on the public. First we will look briefly at some experimental ways to study and measure the impact of the news. Next we will look at how our point of view affects our interpretation of news. Finally, we will look at the effect of news reporting on foreign policy.

MEASURING EFFECTS OF NEWS

Memory for the News

News offers an interesting case to test people's memory in a real-world setting. News stories are typically fairly short, self-contained pieces, unlike longer, more involved TV programs or in-depth magazine articles. As with any verbal material, memory is highly dependent upon the quality of initial comprehension (Findahl & Hoijer, 1981, 1982). For example, Larsen (1983) applied the text processing model of Kintsch and van Dijk (1978; see also van Dijk, 1985a) to radio news stories to study how people integrate new knowledge to information already in memory.

Gunter, Berry & Clifford (1982) reviewed the literature studying the way that visual and auditory information complement or interfere with each other in memory for TV news. The major finding was that memory was best if there was a close fit between the video and the audio component, as when the film illustrated exactly what was being described by the reporter. When the relationship was less clear or when the video and audio portion evoked different previous information from the viewer's memory, comprehension and memory for the new information suffered. See Gunter (1987) for a complete discussion of memory for broadcast news.

Good News–Bad News

Harvey Hornstein and his colleagues (Blackman & Hornstein, 1977; Holloway & Hornstein, 1976; Hornstein, LaKind, Frankel & Manne, 1975) proposed and tested an interesting theory about different effects of good news and bad news. Similarly to the cultivation theorists (Gerbner, et al., 1986) they argued that we respond to news stories by formulating "actuarial statements" about the social reality. These probabilistic judgments concern such matters as how good or bad people are. Hornstein has demonstrated that such evaluations have potentially serious effects on behavior.

A typical experiment had subjects ushered into a waiting room where they were asked to sit for a few minutes until the experiment was ready to start. In this room a radio played music which was interrupted by a news bulletin containing either a "good news" or "bad news" story such as the following:

GOOD NEWS story: A middle-aged man will be saved thanks to a person he as never met. The man, who suffers from a fatal kidney disease, had only a short while to live without the emergency kidney transplant. WWBG had broadcast pleas for help. Late last night a respected clergyman came to the hospital and offered to help. The donor had refused the family's offer to pay his hospital costs. Even in this day and age, some people hear a call for help.

BAD NEWS story: A 72-year-old sculptress, beloved by neighborhood children for her statues of Winnie the Pooh, was strangled in her apartment last night by what appears to be a self-styled executioner. The murderer, who has been identified as a respected clergyman, was a long-time neighbor of the victim. He had the keys to the apartment because he occasionally babysat for the victim's grandchildren and was in the habit of bringing up her mail and packages. (Howitt, 1982, p. 5l)

Afterwards subjects were tested or observed doing some other behavior in some way. Several interesting results were found. Subjects who heard the "good news" were more likely to return a lost wallet than subjects hearing the "bad news" and were also more likely to cooperate rather than compete when playing a game with opportunities for either strategy. In terms of attitude, "good news" subjects were more likely to believe that people lead good decent lives. Interestingly enough, real world bad news overshadowed the laboratory good news. On one occasion when data were collected just after the assassination of Senator Robert Kennedy, both good news and bad news subject acted like the bad news group.

Further exploration showed that good and bad news involving nonhuman agents (e.g., earthquakes, floods) did not show the same differences, nor was it necessary that subjects' mood change. Good and bad news had the consistent effects regardless of mood change in the subjects (Blackman & Hornstein, 1977). This research provides an interesting demonstration of how good or bad news may affect our reality far beyond the story itself.

Suicides: Triggered by News?

A very different approach to studying the effects of news stories has been taken by University of California, San Diego sociologist David Phillips (Bollen & Phillips 1982; Phillips, 1977, 1984; Phillips & Carstensen, 1986), in his studies of the role of media news in triggering suicides. This research examined the frequent recent fear that news coverage of teen suicides may encourage others to take their own lives.

Phillips' basic method is to examine correlations of media reports of suicides with changes in the rates of actual suicides. For example, Phillips and Carstensen (1986) examined seven years (1973–79) of such relations by looking at 12,585 actual teenage suicides in relation to TV news reports and feature stories about suicide. They found that there was a significant increase in suicides 0 to 7 days after such a news story. This increase was correlated ($r = .52$) with the number of news programs carrying the story. This correlation was significant only for teen, not adult, suicides and was stronger for girls than for boys. The experimenters concluded that the news stories (no difference between feature stories and reports of actual suicides) trigger additional teen suicides. In their article Phillips and Carstensen discuss and refute several possible alternative explanations of their findings, although the findings necessarily remain correlational.

In considering effects of news, one important factor is the point of view of the receiver. The meaning that an event has for one person or one nation may be very different than what it means for another, simply because of the different background and experiences.

THE EFFECT OF DIFFERENT POINTS OF VIEW

Part of the reason that people in different nations tend to perceive the same situations so differently is that the reality they construct in response to news is so different. Not only the reporting of such events in the media varies in different places, but even more basically, the interpretaion of the same events differs.

The United States and Nicaragua

As a case study, let's examine the United States versus Nicaraguan views of events in Central America in the 1980s. The same events had drastically different meaning in Managua and Washington (and for citizens in both countries). The 1979 Sandinista revolution that brought down the Somoza regime was greeted joyously by Nicaraguans as the fall of a hated dictator and dynasty but by many in the United States as the loss of a trusted ally. The subsequent influx of Cuban doctors and teachers was seen by the Nicaraguans as efforts to improve their literacy and health care but by the United States as evidence of increasing communist influence. The massive literacy campaign was viewed by Managua as a grassroots educational program but by Washington as a massive propaganda campaign.

The U. S. invasion of Grenada in 1983 was seen by Washington as the noble freeing of a tiny nation from tyranny and anarchy but seen by Nicaragua as blatant imperialism and a trial run for invasion of Nicaragua. The huge Nicaraguan military buildup and the U.S. arming of neighboring Honduras were seen by the acting nations in each case as defensive measures against dangerous aggression by the other. The rise of the contra (anti-Sandinista) rebels in the early 1980s was taken by the United States as proof that the Sandinista revolution had deserted its original ideals and by Nicaragua as evidence of U.S. meddling to overthrow their government. The Nicaraguan elections of 1984 were called a public relations sham by Washington and a proof of democracy in action by Managua. Curiously, elections under very similar conditions in neighboring El Salvador about the same time were called a public relations sham by Nicaragua and a proof of democracy in action by Washington.

The point of this example is not that one side was right and the other wrong. In a sense, both are right, *from their own perspective*. The objective truth, in the cases where that exists at all, probably lies somewhere in between. When news media report events entirely or predominantly through the view of its nation's government and people, those viewers may never have the chance to learn how those same events are perceived in the other countries affected. For example, whatever one's political beliefs about U.S. policy in Central America, it is important that North Americans understand that most Nicaraguans see the United States as a military threat very likely to invade their country, as they in fact have done several times previously in the last 150 years. Thus American troops pouring into Honduras look like a genuine threat. Similarly, Nicaraguans should understand how strongly most Americans feel about the threat of communism and its potential spread. Thus Daniel Ortega's visit to Moscow just after a Congressional vote on contra aid seemed threatening in the United States. This is not to say that either fear is necessarily justified or unjustified, but both are a vital part of the mindset of each of their peoples.

Our understanding of events in faraway places is for most people almost entirely a product of learning from the media, which for most people means television. If U.S. television sees the revolution in Nicaragua only in geopolitical terms (democracy vs. communism), and Nicaraguan television sees it only in terms of a fear of a U.S. invasion, neither people will be able to fully grasp all of the reality of the situation.

Soviet versus U.S. Perceptions

As a second case study, let's examine American and Soviet views of each other. Why can't the United States and the Soviet Union get together better to negotiate arms control and reduction? Why do the two superpowers see human rights so differently? Part of the answer may lie in the different perspectives of the two nations, including how the media present information about the other country.

Arms control. Most Americans see the Soviet Union as a militaristic and totalitarian state eager to export its political system at gunpoint on vulnerable nations. Many Russians see the United States as an arrogant self-righteous country seeking to dominate the world. Americans remember how the Soviets effectively took over several Eastern European countries just after World War II. Soviets remember that the United States is the only nation to have ever dropped an atomic bomb in warfare and fear it may do so again. Americans feel for the Soviet citizens who are intimidated in their closed society with press censorship and denial of the right to leave the country. Soviets feel for the unemployed and homeless Americans whose government does not seem to care enough to guarantee them a chance to earn a living. Americans remember the Soviets' crushing of democratic rumblings in Hungary (1956), Czechoslovakia (1968), and Poland (1981). Russians remember American invasions of Cuba and the Philippines (1898), the Dominican Republic (1965), Grenada (1983), and numerous invasions of Haiti and Nicaragua over a century or longer. Russians remember their 20 million dead in World War II when Hitler invaded shortly after agreeing with Stalin not to do so. All in all, it is not surprising that trust is difficult to build under such circumstances.

Human rights. One of the most frequently discussed Americans on Soviet TV news is unfamiliar to most Americans. He is Leonard Peltier, an American Indian jailed for the murder of two FBI agents on the Pine Ridge Indian Reservation. The FBI's handling of this case and general unrest on Indian reservations in the 1970s was highly questionable (see Churchill & Vander Wall, 1987). Though the Peltier case received very little publicity in the United States, it was widely publicized in the Soviet Union. Much as dissidents like Andrei Sakharov became heroes to the West, Peltier emerged as Moscow's symbol of America's alleged disregard for basic human rights. In June 1987 the U.S.S.R. received permission for two Soviet opthalmologists to examine Peltier in Leavenworth Federal Penitentiary.

In addition to the blatant political motivations of the visit, it also reflected two genuinely different views of human rights in the East and West. While political rights of the individual are supreme in the Western conception of human rights, to the Soviets the economic rights to full employment, housing, and health care take priority. Thus the frequent Soviet views of homeless Americans sleeping on the street or standing around idly unemployed appear as serious a human rights violation to them as press censorship or denial of exit visas seems to Americans. Part of the political socialization of the United States extols political freedoms as enshrined in the Bill of Rights. The Soviet political socialization emphasizes economic rights instead.

Some critics argue that U.S. media badly misread the Soviet press and government (See Box 7.3). However, the issue of different points of view can even operate within a society. See Box 7.4 for an example of how differently the three American TV networks reported events in Poland in 1981. There is also concern worldwide that newsgathering and dissemination has come to be excessively dominated by a few large TV networks and wire services. See Box 7.5 for a discussion of this concern and proposed alternatives.

NEWS AND FOREIGN POLICY

The media's reporting of news affects more than our perceived reality of the world. The act of reporting and the perceived reality interpreted can then actually affect the conduct of foreign policy. The event of reporting the reality becomes a part of the reality being reported. Long after the events themselves, what is remembered is the news coverage of them. "The reality that lives on is the reality etched in the memories of the millions who watched rather than the few who were actually there" (Lang & Lang, 1984, p. 213). Significantly, a few of the "millions who watched" are the policymakers themselves.

Former high-ranking Soviet official later turned defector Arkady Shevchenko (1986) argued that American news media are misreading the Soviets in some serious ways. He says that the American tendency to focus on personalities has caused our media to overemphasize General Secretary Mikhail Gorbachev and underestimate structural and institutional aspects of the Soviet system. The stultifying bureaucracy in the U.S.S.R. is highly resistant to any change, especially rapid change, yet some Western media seem to believe Gorbachev is radically transforming Soviet society in a year or two. Too much attention may be paid to reform-minded pronouncements and too little to the lack of substantive change occurring at a comparable pace. The newsworthy events (see first part of this chapter) capture more attention than the enduring trends. Shevchenko also claims that Western media are very naive about accepting the word of Soviet "scholars" like Georgiy Arbatov or Radomir Bogdanor of the Soviet Institute for the Study of the U.S.A. and Canada. Such spokespersons, he claims, are not at all scholars in the Western sense but rather part of the overall propaganda machine connected to the KGB and its disinformation campaigns.

How Media Affect Foreign Policy

Larson (1986) identified nine propositions about the way that news media, especially television, can have substantial effects on foreign policy and foreign relations.

1. The technology and organizational structures for gathering and disseminating international news are inherently transnational in nature. This transnational character of media necessarily involves it in policymaking issues. The sharing of wire service stories and TV footage is common. Reporters, especially for television, in a foreign locale, depend on local facilities to transmit news stories home, and often must cope with local censorship of such coverage. Governments sometimes try to indirectly manipulate the reality by manipulating the coverage of that reality. For example, when South Africa prohibits photos of protests, demonstrations, or even funerals in black townships or when Israel bars reporters from the West Bank, it is attempting to erase this reality from the consciousness from the world memory.

2. The presence of the press makes private or secret negotiations between governments more difficult. Diplomats negotiating sensitive issues must also consider the implicit third party in the negotiations, that is, public opinion. With television it is harder to keep secret talks secret. Veteran Israeli diplomat Abba Eban (1983, p. 345) went so far as describe the current situation as "the collapse of reticence and

BOX 7.4. THREE VIEWS FROM WARSAW

Walter Karp(1985) in Hiebert & Reuss (1985, pp. 215ff) offers an interesting example of how the three U.S. commercial networks' news departments treated the Polish martial law crackdown on the Solidarity movement in December 1981. "CBS Evening News" spoke of the "Soviet-backed Polish army" exercising harsh repression. Reports played up unsubstantiated rumors of bloodshed, brutality, and heavy resistance, including a "wave of sit-down strikes" broken by tanks. The close cooperation of the Soviets with Polish military junta was repeatedly stressed. No mention at all was made of the collapse of Solidarity. Bill Moyers' commentary assailed the Reagan Administration for not helping to preserve freedom in Poland. When the United States later imposed sanctions, these were played up strongly by CBS, which failed to mention criticism of this policy by Western European Allies and the Polish Catholic church. Finally, CBS was the only network not to show Secretary of State Alexander Haig's failure to explain to a reporter why the United States opposed military dictatorship in Poland but not in places like Chile, the Philippines, and South Korea.

In contrast to this treatment, NBC was far less inflammatory and consistently throughout noted the lack of solid evidence about exactly what was happening. NBC quoted a White House spokesman describing the Polish turmoil as an "internal matter."

Finally, ABC news was calm and detached like NBC but provided a sharper analysis of the situation. For example, they pointed out that the Polish army was not a tool of discredited Polish Communist party but rather was the protagonist in what was in fact the first military coup in Soviet-dominated Eastern Europe. Increasingly, ABC stressed the threat to the United States of the Polish situation and suggested that President Reagan feared that the Soviet Union could crush Solidarity without a costly invasion, possibly even implying that he really wanted an invasion.

What was the reality of what happened in Poland in December 1981? The nature of that perceived reality certainly depended on which station you watched.

privacy in negotiation." While such public scrutiny has probably placed some highly desirable curbs on corruption and extra-legal chicanery (e.g., exposure in late 1986 of Oliver North's secret Nicaraguan contra war), it has also made legitimate secret negotiations in the public interest much harder to keep secret (e.g., talks to secure the release of Western hostages in Beirut).

We have come to expect the presence of television at important events, and, when it is excluded, that in itself is news and the object of

BOX 7.5.   WESTERN BIAS AND THE NEW WORLD
INFORMATION ORDER

As expensive newsgathering and transmission technology has forced print and broadcast media alike to consolidate their efforts, world information transmission has come to be heavily dominated by the "Big 4" (Associated Press–AP, United Press International–UPI, Reuters, and Agence France Presse–AFP). Because most local papers and local TV and radio stations cannot afford their own correspondents around the world, they instead subscribe to the major wire services. Thus knowledge that people around the world have about current events comes disproportionately from the major wire services and the TV networks. Critics, especially voices from the Third World, argue that these wire services and TV networks present an overly positive view of developed countries and perpetuate a cultural domination of lesser developed countries, a sort of "colonization of information", continuing an earlier trend of political domination. There are only a few small alternative wire services (e.g., South–North News Service) that intentionally attempt to redress such imbalances.

Some have proposed an alternative called the New World Information Order (NWIO). Contrary to the Western view of the press and government in a sort of adversarial relationship, this view sees information as a natural resource to be used for political, economic, and cultural development. The press is thus a tool to be used by the government for development. Placing such a priority ahead of Western liberal standards like freedom of the press has made the NWIO perspective anathema to most Western governments and journalists. Specific proposals put forth by NWIO proponents generally support government media more generously than independent media and often limit access to information by journalists or increase government control and licensing of journalists. Strident support for NWIO positions was a major reason for the United States and Britain withdrawing from the United Nations Educational, Social, and Cultural Organization (UNESCO) in the 1980s.

intense criticism and even outrage, as in the 1983 U.S. invasion of Grenada, the 1982 British–Argentine war over the Falklands/Malvinas, or the South African and Israeli prohibitions of news of dissent.

3. Access to appropriate pictures heavily influences current news gathering practices. The availability of relevant and appropriate video material affects the choice of stories. This clearly leads to overcoverage of some photogenic issues and undercoverage of others which are less so, thus covertly setting the agenda toward some issues. It also favors coverage from places where a network has correspon-

dents on site, which usually (for U.S. media) means primarily western Europe, with many other places covered first-hand only if there is a current crisis (Larson, 1984). The Iranian revolution of 1979 caught the United States by surprise in part because on-site reporters in preceding years had been few (see discussion below).

4. News, especially on television, provides episodic accounts, often focusing saturation coverage on a "big story" and resulting, over the long run, in an ahistorical account. Extensive coverage of the Islamic revolution and the taking of the U.S. hostages in Iran in 1979 preceded many years of very meager coverage of that country. Many viewers had the impression that the crisis had come out of nowhere and was completely unexpected and unforeseen. Although it may have been unexpected by many, signs pointing in that direction had been present for years but ignored or unnoticed by the media.

Similarly, the Sandinista revolution in Nicaragua in 1979 catapulted that country into U.S. news for the first time in recent years. Events that followed over the next decade, such as the contra war and the Reagan administration's overt and covert support for that effort were not usually portrayed or perceived in the context of decades of a ruthless dictatorship under the Somoza family and well over a century of U.S. intervention on numerous occasions. United States policy itself took a very ahistorical view, focussing only on perceived current East–West geopolitical concerns.

5. Television network and major wire service news usually follows or reinforces government policy. This occurs not due to slavish adherence to official policy by media but rather because so many of the sources for many of the stories come from inside the government. Also, the focus is so much on individuals that policymakers and spokespersons tend to be followed by reporters more than trends and background are. Policymakers themselves read and watch media and are influenced by them. If media cover primarily certain areas of the world and certain topics, policymakers as well as the ordinary public will think in similar terms. For example, summit meetings between U.S. and Soviet leaders are massively covered in the press, even when it is known in advance there will be little of substance emerge; still, all parties involved and the public see such meetings as pivotal.

6. Media sometimes participate in foreign policy by serving as a direct channel of communications between government officials or policy elites in one nation and those in others. Walter Cronkite's role in bringing Begin and Sadat together (see Box 7.2) was pivotal. In some crisis situations, networks may actually know more than governments and may thus reverse the usual government-to-media flow

of news. For example, early in the crisis of the hijacking of the TWA airliner in June 1985, CBS had more information about what was happening than the U.S. government did (Joyce, 1986). On occasion the press actually briefs the government!

7. Policy problems may be created or exacerbated by lack of media attention to basic processes of social and cultural change in developing nations. The bias in international news coverage by U.S. sources toward heavier coverage of developed nations and those of obvious present geopolitical importance has long been known (Larson, 1984). Western Europe, Japan, and the Soviet Union receive heavy coverage in the United States, while Africa, Latin America, and much of Asia are largely invisible (Larson, McAnany & Storey, 1986; McAnany, 1983). Only in a crisis or when events thrust the United States into immediate involvement does the focus shift to such places, as was seen in Iran in 1979, El Salvador in 1980, or the Ethiopian famine relief story of 1984. Then the perceived reality is largely ahistorical with no background for understanding the puzzling present events.

8. The power of media, especially television, to convey emotions and a sense of intimacy can be a factor in foreign policy. Interest in the African famine mushroomed in 1984 in response to TV pictures of starving children, though the famine had been around for years and was then equally bad in some other countries where the cameras weren't present (Kalter, May 24, 1986). Coverage of Middle Eastern hostage stories is encouraged by the ease with which TV conveys the wrenching emotion associated with such captivity, especially seen in interviews with captives and their waiting families. One reason for the U.S. government's agreement to sell arms to Iran in exchange for hostages in 1986 may have been such coverage, which seemed to make arranging release of the captives a higher priority than other considerations.

9. Media can change public perceptions about foreign affairs, particularly when they convey new visual information and when such information is repeatedly presented over a long period of time. The dramatic change in American public opinion about the Vietnam War from 1965 to 1969 is perhaps the most dramatic example (See Box 7.6), but there are others. Protracted and detailed coverage of the Iran hostage crisis of 1979 to 1981 contributed to the frustration of Americans with that situation and with their President Jimmy Carter, who had failed to have them released. Although it is not clear what he or any other President could have done to bring the hostages home, Carter became a scapegoat in the November 1980 election, which swept Ronald Reagan into office in a landslide.

BOX 7.6.   VIETNAM AS THE TV WAR

As well as being the first war lost by the United States, the Vietnam conflict was the first television war. This aspect is sometimes cited as a major reason why it lost support among the American people to an extent never before seen in the United States. Although there were many other reasons for the lack of public support for the Vietnam War, the fact that we could all see the horrors of war every night while we ate dinner brought home the reality of how violent and deadly it truly was. The romantic ideals that some soldiers take to war and some family members back home cling to simply could not continue to be our reality. This war (like all others) was hell, but this time everybody could see it first hand. The effects of bringing such wars into our living rooms has been a hotly debated topic; see Arlen (1969) and articles in Hiebert and Reuss (1985).

Now let's turn to examining that Iranian hostage situation in more detail as a fascinating case study of the role of media in creating the perceived reality of a major news story.

Case Study: Iran Hostage Crisis 1979–81

Larson (1986) analyzed early evening U.S. television news coverage of Iran by CBS, NBC, and ABC from 1972 to 1981. From the time January 1972 to October 1977, coverage of Iran was very meager, only about 1% of all international news stories. Of those stories that did occur, only 10% originated from Iran itself, others being wire service stories read by the anchor or overseas reports from another country about Iran. The two dominant themes of those stories were oil and arms sales, exactly the focus of the U.S. government in relations with Iran during this period. Although there were occasional hints of widespread discontent, such as anti-shah demonstrations, there was no consistent attention paid to developing unrest. In an analysis of professional writings by foreign policy experts during this same period (*Middle East Journal, Foreign Affairs*, and *Foreign Policy*), little understanding of grassroots discontent in Iran was present there either (Mowlana, 1984).

In the period November 1977 to January 1979 the character of U.S. reporting on Iran changed considerably. The shah's visit to Washington in November 1977 evoked an anti-shah demonstration, which was quelled by tear gas that floated across to President Carter's South Lawn reception for the shah at the White House. After this "newsworthy" event, attention began to be paid to flaws in the shah and his regime. In 1978 all three networks placed correspondents in Teheran, which resulted in over half the stories on Iran originating from there and focussing on antigovernment demonstrations, strikes, and marches.

After the departure of the besieged shah in January 1979, TV served as the major communication between the exiled Ayatollah Khomeini in Paris and the fragile caretaker government of Shapour Bakhtiar in Teheran. After the return of Khomeini to Iran in February, U.S. TV focused on Iran, especially its implications for the United States. In the months April to October, however, coverage of Iran on American TV dropped off sharply.

After the Iranian seizure of the U.S. hostages at the American embassy in Teheran on November 4, 1979, however, all of that changed, with the story receiving extremely heavy coverage (nearly a third of all international news stories in 1980). Several themes emerged, primary among them attempts at communication between the U.S. and Iranian governments. Television, and to a lesser extent newspapers, became major channels of communication between the two governments. Iran allowed an NBC interview with hostage William Gallegos and even took out a full-page ad in *the New York Times* to print the 3500-word text of a Khomeini speech to the American people. U.S. reporters remained in Iran, except for a brief period of exile from January to March 1980.

Besides the theme of communication between governments, the media covered the hostage families, early release of some hostages, continuing activities and death of the shah in Egypt in July 1980, and the effect of the Iran-hostage crisis on the 1980 U.S. Presidential election. The release of the hostages on Reagan's Inauguration Day in January 1981 received heavy coverage, but subsequent stories on Iran that year originated elsewhere or occasionally from correspondents of other nations in Iran. For fascinating analysis of the Iranian media before, during, and after the revolution, see Beeman (1984).

CONCLUSIONS

Television as a medium has become news in itself. The weekly top-10 Nielsen ratings are reported on TV news and in newspaper wire services and feature stories. Certain blockbuster TV entertainment shows become news events in themselves, receiving coverage throughout print and broadcast media. Probably the most striking example of this phenomenon in recent years were two 1983 events, the last episode of M.A.S.H. in February and the nuclear war TV movie "The Day After" in November. ABC's "The Day After" even received coverage as a news story on "CBS' 60 Minutes" the hour before it was to air on another channel! Never before had a network offered a 20-minute promotion of a competitor's program and did so here only because the movie itself had become such a news story. More recently, the broadcast of the strongly anti-Soviet miniseries "Amerika" in February 1987 was preceded by much media controversy over its allegedly inflammatory position harmful to U.S. –Soviet rapprochement.

Sometimes the line between the genres of media news and fiction becomes blurred. A particularly controversial form is the docudrama (See Box 7.7). Is art imitating life, life imitating art or are they both the same?

Yet we must be careful we do not attribute a larger role in the perceived reality of our world to TV news than is appropriate. In an article based on interviews with several researchers on the subject, Kalter (1987) attempts to debunk what she called "media myths" about the role of TV news. While two thirds of the respondents in a recent Roper poll asking where they "usually get most of their news" reported that they did so from TV (twice as many as reported doing so from newspapers), more people responded that they read a newspaper in a typical day than watch TV news (67 vs. 52%). Of those who watched TV news, many watched only local news and a large majority were not attending fully to the newscast. Thus TV is a very important source of news but by no means the only one.

Kalter also presents opinion and evidence that newspapers set more of the agenda on news, and television adopts that agenda. Using the Vietnam War as an example, she argues that critical media coverage, starting around 1967, followed public opinion, rather than preceded it. The change in public opinion away from supporting the war occurred similarly for both Korea and Vietnam and was more due to increases in American casualties than to the nature of news coverage.

Even if television news is not quite the pre-eminent influence it is sometimes heralded to be, TV news occupies a major place in the popular imagination. The television coverage of news itself become news, sometimes bigger news than the event being covered. On the eve of the Iowa Presidential caucuses in early 1984, a voter in the studio was asked if she planned to attend the caucus and thus participate in the selection of a nominee for President. Her reply was to look around the studio and say, "Oh, I guess so, but I hate to miss all the excitement here." In other words, the act of reporting had become the newsworthy event, eclipsing the event being reported.

BOX 7.7. THE DOCUDRAMA AS PERCEIVED REALITY

A fairly recent television art form is a new variation on an old theme. This is the docudrama, or fictional story based on real events. Although it is certainly not new to take some historic events and build a story around them, embellishing where facts are unavailable or undramatic (Shakespeare did it all the time), there is greater concern with such recent TV dramas and miniseries based on recent spectacular crimes, political and international figures, and other stories. Often these dramas are taken as truth by the viewing public. The TV movie "The Atlanta Child Murders" aired in 1985, just three years after the real-life conviction of Wayne Williams for two of those crimes. The program's strong suggestion of Williams' innocence and the city's overzealous desire to obtain a conviction at any cost was not a fair and unbiased presentation of the evidence Still, more viewers saw the docudrama than any lengthy news story of those events. Thus, just as Shakespeare's *Richard III* has become the perceived historical king for many people, so "The Atlanta Child Murders" interpretation of those events becomes the basis of perceived reality for its nearly 50 million viewers.

As reported in Chapter 1, a BBC reporter in Vietnam in 1969, upon seeing his first battle, screamed excitedly into the mike, "Oh, my God, it's just like watching television!" Instead of reality being the standard against which we compare television, television had become his standard against which reality was being compared.

155

CHAPTER 8

Politics

My earliest awareness of politics was my anger that the 1956 Presidential nominating conventions pre-empted "Howdy Doody," "The Mickey Mouse Club," and other shows I wanted to watch on TV that summer. The first election I remember following with serious interest was the 1960 Kennedy-Nixon contest, which occurred while I was in junior high. Our family watched the historic first Presidential TV debates. Nixon looked so shifty but Kennedy seemed so young. Eisenhower was the only President I remembered, and I recall it seemed odd to have two men as young as my parents running for the highest office in the land.

Politics and the media have long been intimately involved with each other. Although television has made some drastic changes in the nature of that relationship, the connection itself is not new. Print media have long covered political campaigns, and the level of political rhetoric has sometimes been far more vicious than is typical today. For example, the Presidential campaign of 1884 saw Democrat Grover Cleveland's alleged fathering of an illegitimate child as a major campaign issue ("Hey, man, where's my pa?" "Gone to the White House, ha, ha, ha,!"). See Box 8.1 for political use of the media by abolitionists in the pre-Civil War United States.

Still, from the first tentative and fragmented radio reporting of Warren Harding's victory in 1920 to today's framing of whole campaigns around the use of television news and advertising, broadcast media have transformed political campaigns beyond recognition from Grover Cleveland's days. Wheelchair-bound Franklin D. Roosevelt was perhaps the quintessential radio President; his lofty

BOX 8.1. ABOLITIONIST MEDIA CAMPAIGNS IN THE 19th CENTURY

One of the major political and philosophical issues in the 19th century America was the slavery issue, a controversy so divisive that it played a major role in leading to the calamitous American Civil War (1861–65). Historical novelist John Jakes (1985) identified several ways that the Abolitionists successfully used pre-electronic media to help reshape the nation's thinking against slavery. Abolitionism was a rather extreme position in its early days of popularity in the 1820s, in that it advocated the end of all slavery, on moral grounds, not merely proscribing its extension to the new Western territories. The Abolitionists ran their own newspapers and had supporters in the editors' chairs at many publications. Probably the most famous was William Lloyd Garrison's *Liberator*, begun in 1831. There was also Frederick Douglass' *North Star* (1847), Horace Greeley's New York *Tribune*, and even a children's newspaper call *The Slave's Friend*.

Also tremendously influential were several books. Narratives of escaped slaves became popular in the 1840s, with the pre-eminent example being Frederick Douglass' autobiography. Far eclipsing all other books, however, was Harriet Beecher Stowe's *Uncle Tom's Cabin* (1852), written more out of religiously motivated concern for treatment of slaves than of any political conviction or true egalitarian sentiment (Mrs. Stowe favored sending freed slaves back to Africa). In fact the novel was based on only one short visit to a Kentucky plantation and contained very condescending portraits of Blacks. Still, it had substantial political impact.

Highly newsworthy events that received wide coverage and polarized already strong opinions helped lead the nation to war. Public meetings led by White clergymen or escaped slaves drew increasing crowds. Protests over the Fugitive Slave Law in the 1850s allowing Southern slaveowners to hunt and retrieve runaway slaves in the North occasionally led to dramatic, even violent, reaction, as when a mob of 20,000 unsuccessfully tried to stop seizure of runaway slave Anthony Burns. Shortly afterward Garrison burned a copy of the U.S. Constitution, calling it "a covenant with death and an agreement with hell." In 1859 Abolitionist extremist John Brown and 21 followers tried unsuccessfully to seize arms from the federal arsenal in Harpers Ferry to arm a slave rebellion. He was caught, tried, and hanged, but coverage of the trial split the country more sharply than ever.

mellow tones electrified listeners in ways that watching his crippled body would never do. In recent decades candidates have had to deal with the visual aspect of television as well. Although it is no longer necessary to be a great orator and physical pressence like William Jennings Bryan or even Jesse Jackson, astute use of television is essential.

Joshua Meyrowitz (1986) argues that television coverage has forever changed politics by lessening the distance between the politician and the voter. Although it is no longer necessary to cross a wide gulf between oneself and the voters by being an imposing physical presence in a crowd or an accomplished orator, it is now necessary to know how to use the more intimate medium of television to one's advantage. Many analysts of different political persuasions have acknowledged that Ronald Reagan was a highly effective television politician, as was John Kennedy in an earlier period. Other recent Presidents and candidates, such as George Bush, Gerald Ford, Richard Nixon, Michael Dukakis, Jimmy Carter, and Walter Mondale, have been criticized for less-than-effective use of television.

There is no longer as effective segmentation of the political audience. A candidate cannot deliver one speech to an audience of factory workers and a contradictory address to a group of lawyers, because both may be reported on the evening news, particularly if reporters perceive any inconsistency. A single unfortunate statement or behavior in one location may have a lasting contaminating effect through the magic of television transferring that one place to all places. For example, Democratic Presidential candidate Edmund Muskie was the frontrunner for his party's nomination in 1972 until he was seen on TV shedding a tear in New Hampshire in response to an editor's unfounded attack on his wife. This feeling, however noble, may have cost him his Presidential candidacy. Nixon Agriculture Secretary Earl Butz' private racist joke that became public and Reagan Interior Secretary James Watt's comment about "a black, a Jew, and a cripple" had costly career effects.

Richard Nixon may have never fully realized why the Watergate tapes were so damning and ultimately cost him the U.S. Presidency in 1974. Meyrowitz (1986) suggests that Nixon was evaluating those tapes as private conversations rather than as public statements. In private most people say things they would not like or not deem appropriate for a public forum. Limited to the private event world, such conversations are not inappropriate. As public discourse, however, they appear highly inappropriate and even shocking. Taping and television technology has broken down that public–private barrier by bringing formerly private discourse into the public world.

In this chapter we will begin by looking at the media news coverage of political campaigns. Then we will see how politicians' can manipulate the news coverage their campaign receives. Finally, we will turn to political advertising, when candidates can pay to say exactly what they want. Politicians consistently hope to use media to create a favorable reality about themselves in the public mind. The examples discussed will be primarily from the United States, because that is the area known best to the author and the one most studied by scholars examining politics and the media. Most of the principles discussed, however, are applicable eleswhere.

COVERAGE OF POLITICAL CAMPAIGNS

In the United States and many other nations, the media set the agenda in such a way that politics is prominently featured. Overall, political campaigns, especially at the national level, receive heavy coverage. Looking at this coverage more closely, however, reveals that some aspects receive more coverage than others.

What is Heavily Covered

Certain aspects of political campaigns are inordinately heavily covered and others lightly covered, in large measure depending on how newsworthy they are, in the sense discussed in Chapter 7. For example, major pronouncements receive press attention, especially formal announcements to run for office or to withdraw from a race. Other types of strong statements like a strident attack on an opponent also have high visibility.

Secondly, any type of major blunder, even if substantially inconsequential in the long run, receive wide attention. Gary Hart's apparent overnight tryst with model Donna Rice received heavy media coverage and led to his temporary withdrawal from the Democratic Presidential race in spring of 1987. When he later re-entered the race, his campaign never really caught on. One of the most notorious blunders was President Gerald Ford's statement in the 1976 Presidential debates about Poland being a "free country." Although this was clearly in error, and so acknowledged shortly after by Ford, the press did not let the country forget. Ronald Reagan's "teflon presidency" has sometimes been held up as an exception to this, in that his many mis-statements did not receive as wide press coverage or public concern as those of others.

Third, any kind of colorful response to a political speech or event captures coverage. Cheering masses or angry demonstrations draw cameras. In many countries rulers of questionable legitimacy regularly pay people to attend a speech and "spontaneously" cheer. Likewise, protests against a leader are carefully orchestrated primarily for the TV cameras, not for the speaker. Many felt that the Philippine revolution of 1986 could never have happened without the press on hand to cover protests against Ferdinand Marcos' apparent stealing of the

February 7 election (Kolatch, 1986a,b). This revolution was broadcast around the world and the lesson was duly noted. In summer 1987 widespread and broad-based popular protests in South Korea were televised over the world and soon forced President Chun Doo Hwan to agree to popular elections for President and a stated return to democracy.

Fourth, meetings of a candidate with important people receive press coverage. This is particular important for candidates without wide experience in some areas. For example, U.S. Presidential aspirants with little foreign affairs background often make visits to foreign leaders, in order to be seen on the evening news shaking their hand and conferring. Once in a great while one is able to pull off a major media coup of some substance as well on such a visit, as when candidate Jesse Jackson met with Syrian President Assad to successfully negotiate the release of captured U.S. flyer Goodman. This tactic, of course, involves some risk; if Jackson had failed, he would have been widely accused in inappropriate meddling in affairs of state.

Finally, any aspect of a campaign that emphasizes the "race" aspect receives coverage. Poll results are reported widely and promptly, as are predictions of experts and any event that "upsets" the relative standing of the "players." Relatively unknown candidates suddenly perceived as serious contenders or front runners receive a rapid and substantial increase in coverage. They don't necessarily even have to *win;* simply a surprisingly good showing is often enough for a media victory. After doing well in the 1984 New Hampshire Democratic primary, Gary Hart suddenly was everywhere in the news, after several months of desperately seeking coverage of his lackluster campaign. Dark horse peace candidate Gene McCarthy's surprising showing in the New Hampshire Democratic primary in 1968 was instrumental in President Lyndon Johnson's surprise decision on March 31 not to seek renomination himself.

The race aspect which has the most coverage is, of course, the result of the actual election. There is a lot of concern that knowledge of the results, or predicted results, in the case of network projections of winners, may actually affect the outcome of the election by influencing voters who have not yet gone to the polls. See Box 8.2 for a discussion of this issue.

What Is Lightly Covered

Just as some aspects of political campaigns are heavily covered, so others are relatively lightly covered. Candidates' qualifications in intangible, but highly important, ways are relatively difficult for press to

BOX 8.2. BROADCASTING ELECTION RETURNS BEFORE THE POLLS CLOSE

The United States has consistently had one of the lowest voter turnout rates in the world, not infrequently less than half the qualified voters. Although there are probably many reasons for this apathy, several of them cluster around the idea that people think their vote doesn't matter. This could be due to the huge size of the national electorate, yet voter turnout is generally highest in elections where one is voting for President and lowest where the races are purely local.

One particularly controversial issue concerns the broadcasting of election results and predictions before the polls have closed in all states. In the days of paper ballots, no substantive results could be had for several hours anyway, but that is no longer the case. Four studies done many years ago assessed West Coast voters' exposure to election results and projections before they voted (Fuchs, 1966; Lang & Lang, 1968; Mendelsohn, 1966; Tuchman & Coffin, 1971). These studies showed only modest exposure to the projections and very small proportions indicating changing their vote or deciding not to vote (1%–3%). Still, however, many elections are decided by such margins.

Since these studies were done, sampling techniques have improved and networks today take "exit polls" by asking voters as they leave the polling places whom they voted for. Assuming appropriate sampling and truthful responses, exit poll results and thus projected winners can be had before the polls close. Networks, in a race to scoop the competition, routinely have delcared projected winners in races with only a tiny percentage of votes counted (less than 10%). Although this may be scientifically sound, based on the statistics of representative sampling, it may convey a very different message to viewers. If results can be had with only 5% of the votes in, it doesn't seem to an individual voter that a single ballot can make much difference. There is not much incentive to go vote after you have already heard the results on television.

In response to such concerns, in 1984, 1986, and 1988 the networks agreed to some degree of withholding or limiting of their coverage until polls had closed at least some places. If that were adhered to nationwide, it would delay projecting winners by several hours in national elections. The 48 contiguous states of the United States span four time zones, with Alaska and Hawaii two hours behind the last of those four!

cover. What someone has gained from being governor of New York or Senator from Iowa, for example, that would help them as President is difficult to determine. Very abstract issues, such as character, are in one sense extremely important but in another sense very difficult to either report on or assess. Coverage that does occur tends to focus on superficial, though not necessarily irrelevant, indicators of integrity (or more often lack thereof), like marital infidelity or possible corrupt business dealings.

Also relatively lightly covered are positions on issues, especially complex ones. Television especially is ill-suited to detailed presentations of positions on complex issues like the economy. Print media can do so much better, as in publication of a candidate's lengthy position paper on some issue. However, few people read such papers; they listen to Dan Rather's 30-second interpretation of it, which may focus on peripheral aspects that are more "newsworthy." Many candidates and incumbents have written scholarly books carefully outlining comprehensive positions on complex issues; such positions may be vitally important to predicting their performance in office, yet they are difficult to cover adequately in the media, especially on television. A 200-page treatise on economic issues simply does not translate well to a 60-second news story.

An exception to television not dealing well with complex candidate positions would seem to be the Presidential candidate debates, held frequently (though not consistently) since the 1960 Kennedy–Nixon faceoffs (Kraus, 1962, 1977, 1988). Here the candidates get a chance to put forward their positions in more detail and in perhaps the only forum where partisans of the other side will actually listen to them. Still, however, the debates are typically analyzed by both media commentators and the public in terms of superficial appearances and performances. No one remembers what Nixon spoke about in 1960, but every commentator writes of how he "lost" because of poor makeup and looking tired and wan. Gerald Ford "lost" the 1976 debates because of his Poland remark. Reagan "won" the 1980 and 1984 debates because he seemed friendly and trustworthy and stuck to generalities. The one exception was the one 1984 debate that he "lost" because he became too bogged down in facts where he was not comfortable, eloquent, or accurate. These debates, which were supposed to be a forum to hear opposing candidates views', have too often become circuses to see who looks smoother or stumbles first. This state of affairs is not necessarily that different from the Lincoln–Douglas debates of the 1850s but the fact that today's oratory is televised nationwide magnifies its impact immeasurably. See Kraus (1988) for a thorough review of the Presidential debates and their effects.

Now let us turn to looking at how politicians can use the media news coverage to their advantage. Later in the chapter we will look specifically at political advertising and its effects.

POLITICIANS' USE OF NEWS MEDIA

Beyond paid political advertising, campaign strategists devote considerable energy to most effectively using news coverage to create a positive and electable image of their candidate. This can be done in many different ways, some of which are an integral part of daily life of newsmakers. For example, an elected official may have more or fewer news conferences, depending on the eagerness for coverage. An incumbent has considerable advantage over the challenger in such matters. For example, while Democratic Presidential candidates were squabbling among themselves in early summer 1972, Republican candidate (and incumbent President) Richard Nixon captured media attention by his historic trip to China. His landmark voyage opening up the world's largest country to America contrasted sharply to the petty bickering of his Democratic opponents attacking each other. Similarly, Ronald Reagan seemed to try to divert media attention from the Iran-contra affair in early 1987 by becoming more active and outspoken in seeking an arms control agreement with the Soviets. His historic trip to Moscow in spring 1988 contrasted to the Democrats' primary squabbles.

In any political system, but especially totalitarian ones, it is not uncommmon for a leader to whip up support and mute discontent by emphasizing or even provoking a foreign "enemy." Iran and Libya invoke the American bogeyman to distract dissatisfaction with failing domestic policies, while Argentina's military government in part provoked the Falklands/Malvinas War with Britain in 1982 to unite the country and mute criticisms of the economy and human rights abuses. Right-wing dictatorships may blame all their problems on communism, whereas communist states may blame the CIA or international capitalism.

Candidates help set an agenda by telling us what issues are important in the campaign. Ronald Reagan in 1980 and 1984 told us that it was important to "feel good" about America, and that struck a responsive chord in a nation weary of inflation, Watergate, and international terrorism. His 1984 opponent, Walter Mondale, tried unsuccessfully to argue that honesty was an important issue, even if it meant saying he might have to raise taxes. It is a reality that, in setting the agenda in terms of issues, candidates must consider not only what they believe is important but also what they believe the public wants to hear. Mondale's bitter defeat after calling for a tax increase was not lost on the Democrats in 1988, when they refused to have any platform mention of a tax increase, even a plank calling for higher taxes for the wealthy. Even so, Republican George Bush tried to make taxes an issue by criticizing Michael Dukakis' refusal to unequivocally promise *not* to raise taxes.

Credible "pseudo-events" may be created to capture media coverage and, in effect, produce hours and hours of free advertising. For example, when Bob Graham ran for governor of Florida in 1978, he began as an unknown state legislator with a name recognition of 3% and 0% of the vote among six candidates. How he overcame this was largely due to his "work days" project. During the campaign he worked for 100 days doing different jobs around the state, apparently to learn the demands and needs of different sectors of the electorate. These were heavily covered by the media and worked greatly to Graham's advantage, in spite of the obvious political motivation behind them. He defused some of the predictable criticism of self-serving gimmickry by dressing appropriately and actually working a full eight hours on each job. The first nine days were done before the media were invited in, so Graham fine-tuned his procedure. Photos from the workdays were of course used in his campaign advertising, but they were also widely covered as news. In his speeches he made references to insights he had gained from these days, and he continued them intermittently after becoming governor, all in all confirming the impression that he had actually learned from them and was not merely exercising in transparent political grandstanding (Jamieson & Campbell, 1988). All in all, it was a brilliant example of the use of news media for one's own political gain; no amount of paid advertising could have done what he had for free in the news.

More and more political ads have the appearance of news. In fact they often use news footage of the candidate doing something important that previously made the news. The "slice-of-life" endorsements by the common man and woman are very much in the style of the news interview of members of the public. The "cinema verité"technique of following the candidate through a little story readily taps into the same mental narrative schema (see Chapter 2) that we use to understand TV sitcom or drama plots, magazine stories, or other media pieces.

The use of sports, battle, and race metaphors in political campaigns also can gain coverage. Candidates perceived as front runners and, to a lesser extent, those perceived as serious candidates naturally receive more press coverage, though this can be a mixed blessing. When Democratic Presidential "front runner" Gary Hart challenged the press in spring 1987 to "follow me," the Miami *Herald* staked out his house and noted that attractive model Donna Rice apparently spent the night in his home. Ensuing events and innuendoes soon caused Hart to withdraw from the 1988 race, though he re-entered with much fanfare a few months later. His campaign never came close to recovering its earlier momentum, however.

One of the most frustrating aspects of the quadrennial U.S. Presidential sweepstakes is the attempt of lesser-known candidates to get the media to take them seriously. If the public does not perceive them to have a realistic chance of winning, the public acceptance or rejection of their stand on issues or themselves as persons is largely irrelevant. Although polls showed large numbers of Americans favored the positions of moderate independent candidate John Anderson in the 1980 Presidential race, less than 10% voted for him, largely because they felt he had no chance to win. Because no one besides a Republican or Democrat has been elected President in the United States since 1848, people perceive such an eventuality highly unlikely, a social perception which can become a self-fulfilling prophecy.

How a political candidate responds to attacks from the opposition can be very important. Although an unchallenged attack may be accepted uncritically, an overly vicious or petty response may actually engender support for the opponent. An incumbent has less flexibility in handling attacks. In some cases it may be better to ignore or brush off an attack than to "dignify" it with a response, e.g. Reagan's famous "Well, there you go again" comment to Jimmy Carter in the 1980 debates. On the other hand, an incumbent's attack on a challenger is not always so easily dismissed by the latter. Candidate Reagan's criticism of President Carter in 1980 for the Iranian hostage crisis became a substantive one, in spite of the fact neither he nor anyone else proposed a good idea of what Carter might have done to bring the hostages home.

Now that we have considered the use of news for one's political advantage, let us now consider that more direct form of political media, namely political advertising.

POLITICAL ADVERTISING

One of the major political issues of our time is the rapidly escalating costs involved in running for office, largely due to the increased purchase of television time and hiring of media consultants. Being independently wealthy has practically become a *de facto* prerequisite for running for national or even state office. In 1984 Reagan and Mondale each spent about $25 million on advertising (Devlin, 1987). The average U.S. Senator spends around $3 million to hold that job, requiring fundraising at a level of $10,000 a week through a 6-year term (Magnuson, 1988)! Some Senate campaigns have run over $1 million in ads alone. The political arguments of the campaign funding debate are outside the major focus of this book so will not be considered further. However, we want to examine the purposes and effects of political advertising, whose aim is to affect the perceived reality of that candidate in our minds.

Purposes

What are the purposes of political advertising? A primary one for lesser-known candidates and those campaigning outside their previous constituency (e.g., a Senator or Governor running for President) is simply awareness and recognition of their name. Voters have to have heard of a candidate before they can be expected to have any image at all of that candidate or form an attitude about them. Name recognition is the perennial problem of "long-shot" candidates for Presidential nominations or "unknown" challengers to a popular long-time incumbent for any office. In this sense the goal of political advertising is not unlike the goal for advertising a new product on the market.

Political advertising also sets the agenda on issues by conveying to us what issues we should feel are particularly important. Obviously a candidate will try to highlight those issues where he or she is strongest. For example, an incumbent President with several foreign policy successes, but economic problems at home, is going to try to position foreign policy issues as being the major ones in the campaign, whereas the opposing candidate may try to slant the campaign toward domestic issues. Sometimes such decisions are not so clearcut. For example, Democrats in 1980 had to decide whether to make age an issue in regard to Republican Ronald Reagan, who would be the oldest President ever elected. On the one hand, they stood to gain if voters became concerned that 69 was too old to begin the job. On the other hand, they stood to lose if voters perceived them to be too mean-spirited and unfairly attacking a nice older gentleman fully capable of competently functioning in office. For better or worse, Democrats chose not to make age an issue, a strategy adhered to in 1984 against then-73-year-old Reagan.

Political advertising seeks to convey an image of a candidate, or perhaps reinforce, soften, or redefine an existing image. This construction of an image is done especially effectively by television. Clearly this is related to setting the agenda. The widespread use of media consultants, such as the character played by Richard Gere in the 1986 movie *Power,* testifies to the importance of image. Polls are taken by a candidate's campaign staff to determine what issues voters are concerned about and what aspects of their own and the opponent's campaigns attract or trouble them. Then the candidate's image is tailored accordingly.

Some studies of candidate image have focused on general affective traits (Patton, 1978; Powell, 1977) or personality or social attributes (Anderson & Kibler, 1978; Bowes & Strentz, 1978; Kendall & Yum, 1984; Nimmo & Savage, 1976) and compared the image a voter has with actual voting behavior. More situational approaches (Husson, Stephen, Harrison, & Fehr, 1988) have demonstrated a relationship between voters' ratings of candidate behaviors and voting preference.

There are limits, of course, to what a media campaign can do; an urban candidate is not automatically going to look comfortable and convincing astride a horse making a political ad for the rural West. Also, one cannot assume that all voters will understand an ad in the same way. The image that the members of the public construct in response to the same ads may be strikingly different because of their different experiences and political predilections. See Box 8.3 for a compelling example.

Ads may develop or explain issues, such as a position on reducing the federal deficit. Such ads are much more conducive to print than broadcast media, particularly direct mail ads, and there is the high probability that a large majority of voters will not read such material. Of course, due to the mass nature of mass communication, even a miniscule percentage of the population reading a newspaper ad might be considered a success for the candidate.

Finally, ads may be used to raise money. George McGovern in 1972 and John Anderson in 1980 successfully paid for their TV ads by including appeals for funds at the end of their long ads (Devlin, 1987). Thus ads, which are a major expense, may also be used as a way of attracting money to met those expenses.

Appeals

Political ads use most of the same types of appeals discussed earlier in Chapter 4 on advertising. Psychological appeals are very common. Basic appeals to security come out both in the "strong national defense" and "law and order" types of appeal. Patriotic appeals are of course especially common, with certain symbols like the American flag very commonly present in political advertising, even for state

Sometimes the reality that one voter may construct in response to a political ad may differ dramatically from what someone else might interpret from the same ad. As discussed in Chapter 2, our different points of view give us cognitive schemas that we used to interpret new stimuli (e.g., political ads) around. To illustrate this point, Patterson and McClure (1976, p. 114) offer several different responses to the same TV spots for George McGovern, Democratic candidate for President in 1972.

Pro-McGovern viewers said:

1. "McGovern had his coat off, and his tie was hanging down. It was so relaxed, and he seemed to be really concerned with those workers."

2. "It was honest, down-to-earth. People were talking, and he was listening."

3. "I have seen many ads where McGovern is talking to common people. You know, like workers and the elderly. He means what he says. He'll help them."

To the same TV spots, pro-Nixon viewers responded:

1. "He is trying hard to look like one of the boys. You know, roll up the shirt sleeves and loosen the tie. It's just too much for me to take."

2. "Those commercials are so phoney. He doesn't care."

3. "He's with all these groups of people. Always making promises. He's promising more than can be done. Can't do everything for everyone."

and local races. Certain other patriotic symbols like familiar public buildings in Washington, the Statue of Liberty, and national historical symbols are widely used.

Family and affiliation appeals are seen in the typical family campaign ad photo of a candidate with smiling supportive spouse and children, as if being married or a parent somehow qualified one to hold public office. It is interesting and ironic that an occupation virtually guaranteed to take enormous amounts of time away from family responsibilities is so heavily "sold" with such family appeals.

Testimonials are often used, sometimes by famous "endorsers" such as a Senator or President coming to town to plug for the local candidate, or by the man or woman in the street saying how much they trust so-and-so to look after their interests in Washington. A popular President of one's party is eagerly sought for testimonial purposes; an unpopular one, such as the recently-resigned Nixon in 1974, may be an embarrassing liability for candidates of their party for other offices.

The issue of how stridently and directly to attack the opponent in one's advertising is a major question that all political campaigns must deal with. Attacks on the opposition may be highly effective *if* they are perceived as fair. Regardless of their merit or lack of it, if they are perceived as mean-spirited "cheap shots," they can disastrously boomerang against the candidate. Fear of such a scenario sends shivers to all politicians and often causes them to not take chances in this area, as seen in the Democrats' decision not to make Reagan's age an issue in 1980 or 1984.

Attacks may be strong without being direct or even mentioning the opponent by name. For example, in 1964 Lyndon Johnson ran a TV ad (shortly afterwards withdrawn due to complaints) showing a little girl in a field of daisies. Suddenly an atomic bomb explodes and we hear Johnson's voiceover, "These are the stakes: to make a world in which all God's children can live, or go into the dark" (Devlin, 1987). Republican candidate Barry Goldwater was never mentioned, but the ad clearly played on viewer's fears of his hawkishness.

Effects of Political Ads

The effects of political ads, as well as other forms of political communication in media, can be of several sorts (Chaffee & Choe, 1980; Comstock, et al., 1978; Klapper, 1960).

Crystallization.   In spite of the perception that the overriding intent of political ads would appear to be to cause attitude change in people, relatively few political ads change anyone's mind, in the sense of causing them to switch loyalties from one candidate to another (Blumler & McQuail, 1969; Comstock, et al, 1978; Trenaman & McQuail, 1961; Mendelsohn & O'Keefe, 1976). This is not to say they are ineffective, however. They frequently help crystallize existing attitudes by sharpening and elaborating them. For example, perhaps someone in 1988 was slightly leaning toward Michael Dukakis for President because of his leadership as Governor of Masachusetts. Political advertising for Dukakis may have helped "flesh out" that attitude, by providing more information about his positions and more intangible impressions about the candidate on which to base an emotional reaction.

Reinforcement.   In a related vein, political advertising may reinforce existing attitudes in voters to "keep in the fold" a voter who is leaning toward a candidate but not strongly committed. Such an attitude that is reinforced is more likely to translate into voting on Election Day and greater resistance to opposing candidate's attempts to change that attitude. Political strategists are always concerned about reinforcing "soft" support from voters who are leaning toward their candidate but not strongly committed. Many ads are targeted heavily at such people.

Conversion. Once in awhile political advertising may actually convert a voter from one candidate to the other, but this is quite rare and has not changed substantially since the advent of television (Campbell, Gurin, & Miller, 1954; Simon & Stern, 1955; cf. Lazarsfeld, Berelson, & Gaudet, 1948; Berelson, Lazarsfeld, & McPhee, 1954, for pre-TV studies). Of course, because many elections are decided by a tiny fraction of the vote, such people are not insignificant. See Comstock, et al. (1978) for a review of this work.

TELEVISION AS CULTIVATOR OF POLITICAL MODERATION

Before leaving the topic of politics entirely, let us examine the arguments of one group of researchers who feel that television in a very general sense is shaping our political attitudes in some less obvious ways than we generally consider. Our perceived reality about politics may be affected by TV viewing in a more general sense. Using their cultivation model, Gerbner, Gross, Morgan, and Signiorelli (1982, 1984, 1986) examine the relationship between television viewing in general and political attitudes. Using data gathered for several years in the late 1970s and early 1980s by the National Opinion Research Center in their General Social Surveys (NORC/GSS), Gerbner et al. looked at the correlation of amount of TV viewing (and other media use) and political self-designation on a liberal-moderate-conservative dimension.

Heavy TV viewers were most likely to label themselves as moderate politically, whereas heavy newspaper readers labelled themselves conservative and heavy radio listeners labelled themselves liberal. This relationship was quite consistent within various demographic subgroups, especially so for the conservatives and the moderates. Among light viewers, there was consistently greater difference of opinion between liberals and conservatives on several different specific issues than there was between the liberal and conservative heavy viewers. Gerbner et al. argue that television, with its mass market appeal, avoids extreme positions that might offend and this cultivates middle-of-the-road perspectives.

Television may interact with political ideology in other ways to subtly support or undercut existing structures in a society. The social and commercial realities of television may sometimes produce politically strange bedfellows. See Box 8.4 for an interesting example.

CONCLUSION

Our perceived reality of the political world is largely a product of the media. The role of the media, especially television, in politics will continue to be hotly debated. The loudest critics will decry how TV has corrupted the democratic process and reduced political discourse to banal superficialities. Its defenders will point out the technical marvels and improved dissemination of information that technology has allowed us to use in the political process. What is certain, however, is that media do create a political world which is the basis of most of our perceived political knowledge and subsequent political behavior, as in voting. That role is not likely to change, so it behooves us to understand it better.

BOX 8.4.   TELEVISION AND IDEOLOGY: BRAZILIAN CASE STUDY

Does television serve to indoctrinate or perpetuate political and social ideologies? The answer is a complex one with no easily generalizable answer. A case study of the Brazilian TV "novela" (soap opera) is an instructive example. In Third World countries, television is typically controlled largely by the economic elites, often with close political ties to right-wing ideologies. This was true in military-ruled Brazil in the 1970s, when the huge Globo communications network thrived and rose to become the world's fourth largest TV network, after the big three in the United States. Globo has come to be acclaimed for its high-quality programming, which is exported to dozens of countries around the world. The most popular shows, both domestically and for export, are the novelas, which typically air for one hour six nights a week for a period of several months. Somewhat like a very long miniseries, they do have a fixed ending, after which they are replaced by another novela.

Increasingly, the content of some of the novelas have reflected some politically left themes. For example, "Isaura the Slave" is set in colonial Brazil and strongly condemns racism and slavery. "Malu, Woman" shows the struggles of a divorced woman and has a strong feminist message. "Roque Santeiro" tells of a small town controlled by political bosses who stop at nothing to maintain power. "Wheel of Fire" tells of a business executive who repents of past corruption. It features characters who were torturers, rulers, and guerrillas during the years of

---

military rule (1964–85). Formerly shunning television as a tool of the rightist elites, leftist artists like "Roque Santeiro's" author Dias Gomes, a self-described Marxist, have now realized the potential of television, particularly through a large and powerful corporation like TV Globo, to reach far more people than theater, films, or print media could ever hope to. On the other hand, Globo's corporate executives are realizing the immense profitability of television dealing with some of these new themes. Maybe there is a place for programming of artistic and technical quality reflecting a wide spectrum of political and social attitudes while still enjoying commercial success (Bacchetta, 1987).

Violence

When I was in junior high, I was the only one of my friends whose parents took them to see "Psycho" . . . Though I felt proud and privileged and very adult at the time, I also remember subsequent childhood fears about some crazed killer lurking with a knife in dark corners of our house . . . In high school I read Truman Capote's "In Cold Blood" and later saw the movie. Before that I never locked the doors when I was home; ever since then I always have.

Although specific figures obviously depend on our operational definition of violence, any way we look at it, a major part of the perceived reality of media, especially television, involves violence. For example, by age 14 the average child has seen 11,000 murders on television. Between 70% and 93% of U.S. television programs contain some sort of violence (Signiorelli, Gross, & Morgan, 1982). In 1984–85 and 1985–86 the figures were 82% and 79% respectively, with more violence in early prime time (8–9 PM eastern time zone, 7–8 central time zone than later (Gerbner, Gross, Signiorelli, Morgan, 1986). On American television, there are 5 violent acts per prime-time hour and 18 violent acts per weekend daytime hour, the latter mostly due to cartoons, which are very high in violence (Gerbner & Gross, 1980). Violence even occurs in programming we do not immediately associate with aggression, such as news and even rock videos (Sherman & Dominick, 1986). For every 10 males on prime time who commit violence, there are 11 male victims. For every 10 violent females, there are 16 female victims (Gerbner et al., 1986).

Probably more than other topics examined so far in this book, media violence has been a hot political issue. Groups as diverse as the national PTA, the American Medical Association, and the consumer-oriented Action for Children's Television (ACT) and National Coalition of Television Violence (NCTV) have taken up the cause of opposing TV violence. Interestingly enough, it may not be the case that people necessarily like violence. Diener and DeFour (1978) found no correlation between the amount of violence and the Nielsen ratings of American TV shows. A violence-edited version of a *Police Woman* episode was liked just as well as the uncut, more violent version, except that the highly aggressive men did prefer the more violent version. For several years in the mid-1980s most of the top-rated network TV shows were sitcoms, one of the genres lowest in violent content.

There has probably been more psychological research on the topic of violence than on all other topics in this book put together. This chapter makes no claim to comprehensively review all of that literature, as more thorough reviews and discussions are available elsewhere (e.g., Andison, 1977; Comstock, et al., 1978; Eysenck & Nias, 1978; Freedman, 1984; Gunter, 1985; Liebert & Sprafkin et al., 1988). Often the discussion of the scientific issues has been clouded and colored by the economic or philosophical perspectives of those involved, and much of the popular writing on the topic has taken the form of either polemical and often unfounded criticism or a besieged defense supported by economic self-interest but ignoring the research. In both cases crucial distinctions among diverse types and contexts of violence and among different populations are often lacking.

In considering the role of television in encouraging violent behavior or attitudes supporting such behavior, we must not make the mistake of imagining TV to be the only factor, or even the major factor, contributing to violence. Negative social conditions like poverty, racism, crowding, drugs, easy availability of weapons, and the ghetto subculture doubtlessly contribute far more than television. Negative family and/or peer role models have substantial effects. Still, however, because of the *mass* nature of mass communication, even a very small effect of media can be substantial in terms of numbers. To take a hypothetical example, suppose a violent movie could be shown to cause .001% of the viewers to act more violently themselves as a result. Although the percentage may be miniscule, .001% of an audience of twenty million is still 200 people!

We will approach the study of media violence in this chapter by looking at the various effects of this violent view of the world presented on television. This study of the perceived reality of media violence will focus on the psychological processes involved and the weight of the evidence supporting the existence of those effects. Later in the chapter we will look at longitudinal studies probing for long-term effects and finally will address the question of what may be done to provide balance to this violent perceived reality and thus mitigate negative effects of media violence. One form of media violence of greatest concern is sexual violence; consideration of this issue will be deferred to the next chapter on sex and the media.

PSYCHOLOGICAL EFFECTS OF MEDIA VIOLENCE

Most of the public concern and scientific study of the perceived violent reality of television centers around the effects of this world of video violence. The effect which many think of first is modelling, when people imitate violent behavior they see on television. However, this is only one of several psychological effects. The following section will separately examine several different effects of media violence and the evidence supporting each of them.

Modelling

This construct comes out of social learning theory (Bandura, 1977), which tries to apply principles of learning to social situations. See Tan (1986) for details on the application of social learning theory to media violence.

How modelling works.   People see a violent act in the media and later, as a result, behave more violently themselves than they otherwise would. First, the relevant behavior of the model must be *attended to.* Second, it must be *retained,* somehow encoded into memory in some form, as it is being analyzed and interpreted through the cognitive processes. Whether the learned behavior is actually *produced* by the viewer will depend on many factors, such as motivation and the strength of prevailing inhibiting factors.

The process of modelling may actually teach new behaviors, much as one might learn a new athletic skilll by watching a teacher demonstrate it. When teenagers killed themselves playing Russian roulette imitating the famous scene of crazed POWs in Vietnam in *The Deer Hunter* (Radecki, 1984), they may not have known or thought to do that behavior before seeing the film. This is a particularly grisly example of the common phenomenon called observational learning. See Box 9.1 for the story of couple of especially tragic cases where legal charges were filed to blame television for teaching violent behaviors.

Most often, however, it is not the behavior itself which is learned from the media. A second process by which modelling can work is where watching violence on TV *disinhibits* one's tendency to commit some violent act that has already been learned. For example, watching a movie with scenes of street fighting might disinhibit one's tendency to fight. The viewer already knew how to fight; the medium cannot be blamed for teaching that behavior. However, it may be faulted for disinhibiting it, that is, breaking down the normal inhibitions we have against engaging in violence. Thus the violent behavior may occur in the future with a lesser provocation than would have been necessary to evoke it prior to the disinhibition. Disinhibition may also occur through the teaching of more accepting attitudes toward aggression. This change in attitude thus leads to the disinhibition which may subsequently and indirectly lead to violent behavior, though such a causal connection is very difficult to empirically demonstrate unequivocally.

Most of the concern with modelling effects of TV violence assumes a process of *symbolic modelling*, whereby one may be violent in one's own behavior in a somewhat different way than the media model did. That is, the effect has generalized from the specific behavior demonstrated in the media. This type of modelling is far more common than the modelling of a very specific behavior.

There are other even more indirect ways that modelling may occur. Violence may alter the general affective responsiveness of the viewer, which could in turn lead to violent behavior. It could raise the overall arousal level, which could prime the person for (among other behaviors) aggression. Now let's turn to looking at some of the research done to test the modelling hypothesis and identify the conditions under which it occurs.

Early "classic" research. The best-known early research studying modelling of media violence were social psychologist Albert Bandura's Bobo doll studies (Bandura, 1965; Bandura, Ross, & Ross, 1963; Bandura & Walters, 1963; see also Hicks, 1965, 1968; Hanratty, O'Neal, & Sulzer, 1972; Savitsky, Rogers, Izard, & Liebert, 1971). In a typical Bobo doll study testing modelling, Bandura had young children watch someone else behave aggressively toward a large plastic inflatable doll/punching bag. The child's own behavior with the Bobo doll later was subsequently observed. Studies of this type consistently

BOX 9.1.   ARE MEDIA CRIMINALLY LIABLE FOR VIOLENCE?

From time to time people concerned with particularly negative events that appear to have been affected by television have sought relief in the courts, where their claims have come up against First Amendment freedom of speech issues. Two particularly dramatic cases were the Zamora and Niemi cases of the 1970s.

Ronald Zamora, 15, killed his next-door neighbor, 82, in a robbery attempt in 1975 in Miami Beach. She was killed after discovering Zamora and threatening to call the police. What was particularly unusual was that the defense attorney argued for temporary insanity at the time of the crime, arguing that Zamora was "suffering from and acted under the influence of prolonged, intense, involuntary, subliminal television intoxication" (Liebert & Sprafkin, 1988, p. 127). He further argued that the shooting was a TV-learned "conditioned response" to the stimulus of the victim's threatening to call the police. Television was thus an accessory to the crime. In the end, however, the jury failed to buy this reasoning, and Zamora, whose hero was Kojak, was convicted of all counts and sentenced to life.

The second case involved the assault on a 9-year-old girl, Olivia Niemi, by three older girls and a boy in 1974. In the process she was raped with a bottle. Four days before, a TV movie, "Born Innocent" had been aired, showing a scene of a girl being raped with a plumber's helper. Olivia's mother then sued NBC for $11 million for alleged negligence in showing the movie in prime time. Her lawyer argued for "vicarious liability" and claimed that the movie had incited the children to criminal activity. The defense argued on First Amendment grounds and also called into question whether the assailants had in fact seen the movie. (They denied it but other witnesses reported their discussing it with them.) After a series of appeals and countersuits, the case was finally thrown out in 1978 when a judge ruled that the plaintiff had to prove that the network had to intend its viewers to imitate the violent sexual acts depicted. However, when NBC aired "Born Innocent" as a rerun, it aired at 11:30 PM and with most of the critical rape scene edited out (Liebert & Sprafkin, 1988).

Nor are such cases unique to television. The magazine *Soldier of Fortune* ran the following classified as:

FOR HIRE—*U.S. Marine and Vietnam veterans. Weapons specialists with jungle expertise for high-risk assignments in United States or overseas. Call—*
————.

Texan Robert Black hired a former marine through this ad, with the assignment of murdering his wife. Her surviving family brought suit against the magazine for negligence and were awarded $9.4 million in damages in a federal court case (Brockhoff, 1988). The legal basis of the judgment was that the magazine should have known that its offer included illegal acts such as murder. How much responsibility does a publisher (or broadcaster) have to anticipate such consequences of its messages?

demonstrated that children frequently imitated violent behavior previously observed in a live model. More important for our purposes, the same effect was found when the aggressive model was on film rather than "live" (Bandura, Ross, & Ross, 1961; Lovaas, 1961; Nelson, Gelfand, & Hartmann, 1969; Rosenkrans & Hartup, 1967; Walters & Willows, 1968).

Although these studies were important, they were not without criticism. Primarily they were attacked for being too artificial and of questionable generalizability to the "real world." Later research moving away from the laboratory also found corroborative evidence for modelling, however (Huesmann, Lagerspetz, & Eron, 1984; Joy, Kimball, & Zabrack, 1986; Lefkowitz, Eron, Walder & Huesmann, 1977; Leyens, Camino, Parke, & Berkowitz, 1975; Parke, Berkowitz, Leyens, West, & Sebastian, 1977). Thus it seems that modelling media violence is not purely an artifical laboratory phenomenon. Other recent research on the media modelling of violence has worked to identify other factors which affect how much the violence behavior will be modelled.

Important interactive factors. There are several important variables that heighten or attenuate a modelling effect. First, several characteristics of the model are important. People are more likely to imitate or be disinhibited by the aggressive behavior of an attractive, respected, prestigious model than one who does not have such qualities. Also, the more we identify and empathize with a model, the more likely we are to imitate them (Huesmann, Lagerspetz, & Eron, 1984). These points suggest that violence by the "good guys," that is the characters we admire and like to identify with, may be a more serious problem and influence than violence by the "bad guys." This has important ramifications for assessing effects of action–adventure and police shows.

It also matters whether or not the violence is reinforced. If acting violently appears to pay off for the violent character (in money, power, relationship, etc.), it is thus reinforced in the context of the story. Some evidence suggests that reinforced violence is more likely to be modelled than nonreinforced or punished violence (e.g., Bandura, 1965). In a typical TV story line, the violence of the hero pays off, that is, is reinforced, more than the violence of the villain. Here is thus a second reason that "good-guy" violence may have more deleterious effects than "bad-guy" violence.

Another important factor is whether the violence is seen as real or make-believe, that is, the degree of perceived reality (Van der Voort, 1986). There is some evidence of stronger effects of violence that is perceived as real than that which is perceived as unreal. For example, the most violence genre of TV show is the children's cartoon, yet it is the most stylized and unrealistic violence of all. Some studies (e.g., Feshbach, 1976) have shown cartoon violence to have less negative effect than more realistic violence.

In understanding the perceived reality of violent televion, it is important to consider the child's cognitive understanding of television at any given time (e.g., Cantor & Sparks, 1984; Sparks, 1986; Van der Voort, 1986). A very young child might think that a violent death on "Miami Vice" actually shows someone dying, rather than merely an actor pretending to die. Children who believe such staged violence to be real are often more disturbed by it than those who understand the convention of acting. Continuing this line of reasoning, the most difficult form of TV violence for children to deal with might be news and decomentaries, because violence there is real and not staged.

A modelling effect may occur but only in people who are somewhat inclined toward violence to begin with (Heller & Polsky, 1975; Parke et al., 1977), though this result has not been found consistently (e.g., see Huesmann et al., 1984). Unfortunately, studies suggesting such conclusions have often been used to argue that the lack of a *general* effect indicates no substantial effects of media violence. Actually, however, a modelling effect on even a tiny percentage of the population may be cause for serious concern. Another important factor in the reality of violence perceived by the viewer may be the thoughts one has in response to viewing media violence (Berkowitz, 1984). See Dorr and Kovaric (1980) for a discussion of individual differences in reactions to TV violence.

Finally, the variable of arousal level of the subject is important. A person who is already aroused for whatever reason is more likely to engage in violence in response to seeing a violent media model than a non-aroused person is (Tannenbaum, 1971, 1980) The arousal may come from the film itself, as violent films tend to be emotionally arousing and exciting, or it may come from some prior and unrelated source, such as that which was tested in experiments that make one group of subjects angry before exposing them to a violent media model (e.g., Berkowitz, 1965; Hartmann, 1969; Zillmann, 1979). This issue of the interaction of arousal and a violent model will become important later when we examine sexual violence in Chapter 10.

Reinforcement

One of the central principles of operant conditioning, and indeed of all psychology, is reinforcement, which refers to any event that follows a response and increases the probability of that response occurring again. The connection (contingency) between the response and the reinforcement is learned; thus the response is made in anticipation of receiving the reinforcement. A dog learns to fetch a stick because he is reinforced with a dog biscuit when he performs the act. A child does her homework each night because she is reinforced by being allowed to watch TV after she is finished. Responses continue to be made for some period of time without the reinforcement, until they gradually diminish and finally extinguish altogether.

In regard to the effects of violence in the media and the nature of its perceived reality by the viewers, reinforcement can work in one or more of four ways. First of all, violence in the media may reinforce violent tendencies already present in the viewer but not be the source of those tendencies *(preobservation reinforcement)*. The more such tendencies are reinforced, the more likely they are to manifest themselves in behavior. This sense of reinforcement is similar to disinhibition, discussed earlier.

The second sense that reinforcement may occur is the sense mentioned earlier, whereby violent behavior that is reinforced in the context of the story is more likely to be modelled than violent behavior that is punished or not reinforced in the story *(vicarious reinforcement)*. For this reason many critics are more concerned about media violence where violence, particularly crime, appears to pay and is reinforced.

A third type of reinforcement is where media, rather than reinforcing behavior or tendencies to behave in certain ways, may reinforce certain values about the use of violence. For example, characters on action–adventure TV shows and movies frequently use violence to settle interpersonal disputes. As such, they are reinforcing the value that such aggressive behavior is a practically viable and morally acceptable manner of dealing with conflict, a value which may become part of the viewer's perceived reality.

Finally, violent behavior or tendencies to be violent may be reinforced purely by virtue of their occurrence in a context that is overall very reinforcing. For example, the violence in "Miami Vice" may be more serious than violence in "Hill Street Blues" because of the glitzy and glamorous overall context of the former show. Because viewers may choose to identify more with the affluent opulence of "Dynasty" or "Dallas" than the gritty seediness of "Hill Street Blues" or "Cagney and Lacey," violence on the more glamorous shows may have a greater effect, even if the actual violence is less in quantity or graphicness. This effect may, however, be mitigated by the fact that the more realistic shows may have a greater impact than the less realistic ones due to their greater relationship to the viewer's own experiences.

Sensitization

Sensitization is in a sense a reverse modelling effect, whereby the viewers react so strongly to some violence and have such a traumatized perceived reality that they are less likely to imitate it as a result. This is most likely to occur with very extreme, even sensationalized violence, as might be the reaction of someone who has never seen anything stronger than a Disney movie to seeing one of the *Friday the Thirteenth* or *Halloween* films. The tendency away from violence might arise from the arousal of anxiety about the violence and/or the arousal of empathy for the victim of the violence. Although sensitization effects are hard to study scientifically for ethical reasons, evidence suggests that sensitization is not too widespread and does not happen nearly as often as its opposite, desensitization. In general, any situation for which one can posit sensitization effects can also be interpreted in terms of desensitization. For example, people have argued that daily news broadcasts of the Vietnam War sensitized us to the horrors of war and eroded public support for the conflict, in contrast to previous wars. On the other hand, others argue that the same news broadcasts desensitized us to war and thus we now are not bothered by conflicts in Central America or Lebanon. See Box 9.2 for a history of the treatment of the Vietnam War in films.

Desensitization

Although we often think of effects of TV violence in terms of increases in violent behavior, it may be that far more pervasive effects are in the area of desensitization. The idea here is that viewing much violence in the media makes us less sensitive to it, more jaded, and less aroused and bothered by it. We become so used to seeing people blown apart and impaled every night on TV that it no longer particularly troubles us. For example, after seeing a violent TV show, sixth graders were less sensitive to violent images in a subsequent film than were subjects who had seen a nonviolent film (Rabinovitch, McLean, Markham, & Talbott, 1972).

BOX 9.2.   HOLLYWOOD GOES TO VIETNAM

The 1966 pro-military film *The Green Berets* starred John Wayne in a stylized epic with clear good guys and bad guys. Its ending of the sun setting in the east fairly accurately reflected the level of realism of the entire film. By two or three years later such a simplistic approach to Vietnam rang very shallow and false and was not often seen again until a new generation became captivated by Sylvester Stallone's *Rambo: First Blood Part II* in the mid-1980s.

Several years after *The Green Berets*, sentiment in the United States had turned completely around and whatever glory there had been to the Vietnam War had long since disappeared. The 1974 oscar-winning documentary *Hearts and Minds* by Peter Davis was very graphic and carried such a strong antiwar message that some newspapers refused to publish reviews of the film.

Although the last American troops left Vietnam in 1973 and Saigon fell in 1975, there were practically no commercially successful film images of Vietnam before 1978, when *The Deer Hunter* won five Oscars, including best picture, and *Coming Home* picked up Oscars for best actor (Jon Voight) and best actress (Jane Fonda). Both of these (along with *Apocalypse Now*) carried a strong antiwar message and reflected the country's disgust with the war in Vietnam, a wound that had started to heal just enough to be able to handle these graphic and realistic films.

Still, these were not followed by others, as had the first World War II movies. The wound of Vietnam was still unhealed in 1986, when Oliver Stone's *Platoon* appeared and became a cathartic experience for the whole nation, particular the vets themselves. First seen as a commercial gamble, *Platoon* took years to acquire the necessary funding. The Pentagon refused to help the producers, though it enthusiastically aided the makers of *Top Gun*, on the grounds that it wanted to insure a "realistic portrayal" of the military! Stone then turned to a private consulting firm headed by a retired marine captain, who ignored the Pentagon's pleas not to help the producers of *Platoon*. Widely hailed as a critical success (including Best Picture Oscar for 1986), *Platoon* astounded everyone with its huge commercial success as well. As commercial successes generally are, it was then followed by a spate of "realistic" Vietnam films like *Gardens of Stone*, *The Hanoi Hilton*, and *Full Metal Jacket*, none of which received close to *Platoon's* critical or commercial success.

By 1988 the wounds of Vietnam had healed enough to allow the production and commercial success of the first Vietnam War TV series ("Tour of Duty) and big-screen comedy—*Good Morning Vietnam*. A comedy about Vietnam would have been unthinkable before that time.

Desensitization may be seen as a straightforward example of classical conditioning (See Figure 9.1) The normal, unlearned responses to being physically hurt includes pain, fear, and disgust. The first time one sees media violence, it probably evokes such emotional responses, due to its similarity to real violence (Figure 9.1a). Such a single occurrence may actually produce sensitization.

What happens with repeated viewing of violence in comfortable surroundings is quite different, however (Fig.9.1b). The normal, unlearned response to sitting at home in one's easy chair is feeling relaxed and happy. When this is repeatedly paired with violence on TV, that vicarious violence in this pleasant home context gradually becomes associated with that situation and itself comes to be seen as entertaining, pleasant, and even relaxing. The natural association of the video violence and real-life violence has been weakened as the new association of video violence with recreation is strengthened. We repeatedly see violence *without experiencing pain or hurt ourselves* and thus the normal negative responses to it weaken. Given what we know about classical conditioning in psychology, it is unlikely that such frequent and repeated exposure to stimuli could *not* have a substantial effect.

Suppose that people are desensitized to violence from the media. What are the implications of that? Becoming jaded to news of war and violence will cause such stories not to bother us so much any more. While we may never actually like violence or act violently ourselves, we may not dislike it nearly so much. It just doesn't seem all that serious. This has important implications for behavior. For example, Drabman and Thomas (1974, 1976) had 8- to 10-year-old

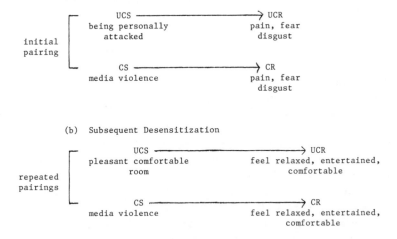

FIGURE 9.1. Desensitization as Classical Conditioning

children watch a violent or nonviolent film and then watch younger children play. When the younger children started to get rough, the older children who had watched the nonviolent film called an adult sooner than did the older children who had watched the violent film.

Another area of concern with desensitization has to do with tolerance of violence toward woman. Sexual violence is one of the major current concerns among media researchers studying violence; we will examine this aspect of violence in some detail in Chapter 10.

Cultivation Theory

Another type of effect on attitudes, which then may indirectly affect behavior, is cultivation. George Gerbner and his colleagues have argued that, the more exposure a person has to television, the more their perception of social realities will match that which is presented on TV (Gerbner, Gross, Morgan, & Signiorelli, 1980, 1986; Gerbner, Gross, Signiorelli, Morgan, & Jackson-Beeck, 1979; see also Leahy, 1987; Pingree & Hawkins, 1981; Weaver & Wakshlag, 1986). Although these researchers are best know for their research on TV violence, the notion of cultivation is much broader. Gerbner et al. argue that cultivation is "part of a continual, dynamic, ongoing process of interaction among messages and contexts" (1986, p. 24). They distinguish cultivation from direct effects and reinforcement by attributing a more active role to the viewer, who is interacting with the medium, not being passively manipulated by it. Nevertheless, there is a coming together of the viewer's outlook and that of the medium, whereby the person's perceived reality gradually approaches that of the TV world.

This social reality takes many forms, including understanding of sex roles (Morgan, 1982), political attitudes (Gerbner, Gross, Morgan & Signiorelli, 1984; Gerbner, et al., 1986), science and scientists (Gerbner, Gross, Morgan, & Signiorelli, 1981a), health benefits and practices (Gerbner, Gross, Morgan, & Signiorelli, 1981b), adolescent career choices (Morgan & Gerbner, 1982), and views of the elderly (Gerbner, Gross, Signiorelli & Morgan, 1980) and minorities (Gross, 1984; Volgy & Schwarz 1980). Gerbner and colleagues typically perform correlational studies to test this model by comparing the attitudes and perceptions of events by heavy and light TV viewers.

Cultivation theory is best known, however, for its research on cultivation of attitudes related to violence (Gerbner & Gross, 1980; Gerbner et al., 1980) Such studies have shown that heavy viewers believe the world to be a more dangerous and crime-ridden place than do the light viewers. This of course could be due either to TV teaching that this is what the world is like or to the fact that more fearful people are drawn to watching more TV. If it is the former, and Gerbner believes it is, TV can induce a general mindset about the position of violence in the world, completely aside from any effects it might have in teaching violent behavior. Finally, cultivation theory speaks of TV teaching the role of victim. From watching lots of crime and adventure shows, viewers learn what it is like to be the victim of violence, and this role becomes very real to them, even if it is completely outside their own experience.

In spite of being very influential, cultivation theory is not without its critics. Several studies have shown that careful controls of certain other sociodemographic and personality variables tend to reduce or eliminate cultivation effects (Carveth & Alexander, 1985; Doob & Macdonald, 1979; Hawkins & Pingree, 1982; Hirsch, 1980; Hughes, 1980; Perse, 1986; Potter, 1986; Wober, 1986). Secondly, cultivation studies have been criticized on methodological grounds, including response biases and problems with the measuring instruments (Hirsch, 1980; Hughes, 1980; Perse, 1986; Potter, 1986; Schneider, 1987; Schuman & Presser, 1981; Wober, 1978; Wober & Gunter, 1986). There have also been criticisms of some of the assumptions underlying cultivation theory. For example, it seems to assume, without demonstrating, that the messages of TV are essentially uniform (Hawkins & Pingree, 1981) and that viewers accept what they see as perceived reality (Slater & Elliott, 1982). See Rubin, Perse, & Taylor (1988) for a review of the critiques of cultivation theory.

To deal with some of these concerns, there has recently been some tendency to reinterpret cultivation theory in line with a uses and gratifications approach, stressing the active mental activity of the viewer while watching TV (Levy & Windahl, 1984; Rubin & Perse, 1987; Weaver & Wakshlag, 1986). Whatever cultivation in fact occurs then grows out of the active information processing and the construction of reality performed by the viewer.

Now let's turn to the final apparent psychological effect of violence—catharsis.

Catharsis

The notion of catharsis extends all the way back to Aristotle's *Poetics*, where he speaks of drama purging the emotions of the audience. In modern times, however, the notion largely developed in psychoanalytic theory. According to Freud, the id, ego, and superego are locked in battle, with anxiety resulting from id impulses trying to express themselves and, in so doing, coming into conflict with the moralistic superego. Threatening unconscious impulses like sex and aggression are repressed from consciousness but may cause anxiety when they creep back into consciousness from time to time. These repressed impulses and the anxiety they produce may be dealt with directly by overt sexual or aggressive behavior or indirectly through some sublimated substitute activity, such as watching others be sexual or aggressive on television.

The emotional release called catharsis comes from "venting" the impulse, that is, expressing it, either directly or indirectly. This emotional purging has been a notoriously difficult concept to operationally define and test, but it has continued to have a lot of intuitive appeal and anecdotal support (people report feeling better after watching a scary movie). Catharsis theory does, however, make one very clear prediction about the effect of TV violence on behavior, a prediction that is exactly opposite to the prediction of modelling theory. Although modelling predicts an increase in aggressive behavior after watching media violence, catharsis theory predicts a reduction in violent behavior (Feshbach, 1955). If the substitute behavior of watching the violence provides the emotional release that would normally require actually being violent, then violent behavior actually ought to decrease after watching media violence. Thus the two models are clearly and competitively testable. When such tests have been done, modelling theory has usually been supported (e.g., Siegel, 1956), whereas catharsis theory seldom has. In spite of consistent failures to provide scientific evidence for catharsis (Geen & Quanty, 1977; Zillmann, 1979), it continues to occupy a place in the popular imagination.

Later refinements of catharsis theory have been proposed (Feshbach & Singer, 1971). It may be that the media violence elicits fantasizing by the viewer, and that fantasizing, rather than the media violence per se, is what leads to catharsis. Another version of catharsis theory argues that watching media violence reduces one's arousal level and thus the person is less prone to violence. There is evidence that a reduction of arousal level is associated with decreased violent behavior. Thirdly, TV violence may elicit an inhibition response, which puts a "brake" on tendencies toward violent behavior. This is very similar to a sensitization hypothesis.

The effects of media violence discussed above are not presented as an exhaustive list but rather as general classes into which most proposed effects fall. Occasionally an effect falls outside those classes, however; see Box 9.3 for some interesting evidence of violent media causing amnesia in viewers.

LONGITUDINAL STUDIES

Although dozens, if not hundreds, of studies have shown some psychological effect of media violence, most of those have been short-term and in the laboratory, often using the methodology of showing subjects a film and subsequently measuring their behavior or attitudes in some way. Although these findings are important, they are not definitive answers about the long-term cumulative effects of watching hundreds of hours of violent television as recreation throughout one's childhood. There have been a few studies that have addressed this issue, most notably those from the laboratory of University of Illinois at Chicago psychologists Rowell Huesmann and Leonard Eron.

Longitudinal studies over 10 years in the United States and Finland provided the first evidence of a causal relationship between real-world viewing of TV violence through childhood and aggressive behavior as a child and a young adult (Eron, Huesmann, Lefkowitz, & Walder, 1972; Lefkowitz, Eron, Walder, & Huesmann, 1977; Pit-kanen-Pulkkinen, 1981). Through careful design and control for other variables, Eron and Lefkowitz concluded that they can rule out other explanations like dispositional violence in people being the cause of both more violent TV viewing and more violent behavior.

In a later 3-year longitudinal study, Huesmann, Lagerspetz, and Eron (1984) further explored the role of several intervening variables on the relation of TV violence viewing and aggressive behavior in American and Finnish children in elementary school. The study collected a mass of data between 1977 and 1980 from the children, their parents, the children's peers, and the school. Data gathered included measures of TV viewing, attitudes, behaviors, ratings of self and others, and family demographics. A few of the highlights are presented below.

As had been found in many other studies, there was a positive correlation of violent TV viewing and peer-rated aggression, stronger for boys than girls and for Americans than Finns; the overall level of violent behavior was higher in the American children. One of the most striking results for both samples was the strong correlation of violent behavior and self-rated identification with the violent TV model, especially for boys. The best predictor of later aggressive

BOX 9.3. VIOLENCE AS LEADING TO AMNESIA

One curious effect of media violence not on the typical lists of effects is amnesia, but just such an effect has been proposed by Loftus and Burns (1982). It has been known for some time that a physical injury to the brain can result in a loss of memory for events immediately preceding the impact. For example, the shock of one's head flying against the headrest in a collision may lead to amnesia for events immediately preceding the impact. It is as if the brain had not yet had time to transfer the event from short-term to long-term memory. Loftus and Burns demonstrated that such an effect may also occur solely from the mental shock of graphic violence on the screen. Subjects saw a 2-minute film of a bank robbery, in either a violent or nonviolent version. In the violent version the fleeing robbers shoot their pursuers and hit a young boy in the street in the face, after which he falls, clutching his bloody face. The nonviolent version is identical up to the point of shooting, at which point the camera cuts to the interior of the bank. Using both recall and recognition measures, subjects seeing the nonviolent version of the film later remembered the number on the boy's t-shirt better than subjects seeing the violent film, although the shirt was shown the same amount of time in both. A second study ruled out that the effect could have been due to the unexpectedness or surprisingness of the shooting.

behavior was the interactive product of violent viewing and identification with the violent character. There was no evidence that violent TV affects only children naturally more predisposed to violent behavior or that children who fantasize more were affected any differently. Neither were there particular effects of level of parental violent behavior or TV viewing on children's aggressiveness. This research is continuing with samples in Australia, the Netherlands, Poland, and Israel.

This positive relationship between violent TV viewing and subsequent aggressive behavior has been the general finding of recent longitudinal studies, with only a few exceptions (most notably Milavsky, Kessler, Stipp, & Rubens, 1982). Although many researchers conclude that a convincing causal link between media aggression and violent behavior has been demonstrated (e.g., Friedrich-Cofer & Huston, 1986), others urge caution in interpreting beyond correlational and suggestive causal results (e.g., Freedman, 1986). Even the most conservative conclusion, however, concerns only behavioral effects and says nothing about attitudinal effects like desensitization and cultivation.

HELPING THE CHILD DEAL WITH VIOLENT TELEVISION

Given the probable negative effects and influences of violent television, what is a parent to do, short of prohibiting viewing altogether? Prohibition would not be totally successful, anyhow, since children see TV at friends' homes and may rent violent videos and movies.

Although mitigating the effects of TV violence has not been a major thrust of the research, there have been some interesting findings addressing this issue. Huesmann, Eron, Klein, Brice, and Fischer (1983) developed a treatment designed to change children's attitudes about violent TV. A total of 169 1st-and 3rd-graders who watched a lot of violent TV were exposed to two treatment sessions over two years. The first session involved showing children TV film clips and having them discuss the violence and alternative nonviolent "realistic" ways that the problems could have been solved. Neither the treatment session nor a control group session discussing other aspects of TV had any effect on the subjects' own aggressiveness or their belief about the reality of TV violence.

However, a second intervention nine months later with the same children had children develop arguments about the negative effects of TV violence, write a paragraph on the topic, and make a group video with everyone reading their essay. This treatment (but not the control) led to reduced aggressive behavior and a weaker relationship between aggression and violent TV viewing. In terms of attitudes, the treatment had a substantial effect on subjects' ratings on two questions ("Are television shows with a lot of hitting and shooting harmless for kids?" "How likely is it that watching a lot of television violence would make a kid meaner?"). The effect occurred most strongly in children who identified least with the violent characters, suggesting the important role of identification with the aggressive model.

A somewhat different approach by Barbara Wilson and her colleagues used systematic desensitization techniques to reduce children's fear reactions to scary media presentations (Wilson, 1987; Wilson & Cantor, 1987; Wilson, Hoffner, & Cantor, 1987). For example, children heard explanations about tarantulas, paraphrased them back, and played with a plastic replica of a tarantula before seeing a scary movie about tarantulas (Wilson, 1987).

The success of Huesmann and Wilson and their colleagues in mitigating the effects of TV violence through training is encouraging if for no other reason than it shows learning is subject to alteration by new learning. This is especially encouraging, since aggression is known to be a behavior that is remarkably stable over time (Huesmann, Eron, Lefkowitz, & Walder, 1984; Olweus, 1979).

CONCLUSION

What, then, may we conclude from these masses of research studies of media violence inside and outside the laboratory? Probably no single study in itself should be seen as thoroughly definitive in establishing a deleterious effect of TV violence on children. However, overall, the evidence converges substantially on the conclusion that TV violence does have harmful effects on children, both in the sense of increasing aggressive behavior and in altering attitudes and values, particularly through processes of desensitization and the cultivation of fear. The laboratory research generally has yielded stronger conclusions than the field studies, and different researchers often interpret the same data very differently (e.g., Friedrich-Cofer & Huston, 1986, versus Freedman, 1984, 1986). Even if the effects turn our to be somewhat more restricted than some would argue today, the cause for concern is still present.

Although most of the longitudinal field studies have shown a significant positive correlation between viewing televised violence and subsequent aggressive behavior, such correlations have typically been small in magnitude (e.g., rs between .15 and .30, accounting for 2.25% to 9% of the variance). The fact that this amount is small, however, should not be surprising. Social learning theory, for example, would predict such a modest effect, since television is, after all, only a small part of the matrix of influences in people's lives (Tan, 1986).

The effects of media violence, however, do not fall equally on all. Some people are affected more than others, and some types of violence and shows have more effect than others. In proposing policy, either legislative regulation or network industry guidelines, such distinctions must be considered. All violence is not equally harmful.

The debate over the effects of media violence has been strident and heated and probably will continue at that level. Predictably, the networks in particular have refuted the conclusions of much of the behavioral research (e.g., Wurtzel & Lometti, 1987a,b). The negative effects of TV are probably neither as widespread and serious as suggested by the strongest critics nor as benign as suggested by the apologists (e.g., Freedman, 1984, 1986; Howitt, 1982).

An approach taken only infrequently in the research has been to examine what attracts viewers to violence and why some are attracted much more than others. Fenigstein and Heyduk (1985) found that aggressive thoughts and behaviors increase one's preference for viewing violence and that the presence of sexual aggressive fantasies increases the desire to view violent pornography. Such a factor may be turned more positively. The induction of affiliation motives by a 10-minute fantasy induction actually increased the preference for viewing affiliation-oriented TV 40 minutes later (Fenigstein & Heyduk, 1985).

We have not yet seriously addressed the type of media violence causing the greatest concern today, that is, sexual violence. We will examine this issue and research on the problem in detail in the next chapter after a look at sex in the media.

Sex

One evening in college I shared some of my deepest fears with my one close female married friends. We met for a couple of hours in one of the library stairwells, the typical place for serious conversations in the winter at that college. I confessed that I did not feel I had as strong a sex drive as the men on TV and the movies and was a bit concerned because I did not always honestly, even deep-down, want to hop into bed with every beautiful woman that I saw. Did that mean that I was gay? Did that mean I was sick? My friend smiled. No, she said, it means you're perfectly normal. Did it ever occur to you that the ultra-horny guys on TV might not be realistic?

Some of our major sources of information about sex come from the media. Everything from the mildest innuendo on a network sitcom to the rawest pornography on X-rated video is contributing to our perceived reality of what sex is all about. We're continually learning about sex and modifying our constructed reality of its nature. How we act on that information may have serious consequences on our lives and the lives of others. After examining the nature of sex in the media, we will examine research on its effects, with particular focus on one of the most controversial varieties, sexual violence.

THE NATURE OF SEX IN MEDIA

Definitional Issues

Whenever we speak of sex in the media, we must clarify what we are considering. There is a class of media (at least in the U.S.) clearly labelled "pornographic," "X-rated" (in the case of movies), or "sexually explicit." These materials are typically marketed separately from nonsexual media and are at least somewhat restricted from children, although just how restricted they are and should be remains a controversial issue. These media are generally recognized as being for sexual purposes only and without recognized literary or artistic merit. One possible exception to this is the relatively tame *Playboy,* which, alone among sex magazines, has some genuine literary respectability. Finally, there is also a class of serious educational and semi-educational materials such as sex manuals like *The Joy of Sex.*

The 1986 Meese Commission (Final Report, 1986) identified five classes of what it called "pornography." (a) *Sexually violent material* portrayed rape and other instances of physical harm to persons in a sexual context. (b) *Nonviolent materials depicting degradation, domination, subordination, or humiliation* constituted the largest class of commercially available materials and portrayed women as "masochistic, subservient, and over-responsive to the male interest." (c) *Nonviolent and nondegrading materials* typically depicted a couple having vaginal or oral intercourse with no indication of violence or coercion. (d) *Nudity* showed the naked human body with no obvious sexual behavior or intent. (e) *Child pornography* involves minors and, though illegal to produce in the United States, still circulates widely through foreign magazines and personal distribution. Because not everyone would agree that all of these classes of materials are "pornographic," and because the term "pornographic" is highly value-laden but scientifically imprecise, we will instead generally refer to such materials arre "sexually explicit" rather than "pornographic."

Clearly, sex also occurs in the media in other than explicitly sexual materials. For example, it is rampant in advertising, particularly for products like perfume, cologne, and after shave, but also for tires, automobiles, and the kitchen sink. See Chapter 4 for a discussion of classical conditioning in advertising. Sex in media is not limited to explicit portrayals of intercourse or nudity but rather may include any representation which portrays or implies sexual behavior, interest, or motivation. The major focus in this chapter, however, will be on the more explicit materials.

History of Sex in Media

Sexual themes in fiction have been around as long as fiction itself. Ancient Greek comedies were often highly sexual in content, such as Aristophanes' *Lysistrata,* an antiwar comedy about women who withhold sex from their husbands to coerce them to stop fighting wars. Literary classics like Chaucer's *Canterbury Tales* and Shakespeare's *The Taming of the Shrew* are filled with sexual double entendres and overtly sexual themes, some of which is missed today due to the archaic language and the "classic" aura around such works. Throughout history, the pendulum has swung back and forth in terms of how widespread and explicit sexual expression in literature can be.

Since the advent of broadcast media, standards have generally been more conservative for radio and television than for print, because it is easier to keep sexually-oriented print media from children than it is broadcast. With the advent of widespread cable and videocassette technology in the 1980s, a sort of double standard has arisen, with greater permissiveness for cable and cassette than for network television, on the logic than cable and rented movies are "invited" into the home, while network programming is there uninvited whenever a TV set is present.

There has been considerable change in regard to sexual expression on television in the last 40 years, as discussed in Chapter 5. In the 1950s it was considered unacceptable to show a married couple sharing the same bed. Thus Lucy and Ricky Ricardo on "I Love Lucy" slept in twin beds and spoke of her condition as "expecting" or "having a baby," but never as "pregnant," a word considered as inappropriate in 1952 as "fuck" or "nigger" would be today.

Media Sex Today

Content analyses (Sprafkin & Silverman, 1981) show that none of the sex on network television is explicit, though innuendoes are rampant. Most of these occur in a humorous context, primarily in sitcoms and variety show in these late-1970s samples. One interesting finding is that references to premarital and extramarital sexual encounters far outnumbered references to sex between spouses (Fernandez-Collado & Greenberg, 1978). Although more sexual references overall occurred in daytime soaps than on prime-time TV, evening programming contained more references to intercourse and sexual deviance (Greenberg, Abelman, & Neuendorf, 1981).

In a study examining the sources from which children and teenagers have acquired information about sex over the last few decades, Gebhard (1977) concluded that children are learning basic facts about sex earlier than was formerly the case. More interestingly, mass media have risen in importance as a source of such information (up to third in the 1975 sample, behind peers and mother).

Sex in media is one area where we clearly accept some limits on freedom of speech. The sharp differences of opinion surface in deciding just where those limits ought to be. Few are arguing that "The Cosby Show" should be allowed to showed frontal nudity or child prostitutes in chains, in the highly unlikely event that the producers would ever care to do so. One important issue in discussion of where the limits should be is the age of the viewer or reader. There is far more concern about the effects of sexual media on children than on adults. Even the most libertarian person would probably not want their 6-year-old reading *Hustler,* whereas even the most puritanical person would have fewer concerns about adults viewing X-rated videos than about children seeing them.

Media are clearly major sources of information about sex, information which we use to construct our reality of what sexuality and sexual behavior and values are all about. To better understand this perceived reality, let's turn to examining some effects of viewing sex in the media. How are we different after exposure to such material?

EFFECTS OF VIEWING MEDIA SEX

What is in one sense the most important effect is that sex draws an audience, a reality that has crucial economic ramifications for all media. As much as many might wish it otherwise, sex does sell, even very raunchy sex. Sexually-oriented media, both print and broadcast, are highly profitable commercially. This economic effect, however, is not the focus of this book; let us turn now to the various psychological effects.

Arousal

A fairly straightforward effect of sex in media is sexual arousal, the drive that energizes or intensifies sexual behavior (Zillmann, 1978, 1984). Sexually oriented media, especially explicit magazines and videos, do tend to arouse people sexually, both in terms of self-rating of arousal level and physiological arousal measures such as penile tumescence (Malamuth & Check, 1980a), vaginal changes (Sintchak &

Geer, 1975), and thermography (Abramson, Perry, Seeley, Seeley, & Rothblatt, 1981). Sexual violence is particularly arousing to sex offenders and much less so to normal men, unless the victim is portrayed as being aroused by the assault; these findings are discussed in more detail later in the chapter.

Sexual arousal to stimuli not naturally evoking such response may be learned through classical conditioning. For example, Rachman (1966) and Rachman and Hodgson (1968) classically conditioned men to be sexually aroused by women's boots by pairing the boots with nude photos, thus providing a model of how fetishes could be learned. More generally, this could account for the vast individual differences in what specific stimuli arouse people sexually. Through our different experiences, we have all been conditioned to different stimuli.

Contrary to what one might expect, the degree of arousal is not necessarily highly correlated with the degree of explicitness of the media. Sometimes one is actually more aroused by a less sexually explicit story than a more explicit one (e.g., Bancroft & Mathews, 1971). Censoring out a sex scene may actually make a film more arousing because viewers can fill in their own completion. Sexual arousal is highly individual. When people are allowed to use their own imaginations to construct the ending of a romantic scene, they are more likely to construct a reality that is more arousing to them personally than if they view someone else's idea of what is arousing. There is some validity to the old truism that the major sex organ is the brain.

Attitudes and Values

Some issues.   A large class of effects of media sex have to do with effects on attitudes and values. One frequent concern is a desensitization to certain expressions of sexuality deemed by someone to be "inappropriate." For example, parents may be concerned that TV sitcoms showing teenagers considering being sexually active may contradict and thus weaken family-taught values against premarital sex. Women may be concerned that car magazines selling shock absorbers by showing a bikini-clad woman held in mock bondage by a giant shock absorber may desensitize readers about violence toward women.

Sometimes the media may actually change one's value or attitude, rather then merely desensitizing or reinforcing an existing one. It may be that teenage girls watching Mallory Keaton on "Family Ties" as she considers having sex with her boy friend may also come to adopt those values. This is especially likely to happen if the TV characters holding those values are respected characters whom viewers identify with. Sexual promiscuity by a prostitute character is less likely to influence the values of a viewer than promiscuity by a respected suburban wife and mother.

Another concern about effects on values and attitudes is that sexual-oriented media may encourage people not to take sexual issues as seriously as they should. When a sex magazine has a regular cartoon called "Chester the Molester" featuring a child molester, many argue that this is an inappropriately light treatment of an extremely serious subject. One article in a sex magazine aimed at male teenagers was entitled "Good Sex with Retarded Girls"; this too is open to such criticism. Although few would probably argue that sex should *never* be comedic, there are for most people some sexual subjects that do not seem appropriate for light treatment.

One type of value of particular concern are attitudes toward women. One of the major criticisms of sexual media is that it is anti-women in a ideological sense. This feminist critique points out that it is usually women, not men, who are the playthings of the opposite sex and the victims of violence in such media. Although this concern spans the gamut of sexual content in media, it is particularly leveled at sexual violence. What are teenage boys going to think women want when they see a picture of a jackhammer in a woman's vagina as the opening photo to a story called "How to Cure Frigidity?" When *Hustler* magazine runs a photo spread of a gang rape turning into an orgy, showing the women appearing to be aroused by the assault, what is being taught about women and their reactions to forcible sex? Research examining this question will be discussed in detail later in the chapter.

Finally in regard to values and attitudes, people sometimes complain that sex in the media, especially the more explicit varieties, removes some of the mystique, some of the aura, from what is a very mysterious, almost sacred, activity. This argument holds that sex is very private and more meaningful and more fun if it is not so public. This is a hard concern even to articulate, even harder to refute or test empirically, but it is one often expressed.

Research evidence.   Several studies have shown effects on attitudes and values about sex as a result of exposure to nonviolent sexually explicit materials. After seeing slides and movies of beautiful female nudes engaged in sexual activity, male subjects rated their own partners as being less physically endowed, though they reported un-diminished sexual satisfaction (Weaver, Masland, & Zillmann, 1984). Using a paradigm of showing subjects weekly films and testing them 1 to 3 weeks later, Zillmann and Bryant (1982, 1984) found that subjects seeing the films overestimated the popularity of sexual practices like fellatio, cunnilingus, anal intercourse, sadomasochism, and bestiality, relatively to perceptions of a control group seeing nonsexually-explicit films. This may reflect the cognitive heuristic of *availability*, whereby we judge the frequency of occurrence of various activities by the ease with which we can generate examples (Taylor, 1982; Tversky & Kahneman, 1973, 1974). Recent vivid media instances thus lead to an overestimation of such occurrences in the real world and a perceived reality substantially at odds with actual reality.

Using the same methodology as Zillmann and Bryant (1982, 1984), Zillmann and Bryant (1988, in press) found effects of this perceived reality on attitudes about real people. Subjects seeing the explicit films reported, relative to a control group, less satisfaction with the affection, physical appearance, sexual curiosity, and sexual performance of their real-life partners. They also saw sex without emotional involvement as being relatively more important than the control group did. They showed greater acceptance of premarital and extramarital sex and and lesser evaluation of marriage and monogamy. They also showed less desire to have children and greater acceptance of male dominance and female servitude. Results generally did not differ for males versus females or students versus nonstudents.

The medium may make a difference. Dermer and Pyszczynski's (1978) subjects were told to think about their mates before *reading* some explicit passages about a woman's sexual fantasies. They later rated their own partner as more sexually attractive. This deviation from the Zillmann and Bryant results may be due to specific procedural aspects of the research or to psychological differences between the media. Nonpictorial descriptions of sex in words in the print medium may be more conducive to fantasizing about one's own partner, while photographic sex may encourage unfavorable comparison to that person.

Catharsis

Another alleged effect of media sex is catharsis, that emotional release so important to psychodynamic models of personality (e.g., Freud). Applied to sex, the catharsis argument says that watching media sex will relieve one's sexual urges, using the magazine or video as a sort of substitute (albeit imperfect) for the real thing. A catharsis argument is frequently used by libertarians to support appeals for lessening restrictions on sexually explicit material (e.g., Kutchinsky, 1973). The research support for catharsis as a function of viewing media sex is meager if not totally nonexistent, however (Comstock, 1985; Final Report, 1986).

Behavioral Effects

Teaching new behaviors.   Another large class of effects are effects on behavior, parallel to the new violent behaviors that may be learned from media. On the one hand, sexual media may actually teach new behaviors. As part of sex therapy, a couple may buy a sex manual in order to learn new sexual positions or behaviors that they did not know before. New behaviors are not always so benign, however. A movie showing a gang rape on a pool table was shown in New Bedford, Massachesetts shortly before a similar event occurred in real life in a nearby bar. The December 1984 issue of *Penthouse* contained a series of photographs of Asian women bound with heavy rope, hung from trees, and sectioned into parts. Two months later an 8-year-old Chinese girl in Chapel Hill, North Carolina, was kidnapped, raped, murdered, and left hanging from a tree limb. (NY *Times,* 2/4/85, cited in Final Report, 1986, p. 208). Of course, such effects are not commonplace and definitively demonstrating a causal relationship in such cases is difficult, but the juxtaposition is nonetheless disturbing.

Some of the rawest material shows extreme sexual violence that might be copied by a viewer. These include very violent and offensive images, including women apparently being killed ("snuff" films) through torturing them with power tools or even such bizarre and twisted images as sexual penetration of eye sockets after death ("skull-fucking"). For obvious ethical reasons, it is difficult to scientifically study effects of such extreme materials.

Disinhibition.   Erotic material may also disinhibit previously learned behavior, such as when watching TV's treatment of premarital sex disinhibits a viewer's inhibition against doing such behavior. Watching a rape scene where a woman is portrayed as enjoying being assaulted may disinhibit some men's secret urge to commit such a crime. This is of particular concern given some evidence suggesting that a surprisingly large number of college students reported they might rape if they were sure they would not get caught (Check, 1985; Malamuth, Haber, & Feshbach, 1980).

Sex crimes. One of the main concerns about a behavioral effect of viewing sexually explicit materials is a possible relationship with sex crimes. There have been many studies looking at rates of crimes like rape, exhibitionism, and child molestation, relative to changes in availability of sexually explicit materials, In a careful review of such studies, Court (1984; see also Court, 1977, 1982, and Bachy, 1976) argues that there is in fact a correlation of availability of sexually explicit materials and certain sex crimes. He claims that earlier studies, especially Kutchinsky's (1973) study claiming a drop in reported sex crimes in Denmark after liberalization of pornography restrictions in the 1960s, are not really valid, due to an inappropriate lumping of rape with nonviolent acts like voyeurism, indecent exposure, and homosexuality.

Most Western nations have experienced a large increase both in the availability of sexually explicit media and the rise in reported rapes in the last 20 years. Court presents some data from the Australian states of Queensland and South Australia that show a sharp increase in rape reports in South Australia but not Queensland after state pornography laws were liberalized in South Australia in the early 1970s. A comparable downturn in reported rapes occurred temporarily in Hawaii between 1974 and 1976 during a temporary imposition of restraints on sexually explicit media. For an interesting and apparent counterexample, see Box 10.1.

Firmly establishing a causal relationship between the availability of sexually explicit media and the frequency of rapes is extremely difficult, due to the many other relevant factors, including the different varieties of sexual material, changes in social consciousness about reporting sexual assaults, and changing norms sanctioning such behavior. Some evidence (Final Report, 1986) suggests a correlation of rape and circulation of sex magazines, particularly those containing sexual violence. For example, Baron and Straus found a correlation of +.64 for rape rates and circulation rates of eight sex magazines in 50 states. While others argue no demonstrated relationship, very few currently support a catharsis explanation that sexually explicit material allows open expression of sexual urges, thus decreasing the rate of sex crimes.

Although no one argues that rape is a victimless crime or should be permitted, pornography and obscenity laws are often attacked in part

Box 10.1. PORNOGRAPHY IN JAPAN

As discussed by Abramson and Hayashi (1984), Japan is an interesting and unusual case study of a society with wide availability of sexual media but very low rape rates. Sexual themes in art and society go back centuries to ancient fertility religious objects and wood block prints called *ukiyo-e*. Although some restriction and censorship occurred after the Meiji Restoration in 1868 and even more after the American occupation after World War II, sexuality continued to be a strong theme of Japanese society and one not associated with shame or guilt. Although there are specific restrictions on showing pictorial representation of pubic hair or adult genitalia anywhere in Japan, there is no restriction of sexual media to certain types of magazines, bookstores, or theaters, as occurs in the United States. Thus nudity, bondage, and rape occur regularly on commercial television and popular movies and magazines, including advertising. Although less explicit sexual scenes with no pubic hair or genitalia are shown in Japan, films portray very vivid scenes of rape and bondage.

Why, then, is the incidence of reported rapes so much lower in Japan than elsewhere (2.4 per 100,000 versus 34.5 in the U.S., 10.1 in England, and 10.7 in West Germany)? Abramson and Hayashi argue that the answer may lie in cultural differences. Japanese society emphasizes order, obligation, cooperation, and virtue, and one who violates social norms is the object of shame. Also, sex is not compartmentalized relative to other segments of society as it is in the United States. Others have suggested that rape in Japan in more likely to be group-instigated, perpetrated by juveniles, and greatly underreported by victims (Goldstein & Ibaraki, 1983).

on the grounds that they proscribe victimless crimes that is not worth police and judicial effort to prosecute. See Box 10.2 for a different perspective on this question.

Prevailing Tone

The perceived reality of media sex and the responses to and effects of sex in the media are not entirely due to the nature of the material itself. They also depend on the context of the material itself and the context in which the person sees it (Eysenck & Nias, 1978; Nias, 1983). This diverse collection of variables is called the "prevailing

204

tone." The nature of this prevailing tone can make enormous difference in the experience of consuming sexual explicit media.

BOX 10.3. PROSOCIAL USES OF SEXUALLY EXPLICIT MATERIALS

Most of the research on sex in the media tends to focus on and test for undesirable effects. However, sexually explicit media may also be used in positive ways to treat sexual dysfunctions such as excessive sexual anxiety or failure to achieve orgasm. For example, videotaped models are presented for observational learning, and systematic desensitization therapy may help reduce anxiety. Such techniques have been successful in changing both attitudes and behavior (Caird & Wincze, 1977; Heiby & Becker, 1980; Heiman, LoPiccolo, & LoPiccolo, 1976).

Secondly, sexual materials are used in diagnosis and treatment of sex offenders. For example, testing one's arousal patterns to different photos might indicate an "inappropriate" pattern, such as sexual arousal in response to children. This arousal pattern may then be modified through behavior therapy. Such techniques have been successful, especially if combined with social skills training (Abel, Becker, & Skinner, 1980; Whitman & Quinsey, 1981). See Quinsey and Marshall (1983) for a review of such approaches.

One of the relevant variables of the prevailing tone is the degree of playfulness or seriousness of the material. Even a highly explicit and potentially controversial topic may not be particularly controversial when presented seriously. For example, a documentary on rape or a tastefully done TV movie on incest may be considered perfectly acceptable, whereas a far less explicit comedy with the same theme may be highly offensive and considered "too sexual." What is really the concern in such cases is not the sex as such, but rather the comedic treatment of it. Highly explicit videos, books, and magazines are used routinely and noncontroversially in sex therapy to treat sexual dysfunctions generally and sex offenders specifically (See Box 10.3).

A second factor in the prevailing tone is the artistic worth and intent. We react very differently to a sexually explicit drawing from Picasso vs. *Hustler* magazine. Shakespeare, Chaucer, *The Song of Solomon* in the Bible, and serious sex manuals like *The Joy of Sex* are seen to have serious literary or didactic intentions and thus the sex therein is considered more acceptable and even healthy. One interesting issue in this regard is how to respond to something written at a time when standards differed from what they are today. For example, should "The Honeymooners" Ralph Kramden's mock threat to Alice, "One of the these days, Alice, Pow, right in the kisser!" be taken as implied violence toward women or seen as the noncontroversial slapstick comedy line that is was in 1955? A parallel concern has been raised in regard to racism, where some people want to remove *Huckleberry Finn* from high school libraries and curricula because the portrayal of the slave Jim seems racist by modern standards.

The relation and integration of sex to the overall plot and intent of the piece is also a part of the prevailing tone. A sex scene, even a mild and nonexplicit one, may be offensive if it appears to be "thrown in" merely to spice up the story but having no connection to it. Something far more explicit may be received much better if it is necessary and central to the plot. Sex scenes in a story about a prostitute may be much less gratuitous than comparable scenes in a story about a female corporate executive. Sex, of course, is not the only common gratuitous factor in media; for example, contemporary TV shows and movies frequently insert car chases and rock video segments completely unrelated to the plot.

Although not the predominant factor many think it is, the degree of explicitness of sex is nevertheless a real factor. Sex may be shown explicitly or implied by innuendo. In the latter sense, one of the sexiest shows was the old TV sitcom "Three's Company," where there were constant remarks and double entendres dealing with sex, but never anything explicit. A study of women's reactions to sex in TV commercials (Johnson & Satow, 1978) found that older women were more offended by the more explicit material, whereas younger women were more offended by innuendo, especially that which could readily be considered sexist.

The context of the viewing also influences the effect of sex in the media. Watching an erotic film with one's parents versus by oneself or in a group of close same-sex friends versus with one's spouse, the reaction to it may be very different as a function of who one watches it with. It was be seen as more or less erotic or arousing and more or less appropriate or offensive.

The cultural context is also a factor. Some cultures of the world do not consider female breasts to be particular erotic or inappropriate for public display. We recognize these cultural differences and thus, at least after the age of 14, most readers do not consider topless women in *National Geographic* photos to be the slightest bit erotic, sexual, or inappropriate. Even in Western culture, standards have changed. In much of the 19th century, knees and calves were thought to be erotic, and the sight of a bare-kneed woman would be as scandalous, perhaps even as sexually arousing, in most settings as a topless woman is today. As societies go, North America overall is a bit more conservative than many Northwest European cultures but far less conservative than Eastern Europe and particularly many Islamic and East Asian cultures.

Finally, the expectations we have affect our perception of the prevailing tone. Sex is less offensive and shocking if it is expected than if it appears as a surprise. Seeing a photo of a nude women being fed through a meat grinder may be less shocking in *Hustler* magazine than if we were to suddenly encounter it in *Newsweek*. The stimulus may be the same, but the perceived reality of the experience of seeing it would differ considerably in the two cases.

Let's look now at some of the major conclusions of the two most comprehensive U.S. reports on the effects of sexually explicit media, the so-called pornography commissions.

THE PORNOGRAPHY COMMISSIONS

National Commission on Obscenity and Pornography

This commission was established by President Lyndon Johnson in 1967 to analyze the (a) pornography control laws, (b) distribution of sexually explicit materials, and (c) effects of consuming such materials, and to recommend appropriate legislative or administrative action. It funded over 80 research studies on the topic, providing important impetus to the scientific study of sexual explicit material. The final report three years later (U.S. Commission on Obscenity and Pornography, 1970) recommended stronger controls on distribution to minors but an abolition of all limits on access by adults. The latter recommendation was based on the majority conclusion that there was "no evidence that exposure to or use of explicit sexual materials play a significant role in the causation of social or individual harms such as crime, delinquency, sexual or nonsexual deviancy or severe emotional disturbance" (p. 58). The report also included a series of minority conclusions, which argued for some curbs on sexually explicit materials.

Although the composition of the commission has been criticized for being overloaded with anti-censorship civil libertarians (Eysenck & Nias, 1978), its majority conclusions were rejected anyway by the new administration of Richard Nixon, who declared, "so long as I am in the White House there will be no relaxation of the national effort to control and eliminate smut from our national life" (Eysenck & Nias, 1978, p. 94). During the same period, the Longford (Longford, 1972) and Williams (1979) Commissions in Great Britain issued reports, followed a few years later by the Fraser Commission in Canada (Report of the Special Committee on Pornography and Prostitution, 1985). The major conclusion of these commissions was a lack of conclusiveness of the research to date. See Einsiedel (1988) for a discussion of these commissions and their social and political context and interpretations of research.

The "Meese Commission"

The nature of sexual media changed greatly from 1970 to 1985, particularly in the great increase of sado-masochistic themes and the linking of sex and violence, themes relatively rare in 1970, or at least not seriously addressed by the earlier U.S. commission. Additionally, technological advancements like cable and satellite TV and VCRs made sexually explicit material available in the home far more easily and privately than formerly was the case. In 1985 1700 new sexually explicit videocassettes were released in the U.S., accounting for about one-fifth of videotape rentals and sales (Final Report, 1986). These changes, plus certain social and political considerations, led to the formation of the new commission.

U.S. Attorney General Edwin Meese charged the newly formed commission in 1985 to "determine the nature, extent, and impact on society of pornography in the United States, and to make specific recommendations . . . concerning more effective ways in which the spread of pornography could be contained, consistent with constitutional guarantees." Although there is a clear political position even in this charge, the part of the Final Report (1986) of most interest here concerns the issue of possible harmful effects of exposure to sexual explicit material. See Paletz (1988) for an examination of the political context and press coverage of the commission.

One of the major conclusions of the commission dealt with the effect of sexual violence, "the available evidence strongly supports the hypothesis that substantial exposure to sexually violent materials . . . bears a causal relationship to antisocial acts of sexual violence, and for some subgroups, possibly the unlawful acts of sexual violence" (p. 40). Evidence for this conclusion will be discussed in the next section.

Groups like the Meese Commission typically have both a scientific and political agenda (Paletz, 1988; Wilcox, 1987). Sometimes, even if there is relative consensus on the scientific conclusions, there is often strong disagreement about the policy ramifications. For example, Linz, Donnerstein, & Penrod (1987) take exception with some of the conclusions drawn by the Meese Commission from those researchers' own work demonstrating deleterious effects of sexual violence (see discussion below). Linz argued that the Commission's call for strengthening obscenity laws was not an appropriate policy change based on the research, because it ignored the strong presence of sexually violent themes in other media and aspects of society other than that which would be legally defined as obscene.

SEXUAL VIOLENCE

Though neither sex nor violence in the media is anything new, the integral combination of the two has become far more prevalent in recent years. Cable and VCR technology has greatly expanded the capability of much of the public to view X-rated material. Although many people are not willing to seek out and visit theaters that show such films, the chance to see such material safely in one's own home make them much more accessible. Sex magazines are not new, but some particularly violent publications are relatively new, and even more "established" publications like *Penthouse* and *Playboy* show some evidence of increasing themes of sexual violence (Malamuth & Spinner, 1980). Dietz and Evans (1982) content analyzed the covers of 1760 sex magazines from 1970 to 1980; they found a huge increase in bondage and domination imagery (up to 17.2% of the covers by 1981). Finally, another old familiar genre, the horror film, has recently evolved into showing frequent and extensive scenes of violence against women in a sexual context (Maslin, 1982). These films are heavily targeted at teenagers, in spite of the R or PG-13 ratings many of them receive. With all of these the major concern is not with the sex or violence in and of itself, but with the way the two appear together. The world constructed in the mind of the viewer of such materials can have some very serious consequences. Let us turn now to examining some of its effects.

Erotica as Stimulator of Aggression

Links between sex and aggression have long been speculated upon, particularly in the sense of sexual arousal facilitating violent behavior. The research has been inconsistent, however, with some studies showing that erotic materials facilitate aggression (Baron, 1979; Donnerstein & Hallam, 1978) and other showing they inhibit it (Donnerstein, Donnerstein, & Evans, 1975; White, 1979). The resolution of this issue apparently concerns the nature of the material. Sexual violence and unpleasant themes typically facilitate aggression, whereas non-violent, more loving and pleasant "soft-core" explicit materials may inhibit it (Zillmann, Bryant, Comisky, & Medoff, 1981). Thus, in considering the effects of sexual media, it is necessary to separate sexual violence from consenting, loving sex and also to consider the affective nature of the material (Sapolsky, 1984).

Effects of Seeing Sexual Violence

Malamuth (1984) reported several studies that showed male subjects sexual violence and afterwards measured their attitudes on several topics. Subjects seeing the films showed a more callous attitude toward rape and women in general, especially if the women victims in the film were portrayed as being aroused by the assault. In terms of sexual arousal, subjects were aroused by the sexual violence only if the victim was shown to be aroused but not if she was not so portrayed.

Individual differences.   Other studies examined convicted rapists and found them to be aroused by both rape and consenting sex, whereas normal subjects were aroused only by the consenting sex (Abel, Bar-low, Blanchard, & Guild, 1977; Barbaree, Marshall, & Lanthier, 1979). A important exception to this occurred if the victim was por-trayed as enjoying the rape and coming to orgasm; in this case normal males (but not females) were equally or more aroused by the rape than the consenting sex (Malamuth, Heim, & Feshbach, 1980).

In further examining this question in regard to individual differ-ences in males, Malamuth (1981) identified one group of college males who were "force-oriented," that is, prone to use force in their own lives. This group, and a group of normal men, were shown a film where a man stops his car on a deserted road to pick up a female. Following this, they either have sex in his car (both consenting) or he rapes her, though she is depicted as finally enjoying the assault. Students were then asked to create their own sexual fantasies to achieve a high level of arousal. Although normal males were more aroused by the consenting scene than the sexual violence, the reverse was true for the force-oriented males!

In another study (Malamuth & Check, 1983), male subjects listened to a tape of a sexual encounter with consenting or nonconsenting sex where the woman showed either arousal or disgust. Where the woman showed disgust, both force-oriented and nonforce-oriented males were more aroused, in terms of both self-report and penile tumescence, by the consenting than the nonconsenting (rape) scene. However, when the woman was portrayed as being aroused, the nonforce-oriented males were equally aroused by both consenting and nonconsenting versions, while the force-oriented subjects showed more arousal to the nonconsenting version.

Donnerstein (1980) showed male students either a nonviolent but sexually explicit film or a film where a woman was sexually abused and assaulted. Subjects seeing the latter but not the former film were more likely to administer electric shocks to a third party in a subsequent "experiment" on learning and punishment, especially so in subjects who had been previously angered. In a similar study (Donnerstein & Berkowitz, 1981), male subjects saw a sexually violent film where a woman is attacked, stripped, tied up, and raped. In one version of the film the woman was portrayed as enjoying the rape. Afterwards subjects were a given a chance to administer electric shocks to a confederate of the experimenter, the same confederate who had earlier angered them. Subjects seeing the film where the woman enjoyed being raped administered more shocks to a female confederate, but not to the male. This suggests that the association of sex and violence in the film allows violent behavior to be transferred to the target confederate.

Several conclusions emerge from this line of research. One is that a critical aspect of the perceived reality of sexual violence is whether the woman is seen as enjoying and being aroused by the assault. Far more undesirable effects generally occur in normal men if the woman is seen to be aroused than if she is seen to be terrorized. This media portrayal of women as being "turned on" by rape is apparently not only a distasteful deviation from reality but also a potentially dangerous one. A second important conclusion is that sexually violent media often affect different men very differently, depending on their own propensity to use force in their own lives. Convicted rapists and other force-oriented men are more likely to become aroused or even incited to violence by sexually violent media, especially if the women is portrayed as being aroused by the assault.

Slasher movies.   Because the studies discussed so far used very sexually explicit materials that would often be termed "pornographic," many might consider them beyond the limits of what they themselves would be exposed. However, explicit sexual violence is by no means confined to X-rated materials or what are often seen as pornographic. For example, more "mainstream" R-rated films are readily available to most teenagers anywhere, in theaters and even more so in video stores. There are the highly successful series like *Halloween, Friday the Thirteenth,* and *Nightmare on Elm Street,* but also many lesser known films. Most are extremely violent with at least strong sexual overtones. For example, *Alien Prey* shows a blood-stained vampire sucking out a dead woman's entrails through a hole in her stomach. *Flesh Feast* treats us to "body maggots" consuming live human beings, starting with the face and working down. *Make Them Die Slowly* promises "24 scenes of barbaric torture," such as a man slicing a woman in half (*Time,* 6/1/87, p. 31). *The Offspring* shows a soldier choking a little-girl captive to death while kissing her.

Although some of these films have R ratings, other are released unrated to avoid the "accompanied by parent" restriction of R movies in the United States. Because no restrictions apply in video stores anyway, the rating is not a major issue. The viewing of such films is widespread among youth. A recent survey of 4500 English and Welsh children found that almost 20% of the 13- 14-year-old boys had seen the sexually violent *I Spit on Your Grave,* a film deemed legally obscene and liable to prosecution in the United Kingdon (Hill, Davis, Holman, & Nelson, 1984)!

The major concern with such films is the juxtaposition of erotic sex and violence. For example, one scene from *Toolbox Murders* opens with a beautiful woman disrobing and getting into her bath, with very romantic music "Pretty Baby" playing in the background. For several minutes she is shown fondling herself, even masturbating, in a very erotic manner. Suddenly the camera cuts to the scene of an intruder breaking into her apartment, with loud, fast-paced suspenseful music in the background. The camera and sound track cut back and forth several times between these two characters until he finally encounters the woman. He attacks her with electric tools, chasing her around the apartment, finally shooting her several times in the head with a nail gun. The scene closes after seeing her bleed profusely, finally lying on the bed to die with the sound track again playing the erotic "Pretty Baby."

Linz, Donnerstein, and Penrod (1984; see also Linz, 1985) were interested in the effects of such films. Their college-student male subjects were initially screened for psychoticism to exclude those who had prior hostile tendencies or psychological problems. Remaining subjects in the experimental group were shown one standard Holly-wood-released R-rated film per day over one week, an admittedly heavy dose. All of the films were very violent and showed multiple instances of women being killed in slow lingering, painful deaths in situations associated with much erotic content (e.g., the *Toolbox Mur-*

ders scene described above). Each day the subjects filled out some questionnaires evaluating that film and also completed some personality measures.

These ratings showed subjects were less depressed, less annoyed, and less anxious in response to the films after a week. The films themselves were rated more enjoyable, more humorous, more socially meaningful, less violent and offensive, and less degrading to women over time. Over time, the violent episodes in general and rape episodes in particular were rated less frequent. A similar study by Krafka (1985) tested women and did not find the same effects. Although these data provide clear evidence of desensitization in men, there is still the question of generalization from the films to other situations.

To answer this question Linz, Donnerstein, and Penrod arranged to have the same subjects participate in a later study which they did not know to have any connection to the movies. For this experiment, they observed a rape trial at the law school and evaluated it in several ways. Compared to a control group, subjects who had seen the slasher films rated the rape victim as less physically and emotionally injured. These results are consistent with those of Zillmann and Bryant (1984), who found that massive exposure to pornography resulted in shorter recommended prison sentences for a rapist. Such findings show that the world we construct in response to seeing such movies can be at variance with reality and can have dire consequences when actions are taken believing that such a world is reality.

Not surprisingly, this study and others by the authors along the same line (See Donnerstein, Linz, & Penrod, 1987, for a review) have caused considerable concern in the public. They have also caused considerable scientific concern. Some of the major effects have not been replicated in later work (Linz & Donnerstein, 1988), and there have been some methodological criticisms. The sharp distinction that Donnerstein and Linz make between the effects of violent and nonviolent pornography has also been called into question (Zillmann & Bryant, 1988). Research findings have been somewhat inconsistent in each area; Zillmann and Bryant argue that Linz and Donnerstein are too quick to cite failures to reject the null hypothesis as support for the harmlessness of nonviolent pornography, yet they all but ignore such results in arguing for serious deleterious effects of sexual violence. There is considerable controversy about the use and interpretation of data from particular studies. How this will be resolved is still unclear; we clearly need more research, especially on slasher-type movies.

Mitigating the negative effects.   Whatever the exact nature of the effects of sexual violence, results from the studies discussed above tend to be disturbing, especially given the widespread viewing of slasher films by children and young teens and the overall increase in sexually violent media. Many of the studies discussed above have developed and evaluated an extensive debriefing procedure which may shed some light on possible ways to lessen the desensitizing effect of such violence.

For example, Linz, Donnerstein, Bross, & Chapin (1986) report an experiment where they "warned" subjects ahead of time about possible desensitizing effects of seeing the slasher films. At this time, many subjects chose to withdraw from the experiment and not see the films; in addition, several dropped out before seeing all five films. Before they dropped out, however, their ratings suggested they were more sensitive to the sexual violence than a control group. Those who stayed and saw all the films showed some desensitizing effects but not others.

Other studies discussed by Linz, Donnerstein, Bross, & Chapin (1986) suggest that a debriefing after seeing the films is highly effective at sensitizing subjects to violence against women. They suggest that an important factor is that the debriefing follow the film and contain specific reference to it. Apparently subjects are much more impressed with the arguments after they have felt themselves excited and aroused by the film and have very specific examples to illustrate the point of the debriefing lecture. In the context of having seen such a film, the specific points of the sensitization lecture have much greater impact. See Box 10.4 for further discussion of ethical issues in such research.

CONCLUSION

What may we conclude from the research on the perceived reality and effects from viewing sexual media? First, it is useful to make a distinction between violent and nonviolent sexual media. The picture regarding nonviolent media is least clear. Aside from the effect of arousal, the research is inconsistent. Although there may be some negative effects of nonviolent material (e.g., Zillmann & Bryant, 1988, in press), the research is inconsistent and clearly calls for further study.

On the issue of violent sexual media, however, some clearer conclusions are possible. Sexual violence is arousing to sex offenders, force-oriented men, and sometimes even to "normal" young men if the woman is portrayed as being aroused by the attack. Repeated

BOX 10.4. ETHICS OF SEX RESEARCH

The more potential harm is identified from viewing sexually explicit (especially sexually violent) materials, the more question is raised about the ethics of doing research by exposing people to such materials. Although we have clearly learned some valuable information, what will be the cost of this knowledge in terms of the lives of the subjects? This issue has been taken seriously by Malamuth, Heim, and Feshbach (1980) and others, who have offered subjects an extensive debriefing, complete with information on the horrible reality of rape and the complete unreality of someone enjoying it. Malamuth and associates even included a discussion of why the myth of enjoying being raped was so prevalent in sexually violent media. Some studies have included evaluations of such debriefing sessions and shown that, compared to a control group not in the experiment, debriefed subjects showed less acceptance of rape myths (Donnerstein & Berkowitz, 1981; Malamuth & Check, 1980b). It is, of course, unethical to have an "ideal" control group that views the sexual violence in the experiment but is not debriefed!

exposure to sexual violence may lead to desensitization toward violence against women in general and greater acceptance of rape myths. In this sense the "no effects" conclusion of the 1970 commission must be revised. Not only does this suggest that the combination of sex and violence together is considerably worse than either one separately, but it also matters further what the nature of the portrayal is. If the woman being assaulted is portrayed as being terrorized and brutalized, negative effects on normal male viewers are less than if she is portrayed as being aroused and/or achieving orgasm through being attacked. Perhaps more that any other topic discussed in this book, this is an extremely dangerous reality for the media to create and for us to accept as real. There is nothing arousing or exciting about being raped, and messages to the contrary do not help teenage boys understand the reality of how to relate to girls and women.

Not all the themes of sexual aggression against women are then limited to X-rated material or even very violent movies. These images are found in mainstream television. For example, in a content analysis study, Lowry, Love, and Kirby (1981) found that, except for erotic touching among unmarried persons, aggressive sexual contact was the most frequent type of sexual interaction in daytime soap operas. A few years ago several episodes of "General Hospital" focused on the rape of one main character by another. Although the woman first appeared humiliated, she later fell in love with the rapist and married him. *Newsweek* (1981, p. 65) reported that producers and actors in soap operas believe the increase in sexual aggression in that genre has attracted more male viewers, "[males] started watching us because we no longer were wimps. When a woman was wrong, we'd slap her down." A content analysis of detective magazines found that 76% of the covers depicted domination of women, whereas 38% depicted women in bondage (Dietz, Harry, & Hazelwood, 1986), all of this in a publication never even considered sexual, much less pornographic!

The perceived reality of some of these media is that men dominate women and even brutalize them. The seriousness may be lessened if the women are, after all, turned on by being raped or tortured. That's what much of the media is saying about how men treat women, but what is the cost of this message on those in the public who may not realize that this picture deviates so significantly from reality?

Prosocial Uses
of Media

One of my earliest childhood memories from the 1950s involves watching a local young man named Fred Rogers and a young woman named Josie Carey host a local children's show on WQED, the new educational channel in Pittsburgh. Every afternoon after school we would turn on Channel 13 to see the pair visit the "attic" full of friends like the talking potted plant couple Phil and Rhonda Dendron. One very special day we were able to visit the studio and watch the show in person. Only later did its creator go national, and I realized I had seen the formative beginnings of "Mister Rogers Neighborhood."

Although it is too simplistic to say that media are all good or all bad, much of this book has focused on rather negative types of perceived realities gleaned from the media—worlds of excessive violence, deception, stereotyping, and misleading distortion. However, media can clearly be used in more positive ways, some of which we have already examined. Sometimes the overriding purpose of a major media enterprise is prosocial in nature, that is, specifically intended to produce some socially positive outcome. In this chapter we will examine some such projects, where the media are explicitly used to attempt to create a better world than what would exist otherwise. Although prosocial activity has been considered elsewhere in the book (e.g., in the chapter on values there was an emphasis on using the media to teach positive values), this chapter considers primarily efforts to teach skills, attitudes, knowledge, and behaviors, as well as values. The three major areas of focus will be educational television for children, social marketing to adults, and curriculum projects to teach better media

219

use. All of these projects attempt to alter the perceived reality we acquire from media in ways that have socially positive effects on individuals and society.

THE CHILDREN'S TELEVISION WORKSHOP PROJECTS

Given children's massive exposure to television, it is all but inconceivable that they are not learning anything from TV. Just what their perceived reality is and what they are learning requires careful examination of both the content of the programs and the cognitive processing that the child is capable of at different developmental stages. For a careful review of such issues, see Huston and Wright (1987). Here, however, we will focus on some specific projects to teach through television.

Although there had been some specifically children's shows on the networks going back to the 1950s ("Ding Dong School," "Romper Room," "Captain Kangaroo"), by the mid-1960s there was increased concern in developing some children's television programming that would be more explicitly educational and socially positive. In the United States the Corporation for Public Broadcasting was founded in 1967, followed by the Public Broadcasting System (PBS) in 1970. Although there had been some educational TV stations since the early 1950s, programming tended to be local and of relatively low budgets and low artistic and technical quality. This situation changed drastically with the founding of the Children's Television Workshop (CTW) in 1968, supported by both public and private funds.

Sesame Street

The next year saw the debut of "Sesame Street," one of the most important television shows of all time. Though only the first of several such shows, "Sesame Street" is still by far the most successful and popular young children's show worldwide; it has been translated into many languages but is always locally produced with adaptation to local culture. Its major purpose was to provide preschoolers with an enriched experience leading to prereading skills. The creators especially hoped to target so-called "disadvantaged" children who often enter school less prepared to learn to read.

The technical quality of "Sesame Street" has been consistently very high, using much animation, humor, and movement. Recognizing that commercials appeal to children, "Sesame Street" drew on many technical characteristics of ads, even going so far as to say things like "This program has been brought to you by the letter *H* and the number 6." The intentional use of a multiracial, multiethnic, multi-class cast ensemble has set a valued social model for children as well. Practically all people now reaching adulthood in many societies of the world have had some exposure to "Sesame Street," and many have had very heavy exposure. According to the 1981 Nielsens, 78% of 2- to 5-year-olds saw it weekly, making it by far the most watched educational TV program in history.

Besides being the most watched young children's TV show, "Sesame Street" has also been the most carefully evaluated show, in terms of research. Let's look now at some of the effects of watching "Sesame Street" (Ball & Bogatz, 1970, Bogatz & Ball, 1971; Cook, Appleton, Conner, Shaffer, Tabkin, & Weber, 1975).

As most parents can tell, the attention and interest level of "Sesame street" is high; preschoolers really do like the show. In terms of more substantive effects on learning, the results are mixed. There is some solid evidence for short-term effects, both in the sense of acquisition of pre-reading skills and positive social skills and attitudes, such as showing evidence of nonracist attitudes and behavior. Longer-term effects are less clear, and some studies have shown the advantages of "Sesame Street," compared to a control group not watching it, disappear after a few months or years (Bogatz & Ball, 1971).

Some interesting qualifications of these effects have been found. The positive effects are stronger if combined with parental discussion and teaching (Cook, Appleton, Conner, Shaffer, Tabkin, & Weber, 1975). This suggests that, among other functions, the program can serve as a good catalyst for informal education within the family. Another interesting finding was that "Sesame Street" helped higher socioeconomic status children more than lower socioeconomic status ones (Ball & Bogatz, 1970). Thus the show had the ironic effect of actually increasing the reading readiness gap between the higher and lower socioeconomic status children, when its stated goal had been to decrease that gap. In another sense, though, this should not have been unexpected, because any kind of intervention generally helps those who are most capable to begin with and thus more able to take full advantage of what it has to offer.

There were also positive social effects. Minority children watching "Sesame Street" showed increased cultural pride, confidence, and interpersonal cooperation (Greenberg, 1982). Also, after two years of watching "Sesame Street," White children showed more positive attitudes toward children of other races (Bogatz & Ball, 1971; Christensen & Roberts, 1983).

Other CTW Projects

In the fall of 1971 the Children's Television Workshop launched a second major programming effort with "The Electric Company", which used much of the successful "Sesame Street's" format but was aimed at improving the reading skills of older children (around second grade). "The Electric Company" was heavily used in the schools as well as at home. Evaluative research (Ball & Bogatz, 1973) found that viewing "The Electric Company" led to improved scores on a reading test battery in children who had watched in school but no improvement compared to a control group in those who had merely watched "The Electric Company" at home. This suggests that the show was helpful in teaching reading but primarily so in conjunction with the experiences offered in the classroom by the teacher and curriculum. Never as popular as "Sesame Street," it later operated in reruns and was finally cancelled in 1986.

A third CTW project, "3–2–1 Contact," debuted in 1980 with the goal of teaching scientific thinking to 8- to 12-year-olds. It attempted to help children experience the excitement of scientific discovery and encourage all children, particularly girls and minorities, to feel comfortable with science as an endeavor (Mielke & Chen, 1983).

There have been other CTW projects (e.g., "Feeling Good," "The Lion, the Witch, and the Wardrobe," and, most recently, "Square One TV"), as well as independent prosocial programs like "Freestyle," "Vegetable Soup," and "Infinity Factory." A continuing concern is obtaining funding for such productions, especially in the era of decreased federal assistance and general budget-cutting in the United States. Some have criticized newer programs such as "Square One TV" as being more entertainment than education, due to economic pressures. For reviews of these programs and their effects, see Bryant, Alexander, and Brown (1983) and Watkins, Huston-Stein, and Wright (1980).

Changing Sex-Role Attitudes

A series called "Freestyle" was produced for U.S. public television with the intention of changing sex role attitudes in 9- to 12-year-olds. The half-hour show presented episodes showing boys and girls learning nontraditional sex role behavior, for example, boys expressing nurturance and emotion, girls being independent and athletic. Evaluative research showed that sex-role attitudes changed in a less traditional direction after watching the show, particularly when the show was viewed at school and followed up with class discussion and exercises (Greenfield, 1984; Johnston & Ettema, 1982, 1986). Such a project suggests the considerable and still largely untapped potential of prosocial television in changing social norms.

Similar effects may occur in responses to regular programming. Corder-Bolz (1980) showed 5- 11-year-old children an episode of the old sitcom "All in the Family," which featured a neighbor family where the husband and wife performed many nontraditional sex-role activities. Children were interviewed about sex-role attitudes before and after viewing. Children over age 5 showed decreased sex-role stereotyping after viewing the show, especially if an adult viewing the show with the child made supportive comments about nonstereotypical behavior.

Commercial TV Contributions

The commercial networks also have a limited amount of prosocial programming for children, primarily for those older than the "Sesame Street" audience. CBS' "In the News" provides brief news features to children during their Saturday morning cartoon diet. Some such recent efforts, such as NBC's "Main Street," ABC's "After School Specials," and CBS' "Schoolbreak Specials" have received critical plaudits, even if not attracting huge audiences. Through group discussion or dramatic stories, lessons are taught on a variety of issues. For example, "Schoolbreak Specials" have presented stories on dealing with a high school classmate who is gay or who has AIDS. The same type of program has also been developed for adults; see Box 11.1

An International Perspective

Prosocial programming for children is hardly a uniquely American phenomenon, however. A particularly intriguing example is the Soviet "Spaconi Nochi Malashi" (Good Night, Little Ones), a sort of Russian "Mister Rogers Neighborhood" appearing for 15 minutes every night at 8:00 PM. Hosted by the attractive young mother Tatiana Vedeneeva, "Spaconi Nochi Malashi" uses a spartan studio set, plus lots of high-tech puppets and animation. A favorite theme is teaching nonviolent and constructive means to resolving personal conflicts, as when puppets Karusha the pig and Stepashka the rabbit learn to set

BOX 11.1. CASO VERDADE

In spite of being overwhelmingly entertainment-oriented, Brazil's giant TV Globo network some years ago initiated a half-hour daily late afternoon show with a primarily prosocial message presented in an entertaining fashion. Each week presented a 5-part story of a *caso verdade* ("true case") of people dealing with some particular social issue. Some of the issues included accepting the birth of a Down's syndrome child or the crippling disease of a family member, adjusting to a wheelchair after an accident, and remarrying after a divorce. Other shows included a group of student journalists doing a story on drug dealers and a Christmas week show about a Brazilian Mother Teresa-like figure. Each episode featured a piece of continuous 5-part story, with narration and contextual comments by a professional (psychologist, physician, etc.) on the story and how viewers might deal with that particular issue.

aside their differences and help each other pick up their toys. Vedeneeva and Fred Rogers became a part of *glasnost* and the thaw in U.S.–Soviet relations in late 1987 when "Spaconi Nochi Malashi" and "Mister Rogers Neighborhood" broadcast cooperative shows from Moscow and Pittsburgh. The real hope of arms control talks was brought down to the preschool level (Townley, 1988).

Educational television is used as an integral part of literacy programs for both children and adults in many Third World countries, sometimes in part compensating for a lack of qualified teachers or the funds to pay them. For example, the Teleniger project in the West African country of Niger uses TV lessons and grade-school-educated teachers with three months special training. They are trained in how to interact with the students to maximize the learning from the television. Reports showed impressive gains in reading (Egly, 1973; Pierre, 1973; Schramm, 1977). See also reports of projects in Mexico (Diaz-Guerrero, Reyes-Lagunes, Witzke, & Holtzman, 1976; Himmelweit, 1978) and El Salvador (Mayo, Hornik, & McAnany, 1976).

The target of prosocial media is not always children, however, and the purpose is not always connected with reading or literacy. The media may be used for other socially positive purposes appealing to adults as well. Let us now examine some of these.

MEDIA USE IN SOCIAL MARKETING

A traditionally underemphasized but currently booming area of marketing is *social marketing,* which involves the "selling" of socially and personally positive behaviors like taking steps to insure or improve one's health or safety (Barach, 1984; Bloom & Novelli, 1987). Many social critics, researchers, and practitioners long concerned with selling products are now turning their attention to how to sell healthy, safe, and socially positive behaviors. Clearly mass media are a major, though not the only, component of social marketing. The perceived reality of the medium is intended to be a catalyst for some behavior or attitude change.

Obstacles to Social Marketing

Although selling good health or safety is in many ways not unlike selling soap or automobiles, there are some difficulties that are particularly acute for social marketing. Schlinger (1976) discussed several obstacles facing public health advertisers with which commercial advertisers less often must deal.

First, social marketers often set unrealistically high goals, such as changing the behavior of 50% to 100% of the public. Although a commercial ad that affects 1% to 10% of the consumers is hugely successful, social marketers often have not fully appreciated that affecting even a very small percentage of a mass audience is a substantial accomplishment. Persons preparing social marketing campaigns are often less thoroughly trained in advertising, media, and marketing than those conducting product ad compaigns.

Secondly, social marketing appeals are often aimed at the 15% or so of the population that is least likely to change. These may be the least educated, most traditional, or most backward segment of the population, precisely the people least likely to stop smoking, start wearing seatbelts, or request medical checkups. Just as political media strategists target advertising at the few undecided voters, so might social marketing better target those people most conducive to attitude and behavior change in the intended direction, rather than the group that is least likely to ever change at all.

Third, particularly in regard to health, the beliefs, attitudes, and motives for unhealthy practices are deeply rooted and highly emotionally laden and thus very resistant to change. For example, trying to convince women to self-examine their breasts for lumps flies against their horrendous fear of cancer and the potential damage to one's sexual self-image by the contemplation of possible surgery. Convincing people to wear seatbelts when they have driven for 50 years without them is not easy. Encouraging people to sign an organ donor card forces at least a fleeting contemplation of one's mortality and thus is requesting something very unpleasant. People are particularly resistant to change if such anxieties occur also in the context of unrealistic fears, for example, fear of being declared dead too soon in order to acquire organs for transplantation (Hessing & Elffers, 1986; Prottas, 1983).

Fourth, social marketing typically is relatively poorly funded and supported, often with opposing forces holding much of the economic and political power. For example, the Tobacco Institute, the oil industry, and National Rifle Association are tremendously powerful lobbies set to oppose media messages against smoking or excessive fuel consumption or favoring firearm restrictions. Public Service Announcements (PSAs), whether print or broadcast, often are noticeably poorer in technical quality and appear less frequently than commercial ads, because of budget limitations. Although radio and TV stations air a certain number of unpaid PSAs, they generally do so at the hours when they are least able to sell lucrative advertising. We see many PSAs during the late late movie and very few during the Super Bowl or "The Cosby Show." Thus specific viewers market cannot be targeted as well as they can by commercial advertising.

Finally, often there is great physical, or at least psychological, distance between the "consumer" and the "product." Selling toothpaste can stress how much sexier your breath will be for that big date tonight. Selling quitting smoking has a much less immediate payoff. Teen smokers think much more about looking cool with their friends this weekend than dying from lung cancer or emphysema in 30 to 40 years. Young healthy adults do not typically feel much urgency to sign an organ donor card; the need is very distant psychologically. Often in social marketing, the consumer is not all that opposed to the message and may even support it; they simply do not feel the immediacy of it and thus are not particularly inclined to act on the message.

Considering the Audience

Knowing the audience well and targeting it as specifically as possible is helpful. Targeting a reasonable audience, not the ones least likely to change, and setting realistic goals and targets are useful. Trying to see the issue from the audience's point of view will make a more convincing message. Frequently social marketers are fervently convinced of the rightness of their message and fail to see how anyone else could view the issue differently. Self-righteousness tends not to be convincing. The attitudes, desires, motivations, and reasonable beliefs of the audience may be used to drive the character of the message. A serious consideration of what kinds of psychological appeals will be the most effective in motivating the particular target audience will be helpful; see Box 11.2 for an unusual approach using shame as a motivator for a PSA. Sometimes the most obvious motivations may not in fact be the most effective; see Box 11.3 for an example of such a case.

Focusing on specific behaviors the audience may take, one small step at a time, is often more useful than a general exhortation aimed at changing attitudes. Very often people know they should stop smoking, wear seat belts, or whatever. What they most need are some specific realistic behaviors than they may do to meet that end. Often existing motivation may be harnessed and channeled to build confidence in taking appropriate specific actions. Merely exhorting people to stop smoking may be of limited use. Showing a PSA of a young child smoking and talking about how cool he looks, "just like Daddy" might reach the smoking parent more effectively. For further discussion of the particular problems facing social marketing, see Barach (1984) and Bloom and Novelli (1987).

Positive Effects of Social Marketing

In spite of the obstacles, there are several clear positive effects that social marketing media campaigns have (Barach, 1984; Bloom & Novelli, 1987; Schlinger, 1976). The first effect is an altered perceived reality which includes a heightened awareness of the problem. Virtually everyone in North America is aware of the health dangers of smoking; this was not the case 30 years ago. Unlike 10 to 20 years ago, most people today are aware of the need for organ donors (Prottas, 1983), largely due to media publicity. Also, sometimes a media campaign on some specific health issue can raise the level of awareness about health topics generally.

A second positive effect is making the problem more salient, thus increasing receptivity to other influences in the same direction later. Even though a particular PSA may not immediately send a person to the doctor to check a suspicious mole for possible melanoma, that person may pay more attention to a later message on that topic. An eventual behavioral effect may actually be a cumulative effect from several influences. This, of course, makes it very difficult to scientifically measure such effects of media campaigns.

A third effect of media campaigns is the stimulation of later conversation with one's family, friends, or doctor. Publicity about the dangers of smoking may encourage supper table conversation between parents and teens encouraged by peers to smoke. Though a

Although positive motivations and emotions are the most typical psychological appeals in any kind of advertising, with the exception of fear appeals (see Chapter 4), negative motivators can on occasion be effective. Tony Schwartz (1981, pp. 100–101) wrote an advertisement employing a very strong shame appeal to exhort people not to let their dogs mess up the sidewalks:

> Let me ask you something. Have you ever seen someone allow his dog to go on the sidewalk? Sometimes right in front of a doorway, maybe your doorway? Did it make you feel angry? Well, don't get angry at the poor soul. Feel sorry for him. He's just a person who's not able to train his dog. He's just not capable of it. In fact, after he's had his dog for a short time, what happens? The dog trains him. So the next time you see a person like that on the street, take a good look at him, and while you're looking, feel sorry for him because you know he just can't help himself, even though he might like to. Some people are strong enough and smart enough to train their dogs to take a few steps off the sidewalk. Other people aren't. Makes you wonder, doesn't it, if the master is at the top of the leash or the bottom of the leash.

Sometimes what people at first think would motivate someone does not in fact do so. Schwartz (1981) offers another example where New York City police wanted to encourage elderly crime victims to report the crimes more faithfully. Appeals to deal with the presumed fear of retribution from the young hoodlums were largely ineffective, until someone discovered that the real reason for lack of reporting was a fear by the residents that reporting crimes would cause *their own children* to insist that they move from the neighborhood that they considered their home. Schwartz then suggests an appeal based on keeping the neighborhood safer and thus not having to move away.

decision not to smoke may result more from the personal interaction than directly from the message, the latter may have partially laid the groundwork for the discussion.

A fourth effect is the generation of self-initiated information-seeking. Someone may seek additional information on some topic as a result of their interest being piqued by media attention to that issue. They might ask the doctor about it on their next visit; they might read an article in the newspaper on the topic that they would not have noted before.

Finally, prosocial media campaigns can reinforce positive existing

BOX 11.3. SELF- AND-ORIENTED APPEALS TO DONATE ORGANS

What type of appeal in a PSA would be the most effective in persuading someone to become a kidney donor? Barnett, Klassen, McMinimy, & Schwarz (1981) came up with a surprising answer. Subjects heard a PSA from the (fictitious) National Kidney Association that stressed either self- or other-oriented reasons for donating a kidney. The other-oriented PSA included the following:

> Few decisions in your life will have such a dramatic effect on the lives of others. A donated kidney provides immeasurable benefit to those who receive the donation. It will help others overcome a debilitating and potentially life-threatening kidney disease. Just imagine how they will feel to be healthy and to live a normal life again with their family and friends. Please consider the decision to donate. Do it for them.

The self-oriented PSA was identical except for the following:

> Few decisions in your life will be as meaningful to you as this one. Donating can be extremely beneficial to you, the person who makes the positive decision to donate. It is an important personal decision that will make you feel better about yourself and says something very positive about you as an individual. People who learn of your decision will undoubtedly think of you as a good and caring person. Please consider the decision to donate. Do it for yourself.

In a subsequent questionnaire, college-student subjects rated the other-oriented PSA as presenting the reasons for donating more clearly but found the self-oriented PSA more convincing, in terms of reported inclination to donate one's own or next-of-kin's kidneys upon death. This suggests that, even though people most often volunteer other-oriented, altruistic motives for organ donation (Fellner & Marshall, 1981; Hessing & Elffers, 1986; Prottas, 1983), they may in fact be more convinced by more self-centered appeals.

attitudes and behavior, such as encouraging the ex-smoker trying hard not to succumb or reinforcing one's feeling that someone really should see a doctor about some medical condition. Often people know what they should do but need a little encouragement to actually do it.

Now let's examine one of the major types of social marketing campaigns, that of public health.

Public Health Media Campaigns

Breslow (1978) identified three methods of risk-factor intervention in medicine. *Epidemiological* intervention involves identifying the characteristics correlated with increased frequency of the disease and taking steps to reduce those characteristics, for example, identifying cardiovascular risk factors like smoking, obesity, cholesterol level, and hypertension, followed by screening people with blood pressure and blood chemistry tests.

Environmental intervention involves taking steps to change the environment in a healthier direction. For example, legislation restricting smoking in public places or reducing industrial emissions into air or water, and adding fluoride to drinking water illustrate such intervention. Making safer cars or lower-fat foods also manipulate the environment.

The third type of intervention, *educational* programs through the media, are of most concern for our purposes here. Such programs may aim to alter the perceived reality by changing knowledge (providing more information about risk factors) or providing an impetus for changing behavior (persuading people to stop smoking). Often changes in knowledge are easier to effect than changes in behavior. For example, even though most smokers are well aware that the practice is bad for health, their own perceived reality, at least at an emotional level, it that *they* won't develop lung cancer.

Stanford Heart Disease Project.   Media campaigns for public health generally are most successful when used in conjunction with other types of intervention. See Solomon and Cardillo (1985) for a discussion of the components of such campaigns. A good example of such a campaign is the extensive and relatively well-controlled project conducted by Stanford University to reduce the instance of coronary heart disease (Maccoby & Farquhar, 1975, 1977; Maccoby & Solomon, 1981). This project involved three towns of population 12 to 15 thousand each in central California. Two of the town received multimedia campaigns about coronary heart disease (CHD) over a 2-year period. One of those towns also received intensive interventions targeted at the high-risk population. These interventions involved both the media and medical community. Screenings were held, specific behavior-modification programs were set up, and people's attempted reduction of high-risk behaviors and characteristics were monitored.

Changes in both knowledge and behavior were monitored in both of the experimental towns and in the control town, which received no media campaign and no other intervention at all. Results showed that media campaigns by themselves produced some increases in knowledge but only very modest, if any, changes in behavior and or decreases in the overall percentage of at-risk people. Media campaigns, coupled with specific behavioral interventions and health monitoring, produced substantial improvements and reduction of the numbers in the at-risk population.

A similar project in rural eastern Finland, which had one of the highest CHD rates in the world, had national and local government cooperation. Along with media campaigns and medical intervention, environmental interventions were instituted, including restrictions on smoking, selling more low-fat dairy foods, and substitution of mushrooms for fat in the local sausage. After 4 1/2 years of the project, there were dramatic reductions in systolic blood pressure and stroke incidence (Breslow, 1978).

Now let us turn to the third major area of this chapter by addressing the practical concern of what may be done, in a general sense, to help children better deal with media, especially television, which they are inevitably going to be exposed to.

HELPING THE CHILD GET THE MOST FROM TELEVISION

As children mature and experience more TV, part of the perceived reality naturally arising from that experience is the development of what Greenfield (1984) called "television literacy." This involves (among other things) knowing how to interpret the cuts, fades, dissolves, and general montage techniques used in the editing of film to make a TV show. Very young children may misinterpret things they see on television because they fail to understand such techniques. Merely having acquired such television literacy, however, does not insure a critical processing of program content or a careful comparison of such material with external reality. These skills must be taught more intentionally, either in the school or the home.

Curriculum Development

Some attempts have been made to develop curricula for use in schools to help children become more critical viewers of television. One of the most extensive is that developed by Dorothy and Jerome Singer and their colleagues at Yale University starting in the late 1970s. They developed eight lessons to be taught twice a week over a 4-week period to third-, fourth-, and fifth-grade children. Topics included Reality and Fantasy on TV, Camera Effects, Commercials, Stereotypes, Identification with TV Characters, and Violence and Aggression. Evaluation studies showed sizable increases in knowledge by the experimental group, particular at immediate testing. The program was then extended to kindergarten, first, and second-grade children; extensive pilot testing suggested that such children could be taught considerable amounts about the nature of television through such a curriculm (Singer & Singer, 1981, 1983; Singer, Singer, & Zuckerman, 1981; Singer, Zuckerman & Singer, 1980).

A second project was developed by Dorr, Graves, and Phelps (1980). Their materials used taped TV excerpts and group discussion, role playing, games, and teacher commentary. One emphasis was on the economic bases of the broadcasting industry, stressing, for example, that the "bottom-line" purpose of television is sell advertising time to make money. A second emphasis, very much in line with the theme of this book, stressed how TV programs vary greatly in realism. It encouraged children to critically evaluate the reality of each show in several ways. In evaluative research, Dorr's curriculum was shown to engender a questioning attitude about television and skepticism about its accurate reflection of reality.

What Can Be Done in the Home

Media education should not be limited only to the classroom, however. Whatever the negative effects of television on children, they can be mitigated, and perhaps even turned to positive changes, through dialogue in the home (Corder-Bolz, 1980; O'Bryant & Corder-Bolz, 1978), leading to development of what have sometimes been called "receivership skills." Although it is obviously not possible to always be with the child when he or she is watching television, an effort to be there at least some of the time may pay off. As the family watches television together, conversation may occur about deceptive advertising, stereotyped group portrayals, antisocial values, or excessive sex or violence. Parents can question the children about their reactions to what is on TV, thus better understanding the perceived reality held by the child. They may comment about their own reactions, thus providing a balance to what may be a skewed portrayal on TV. For example, during my preteen period of being enamoured with game shows, I remember my father commenting, as I watched "The Price Is Right," that the winners had to pay lots of taxes on all of their prizes; it was Dad's way of teaching some anti-materialism values. Johnsson-Smaragdi (1983) found some evidence that family interaction, especially for children around age 11, was facilitated by television viewing, which was seen as an important family interactive activity.

Such parental discussions may help the child deal with troubling material, such as extreme sex or violence, or with a theme that is cognitively too difficult to follow without some adult "translation." Such discussion during the news may help the child learn about events of the world. Television may be used as a catalyst for discussion of important issues within the family. Although it may be difficult for a parent and child to discuss sex or drugs, for example, it may be easier in the context of discussing a TV program on that theme, even if the program was not particularly well done or consistent with the family's values. It still may serve as a relatively non-threatening entree to the topic.

Television need not be an antisocial medium that isolates one family member from another (the "shut-up-I'm-trying-to-watch" model). It can also be an activity that brings them together to watch together but also to talk about the content and other topics that leads to (the "hey-look-at-this" model). It can help family members learn each other's reactions to many topics and situations. It can be a stimulus to cognitive, emotional, and personal growth. All of this is not to say that it *will* be such a positive influence, just that it *can* be. The more carefully programs are selected and the more intentional the parent is about discussing the content, the better the outcome.

Using television as a springboard for productive discussion and psychological growth is not limited to children and families. See Box 11.4 for an unusual example of using television shows as an integral part of psychotherapy.

It is almost a truism that television and other media may be a force for ill or good. Much of the writing and research has focused on the ill wind of TV. The institution of television is with us for good; we cannot isolate our children from its influence. We can, however, take steps to make that interaction a more positive, even rewarding, experience than it would be otherwise.

CONCLUSION

A recurring theme throughout this chapter on prosocial television, if not throughout the entire book, is that the effect that television has depends on more than the content of the programming. What goes on around the viewer during and after the show is also important in the perceived reality developed by audience members as their minds interact with the program. Programs like "Sesame Street" have more positive impact if buttressed by related conversations and work in the home or school. Frightening or troubling aspects of television may be

A few psychotherapists think so highly of at least one network TV show that they use tapes from it in their group and individual therapy. The ABC drama "thirtysomething" features seven urban upper-middle-class characters in their thirties trying to make sense out of today's world. Although the show was roundly criticized by some after its fall 1987 debut for being an unseemly display of self-indulgent yuppie *angst,* it struck a responsive chord with many more viewers and developed an extremely loyal following, as well as receiving critical praise for its scripts and acting.

Among those who were impressed were some therapists, who have found "thirtysomething" episodes very useful in stimulating thought and discussion in clients. Family therapist Bruce Linton has his therapy group for new fathers watch a segment where Michael tells his wife Hope that he has mixed feelings about the arrival of their baby. Although he loves the little girl, he regrets some ways in which the marital relationship seems to have changed.

Linton uses another episode which focuses on the nightmares of 7-year-old Ethan after his parents' separation, to help divorcing parents get in touch with the emotional effects on their children. Another episode, where one couple has an argument in front on another couple, later "replays" the scene from the perspective of each of the four participants. This episode is used by therapists to show clients how different individuals interpret and remember the same interpersonal encounter so differently. Episodes dealing with Elliot and Nancy's on-again-off-again marriage have been useful for clients trying to sort our similar ambivalent relationships. Series characters express their feelings and often effectively model such expression for client-viewers. These clients receive some affirmation that they are not alone in their concerns, but also receive some direction on how to deal with these concerns (Hersch, 1988).

made less threatening by sensitive adult discussion with the viewing child. Media exhortations to live a healthier lifestyle are more effective if combined with behavioral interventions with specific tips on how to do so and support for efforts in that direction. See Wober (1988) for an examination of the systems available for maximizing the benefits of television.

This idea is not unlike research on how children and adults survive traumatic life experiences in general. The ones who survive and grow, rather than be defeated and traumatized, are those who have support in the rough times, those who can talk over the troubling events and have countervailing positive influences to partially balance the strong negative ones.

Cognition and
Media Revisited

During the course of writing this book, I got married and began to share a house after many years of living alone. One adjustment we both had to make was in our media use habits and experience. I watched television far more than my wife, especially sitcoms, while she favored science and medical documentaries. She listened to the radio more, and more to classical and talk shows than to my rock-and-roll. I read the newspaper after dinner with TV in the background; she read it with breakfast and National Public Radio, a meal I was used to sharing with the "Good Morning, America" or "Today" show families. She read magazines early in the evening, while I watched television and later read magazines before bed. Sitcom characters, news anchors, and detective sleuths were significant people in my life. "All Things Considered" regulars and the folks at Lake Woebegone were important in hers. After awhile I noticed, however, that some of my favorite TV shows didn't seem as entertaining as they had been before, possibly because I didn't need them as "family" so much any more.

In this book we have examined the way that the perceived reality, which we create from the media, may or may not correspond well to the reality of the world. The perceived reality of what the world is like is often far more heavily influenced by the media than we realize. It greatly affects our attitudes and behavior when we implicitly assume the world of the media to reflect the real world. In much of this book we have discussed the media in a global fashion that may have inadvertently suggested that the differences among television, radio, and print are nonexistent or irrelevant. Most of the research that has been done, as well as most of the public concern, has focused on television. Nonetheless, it is worthwhile to examine some of the differences between the media. In this final chapter, we will examine some of those differences, as they relate to the perceived reality theme. Following that, we will conclude with a brief look at how the public can influence media and the way that the reporting of media news in the press may affect the perceived reality constructed in the minds of the public.

235

COMPARISON OF DIFFERENT MEDIA

Although fiction occurs in both written and television format, children recognize at an earlier age that books are fiction (Kelly, 1981); television *looks* more like real life. Thus the reality created by television is more easily confused with reality itself than is the printed construction of reality. The medium itself affects how the child can extract information from that medium and represent it in memory (Salomon, 1979, 1983). Lower socioeconomic status and minority children are even more likely to accept the TV reality as accurate than are White middle class children (Dorr, 1982).

Greenfield (1984) offers an insightful discussion of the historical development of media in regard to the psychological processes engaged by each medium. The onset of print media several centuries ago permitted the tangible storage of information for the first time. People who had acquired the skill of literacy thus had access to vast amounts of information previously unavailable except through oral tradition. Literacy also had a social implication, in that it was the first medium of communication that required solitude for its effective practice. Critics of television who fear its advent has isolated children from social interaction are in fact concerned about an effect of the onset of print media; television only continued the requirement of physical isolation, but did not initiate it. In fact, research has shown no relationship between amount of television watched and time spent in interpersonal activity (reviewed in Murray, 1980).

Information Extraction

In some ways radio and print may have more in common cognitively than either does with TV. Both radio and print are exclusively verbal media, whereas television involves the pictorial dimension as well. There is a positive correlation between comprehension of a story read from a book and one heard on the radio but not between a story read and one seen on television (Pezdek & Hartman, 1983; Pezdek, Lehrer, & Simon, 1984; Pezdek & Stevens, 1984). This suggests that skills for extracting information from television are different from those used to extract information from the words of radio or print. Studies of television show that children derive more information from the visual component than from the verbal one (Hayes & Birnbaum, 1980). Overall, comprehension of the same information presented via television was better than the same story presented via radio to second and sixth-grade children (Pezdek, et al., 1984). Thus television is a very efficient way to transmit information to children, suggesting both greater potential and greater concern regarding this medium.

Beagles-Roos and Gat (1983) had children retell a story heard on the radio or seen on television. The style of the retold stories differed in an interesting fashion. Retold TV stories contained more vague reference, such as the use of pronouns without identifying the referent, the use of definite articles (*"the" boy. . . .*) without first introducing the referent, and other forms presupposing more shared information with the hearer. Retold radio stories provided more information, much as a radio play-by-play provides more information than a televised play-by-play. Having children write a story from either "TV" or "real life," Watkins (1988) found that the amount of television the child watched determined how elaborate and complex the "TV story" was. Greenfield (1984) suggests that one subtle effect of watching much television could be to learn a verbal style which is relatively vague in reference, much like talking face to face. In both cases much shared knowledge may be assumed and thus less must be explicitly explained. With radio and print, however, the language must be more explicit to compensate for the lack of a pictorial component.

Baggett (1979) found that adults recalled information from either a silent movie (*The Red Balloon*) or a constructed spoken version equally well, whereas young children remembered the silent film version better. This visual advantage in memory may be part of the appeal of television. Although it decreases somewhat with age, it is a natural characteristic of our information-processing systems, rather than one which is subtly induced by television exposure. The visual continues to have some advantage even with adults, however. In delayed testing a week later, Baggett found that the adults also showed better memory for the visual than the verbal story.

One sometimes hears the claim that radio is the medium requiring the most imagination, due to the need to mentally fill in the missing visual aspect. A fascinating study by Greenfield and her colleagues, reported in Greenfield (1984), had children complete interrupted stories told via radio or television. Results showed that radio stories evoked more novel elements in the imagined story endings than did the televised versions of the same stories. Singer and Singer (1981) found that preschool children who watched more TV were less likely to have an imaginary playmate and showed lower scores on imaginative play. It may depend on the nature of the program, however.

"Sesame Street" and especially the slower-paced "Mister Rogers' Neighborhood" have been shown to stimulate imaginative play (Singer & Singer, 1976; Tower, Singer, & Singer, 1979), while action–adventure shows are associated with the lowest imaginative play scores (Singer & Singer, 1981). Of course, television does teach visual information-processing skills and is overall a very efficient way to transmit information, especially to children.

Media as Agents of Socialization

More generally, the media, particularly television, are extremely important socializing agents in most societies of the world. Children's perceived reality about the culture they live in is in part a media creation. This socialization role of television may be especially crucial in cases where a child finds him/herself in a different culture from birth. In an interesting study comparing U.S. children and foreign children residing in the United States, Zohoori (1988) found that the foreign children found TV more interesting, spent more time watching it, identified more with TV characters, and used TV more for learning than did their U.S. counterparts. Not surprisingly, they also expressed stronger beliefs in the social reality portrayed by television, that is, the perceived reality of TV seemed to them more real, consistent with the fact that they had fewer real personal experiences in that culture upon which to draw. There is also evidence that adult immigrants draw heavily on television to learn about the United States, both before and after their arrival (Littwin, April 9, 1988). See Box 12.1 for some examples of how three very different societies use television as a socializing agent in their cultures.

Most of the focus in this book has been on the perceived reality that we construct through the interaction of our minds with the stimulus material from the TV, radio, magazines, or newspapers. If we want to change the reality of the media, we can sometimes do that as well. Although not the focus of this book, this issue is worth examining briefly as a complement to our basic thesis.

INFLUENCING THE MEDIA

Very often when we critically examine media we are left with the feeling that there is much we do not like, for whatever reason, but that there is little we can do about that state of affairs other than

BOX 12.1.   TV AS SOCIALIZING AGENT IN THREE CULTURES

Singapore. One of the emerging East Asian economic powerhouses very explicitly uses televison to further its social ends. A prosperous, multiethnic, multiracial, multireligious society, Singapore aims to stay that way—happily. Television faces censorship in four areas—racial, religious, moral, and political. No criticism of any race or religion is allowed. No sexual expressions that might offend the Buddhist or Muslim communities are allowed. No religious programming at all is allowed. News of religious or racial strife elsewhere is played down to avoid inflaming local latent grievances. An orderly and harmonious society is deemed to be a higher priority now than Western-style press freedoms. So far, this perceived reality of social harmony has largely been the actual reality as well (Hickey, January 2, 1988).

India. One of the most popular programs on Indian television uses the new medium to tell age-old Hindu stories. "Ramayana" uses live actors to dramatize the ancient Hindu epic of the same name. Devout Hindus place garlands and incense on the TV set every Sunday at 9:30 AM when the show comes on (Panitt, 1988). This show is performing an ages-old anthropological function of cultural continuity (Dorris, 1988), whereby each generation participates in the telling and relearning of the archetypal tales of that culture. The only difference is that the modality has changed from oral (or written) to broadcast tradition.

Ivory Coast. The West African nation of Ivory Coast has two government-run TV stations employing about 600 people. As well as importing French movies and serials and shows like "The Cosby Show" (Papa Bonheur) from the United States, Ivorian TV is increasingly producing its own programming to meet the unique needs of its developing society. Recently it has produced documentaries on traditional African life and health documentaries on AIDS. It is also producing music videos of local artists like reggae star Alpha Blondy. Though not a large country, Ivory Coast is nonetheless a multilingual nation only superficially unified linguistically by the national language of French. To deal with this diversity, the TV broadcasts the first nightly newscast each evening in a different African language each night of the week, followed by a French broadcast. Although most educated Ivorians understand French, the station would like to reach more than merely the upper socioeconomic status people (*Manhattan Mercury*, 1987).

choose not to use the medium (watch the program, read the paper, etc.) we do not care for. This passive model of person-media interaction is not really entirely accurate, however.

Individual Efforts

Individual complaints do have disproportionate impact, in that those who receive them assume that each complaint represents a similar view of many others who did not write. Certain types of letters are more effective than others. A reasoned, logically argued case has a lot more impact than an angry tirade. One brand of club cocktails recently advertised in *Ms* magazine with the slogan "Hit me with a Club." The company received over a thousand letters of protest, arguing that the ad contained a subtle suggestion of physical abuse of women. The company responded that such a connection was never intended or imagined, yet they were concerned enough by the letters to withdraw the ad. Responses do make a difference! (Will, 1987).

Jamieson and Campbell (1988) suggest three types of arguments that are particularly effective when writing to a network, TV, or radio station, or publication. First, a claim of inaccuracy or deception evokes immediate concern. Publishing or broadcasting inaccurate information is seldom intended and must be quickly corrected or balanced to avoid a loss of credibility and possibly legal trouble as well. Second, a claim that an item violates community standards or general good taste causes concern. The press is very loath to offend, by overly explicit sex, violence, language, for example. A sufficient number of people with such concerns may lead to the loss of advertising dollars, which may be the lifeblood of the enterprise. See Box 12.2 for an example of an ad that offended people and was withdrawn due to their complaints.

Third, a claim of lack of balance or fairness is serious. This includes obvious concerns like lack of fairness in covering a political campaign or the use of an unfairly misleading ad, but also claims such as unfairly stereotyping some group or unfairly exploiting the cognitive immaturity of children to encourage them to request certain products from their parents.

Once in a great while the efforts of a single individual can result in policy change or the emergence of organizations to counter heavy media use to promote particular views. For example, John Banzhaf III persuaded the FCC that the Fairness Doctrine required television to run antismoking ads to counter cigarette ads on TV at the time (They ended in the U.S. in 1971). Pete Shields, who lost a son to handgun homicide, and Sarah Brady, whose husband Jim was permanently injured in the assassination attempt on President Reagan in 1981, became active media users in handgun control lobbying efforts through agencies like Handgun Control, Inc., founded by Shields.

For some addresses or organizations and agencies to contact to express media concerns, see Box 12.3.

Group Efforts

Individuals working together can often have even more impact than isolated individuals. One corporate method is the *boycott*, whereby people refrain from buying some product or using some publication or station until changes are made. Even the threat of a boycott sends chills up the spines of advertisers, publications, or radio or TV stations. Newspapers have gone under when certain key economic interests have pulled their advertising. Convenience stores have stopped selling sex magazines in response to public complaints and threat of a boycott by the religious right. Nestle's changed its infant formula marketing in response to a public outcry and boycott. Fear of adverse and organized public reaction is major reason that television stations in the late-1980s were so slow to accept condom ads, even in light of the AIDS scare and a majority of public opinion favoring such ads (This concern did eventually win out over the fear of complaints in most markets.).

In occasional cases a group may file legal action against a media

241

organization. For example, when the FCC periodically reviews applications of radio and television stations for renewal, opportunity is available to challenge such renewal. Although the actual failure to renew is extremely rare in the United States such pressure may have substantial effects on subsequent station policy. For example, civil rights groups in the 1960s used this approach to force broadcasters to be more responsive to Black concerns in their communities. Sometimes the mere threat of legal or legislative action is enough to produce the desired change. For example, consumer groups like Action for Children's Television (ACT) have put pressure on the broadcast industry's National Association of Broadcasters (NAB) to limit the allowable number of minutes of commercials per hour on children's television. Their appeals to the FCC to regulate such numbers have led to the NAB limiting commercial time itself, a move it apparently considered preferable to governmentally-mandated regulation.

Certain organizations have established themselves as watchdogs on certain kinds of issues. For example, the national PTA has at different times monitored children's advertising and violent and sexual content on television. Resulting public awareness, as well as the latent threat of a boycott, has probably had some subtle effects. Many local citizens' groups protesting pornography have pressured convenience stores to stop selling sex magazines.

Sometimes social science research itself may have important impact on policy making. For example, the laboratory research finding that people could not perceive or be affected by backward audio messages (Box 4.3) led several states to withdraw pending legislation requiring record companies to put warning labels on album jackets (Vokey & Read, 1985). The recent research on sexual violence (discussed in Chapter 10) has tremendous potential impact on legal, policy, filmmaking, and even lifestyle issues. For a careful discussion of how research on sexual violence may be used to effect legal and policy change, see Penrod and Linz (1984) and Linz, Turner, Hesse, and Penrod (1984).

Before such research can have much impact on public opinion or public policy, the findings from that research must somehow be communicated to the world beyond the scientific community. This act in itself can often affect the perceived reality about that issue in the mind of the public.

REPORTING MEDIA RESEARCH TO THE PUBLIC

In the reporting of science, the scientist's "truth" and the reporter's "news" are often far from the same. For example, an editor may not consider a particular story about pornography research as news-worthy because the paper has already carried two stories this week on that topic. The scientist looking at the same situation may not be convinced of the overlap, in that one was a story about citizens seeking a ban on sales of *Playboy* in the town, and the other was a feature story about a woman involved in acting in X-rated movies, neither of which at all overlapped with a report of behavioral research on the topic.

In their desire to fairly present all sides of an issue, journalists may emphasize controversy and thus (perhaps inadvertently) play up and legitimatize a fringe position given little credibility in the scientific community. As discussed in Chapter 7, conflict and controversy are highly newsworthy. For example, subliminal advertising greatly in-trigues and even alarms the general pubic, although the research community realizes that its feared effects are vastly overrated or even nonexistent (Moore, 1982; Saegert, 1987). Such a topic may make good journalism but bad science. The perceived reality of readers of such stories may be significantly at variance with the scientific reality.

Journalists and scientists use language in very different ways. As Tavris (1986, p.25) says,

To the academician, the language of the reporter is excessively casual, trivializing, and simple-minded, if not downright wrong or silly. To the journalist, the language of the academicians is excessively passive, technical, and complicated, if not downright wordy or pompous . . . Academic language strives to be informative and accurate . . . To the reporter, though, the result sounds like nit-picking; it encumbers the research with so many qualifications and exceptions that the results seem meaningless.

It is not unusual to encounter the feeling that social science is inferior, underdeveloped science. Not surprisingly, this feeling is common among journalists trained in science. More surprising, however, is that this view is also not unusual among social scientists themselves, some of whom see themselves as doing work which is inferior to that of their colleagues in physics or biology. If many social scientists do not see themselves as true scientists, is it surprising that many others do not so perceive them? This collective inferiority feeling may stem from the fact that social science is by its very nature probabilistic, not deterministic. One can never predict *for sure* what the effect of seeing a violent movie on a particular person will be, in the sense that one can predict with absolute certainty that $2 + 2 = 4$.

Still, social science stories hold much interest for many readers and even journalists. In a study by Dunwoody (1986), newspaper editors actually reported a preference for social science topics to "hard" science. However, the reverse preference was found in reporters. Thus there may often be a situation of an editor selecting a social science topic but assigning it to a reporter who has less interest in it and thus may not treat it as "science," thereby resulting in more sloppy treatment than would be given a "real" science story. For a fascinating series of papers considering how the media report scientific research about media, see Goldstein (1986).

Through most of this book we have focussed on the perceived reality of the *receiver* of media input. It is even more magical to *appear* in the media (See Box 12.4).

ON TO THE FUTURE

One of the most difficult aspects of writing this book is that mass communication is a constantly changing arena. Today's blockbuster miniseries is barely a memory in three months. The next new trend of hit shows are but an idea in some producer's mind now. Broader trends are ephemeral as well. In early 1984 pundits were saying the sitcom was a dying genre; a few months later "The Cosby Show"

BOX 12.4. BEING ON TELEVISION AS A MAGICAL EXPERIENCE

There is something magical for most people about being on television. Because it is a very intrusive medium, being on television makes someone either very excited or very uncomfortable or perhaps both. The importance seems to be the act of being on TV more than what you do there. People are very happy to look perfectly foolish singing a song for Johnny Carson on "The Tonight Show" or even exposing personally embarrassing information on "The Newlywed Game." In the early 1980s there was a popular genre of show featuring people from the "real world," usually doing very strange things ("Real People," "That's Incredible"). In an earlier era we had Allen Funt's classic "Candid Camera," a show which still reappears occasionally in a reincarnated special.

It is hard to "act natural" if the cameras are running, sometimes even if the camera is a family member's camcorder. Anthropologist Edmund Carpenter reported an interesting example of what happened when a Lowell Thomas visited a remote New Guinean village some years ago: "The instant they saw cameras they rushed about for props, then sat in fromt of the cameras, one chopping with a stone axe, another finger-painting on bark, a third starting a fire with bamboo—Santa's workshop." (Kenner, 1973, p. 7).

turned that around and 2 or 3 years later almost all of the top-10 Nielsen shows in the United States were sitcoms. Many people scorned the introduction of "USA Today," saying a national paper using such a colorful magazine format could never last. Not only were they wrong, but it spawned a TV version in late 1988.

Practically no place is beyond the reach of radio and television. Isolated mountainous Nepal was one of the last countries to introduce television, in late 1985 (Foote, 1988). Even the isolated valley town unable to receive TV as late as the 1970s is virtually nonexistent today. Satellite dishes and VCRs running off generators now allow video experiences in places out of the normal reach of broadcast signals. See Williams (1986) for a collection of papers studying the effects of the late introduction of television in the mid-1970s to an otherwise normal Canadian town. Such a study can probably never be conducted again because no such TV-less place will exist.

Changing technology is accelerating more fundamental structural changes in television and other media. The slow but sure decline in the audience percentage of network TV relative to cable will have an enormous, but still unclear, effect on TV programming, economics, and viewing habits. Proliferating cable channels and satellite technology are vastly increasing the number of offerings available. By 1988 cable had reached 51% of U.S. television homes, with channels attracting 20% of the audience (Zoglin, 1988). VCRs have greatly increased audience control in program selection and timing; the total effects of VCRs on quantity and quality of viewing are not yet clear (Gunter & Levy, 1987; Levy, 1987).

Although most of the discussion of television in this book has focused on network television, such stations are already a minority of the number of channels offered in many markets. The network share of the viewing audience is still a large majority but has been rapidly falling in recent years. Interactive television has already arrived in children's TV, where full enjoyment requires purchase of an interactive toy like the Power Jet weapon for "Captain Power and the Soldiers of the Future." Rapid proliferation and dissemination of such interactive media could totally revolutionize the psychological experience of mass communication in ways only vaguely imagined today.

All of this brings us back to the question of "why a *psychology*, especially why a *cognitive* psychology, of the media?" At heart media offer an *experience*, which emerges from the interaction of our minds with the content of the communication. Media affect our minds—they give us ideas, change our attitudes, tell us what the world is like. These mind-changes, that is, our perceived reality, then become the framework around which we interpret the totality of experience. Thus media consumption is basically a cognitive phenomenon.

In one sense media production is art, a creation, a fabrication, but yet, as Picasso once said, "Art is a lie through which we can see the truth." Performing in media is acting, is pretending, is taking a role, yet, as Oscar Wilde once said, "I love acting. It is so much more real than life." One might say the same about media. Life imitates art, and art imitates life. After awhile, it is hard to tell which is which.

References

Abel, E. (1981). Television in international conflict. In A. Arno & W. Dissayanake (Eds.), *The news media and national and international conflict* (pp. 63–70). Boulder, CO: Westview Press.

Abel, G.G., Barlow, D.H., Blanchard, E.B., & Guild, D. (1977). The components of rapists' sexual arousal. *Archives of General Psychiatry, 34*, 895–903.

Abel, G.G., Becker, J., & Skinner, L. (1980). Aggressive behavior and sex. *Psychiatric clinics of North America, 3*, 133–151..

Abramson, P.R., & Hayashi, H. (1984). Pornography in Japan: Cross-cultural and theoretical considerations. In N.M. Malamuth & E. Donnerstein (Eds.), *Pornography and sexual aggression* (pp. 173–183). Orlando: Academic Press.

Abramson, P.R., Perry, L., Seeley, T., Seeley, D., & Rothblatt, A. (1981). Thermographic measurement of sexual arousal: A discriminant validity analysis. *Archives of sexual behavior, 10*(2), 175–176.

Alesandrini, K.L. (1983). Strategies that influence memory for advertising communications. In R.J. Harris (Ed.), *Information processing research in advertising* (pp. 65–82). Hillsdale, NJ: Lawrence Erlbaum Associates.

Alsop, R. (1988 January 26,). Advertisers retreat from making direct pitch to the gay market. *Wall Street Journal*, p. 33.

Altheide, D.L. (1976). *Creating reality: How TV news distorts events.* Beverly Hills: Sage.

Amador, O.G. (1988). Latin lovers, Lolita, and *La Bamba. Americans, 40*(4), 2–9.

Andersen, P.A., & Kibler, R.J. (1978). Candidate valence as a predictor of voter preference. *Human Communication Research, 5*, 4–14.

Anderson, D.R. (1985). Online cognitive processing of television. In L.F. Alwitt & A.A. Mitchell (Eds.), *Psychological processes and advertising effects* (p. 177–199). Hillsdale, NJ: Lawrence Erlbaum Associates.

Andison, F.S. (1977). TV violence and viewer aggression: A cumulation of study results: 1956–1976. *Public Opinion Quarterly, 41*, 314–331.

Ang, I. (1982). *Watching Dallas: Soap opera and the melodramatic imagination.* London: Methuen.

Arlen, M.J. (1969). *Livingroom war.* New York: Viking Press.

Arms, R.L., Russell, G.W., & Sandilands, M.L. (1979). Effects on the hostility of spectators of viewing aggressive sports. *Social Psychology Quarterly, 42*, 275–279.

Aronoff, C. (1974). Old age in prime time. *Journal of Communication, 24*(1), 86–87.

Assman, H. (1987a). *La iglesia electronica y su impacto en America latina* [The electronic church and its impact in Latin America]. San Jose, Costa Rica: DEI.

Assman, H. (1987b, April 30). Phenomenal growth of sects, electronic church related to continents poverty. *Latinamerica Press, 19*(16), 5–6.

Atkin, C., Greenberg, B., & McDermott, S. (1983). Television and race role socialization. *Journalism Quarterly, 60*(3), 407–414.

Bacchetta, V. (1987). Brazil's soap operas: "Huge dramas where the country portrays itself." *Latinamerica Press, 19*(9), 5–6.

Bachy, V. (1976). Danish "permissiveness" revisited. *Journal of Communication, 26,* 40–43.

Baehr, H., & Dyer, G. (Eds.) (1987). *Boxed in: Women and television.* London: Pandora.

Baggett, P. (1979). Structurally equivalent stories in movie and text and the effect of the medium on recall. *Journal of Verbal Learning and Verbal Behavior, 18,* 333–356.

Ball, S., & Bogatz, G.A. (1970). *The first year of Sesame Street: An evaluation.* Princeton, NJ: Educational Testing Service.

Ball, S., & Bogatz, G.A. (1973). *Reading with television: An evaluation of The Electric Company.* Princeton, NJ: Educational Testing Service.

Bancroft, J., & Mathews, A. (1971). Autonomic correlates of penile erection. *Journal of Psychosomatic Research, 15,* 159–167.

Bandura, A. (1965). Influence of model's reinforcement contingencies on the acquisition of imitative responses. *Journal of Personality and Social Psychology, 1,* 585–595.

Bandura, A. (1977). *Social learning theory.* Englewood Cliffs, NJ: Prentice–Hall.

Bandura, A., Ross, D., & Ross, S.A. (1961). Transmission of aggression through imitation of aggressive models. *Journal of Abnormal and Social Psychology, 1,* 575–582.

Bandura, A., Ross, D., & Ross, S. A. (1963) Imitation of film-mediated aggressive models. *Journal of Abnormal and Social Psychology, 66,* 3–11.

Bandura, A., & Walters, R.H. (1963). *Social learning and personality development.* New York: Holt Rinehart & Winston.

Barach, J.A. (1984). Applying marketing principles to social causes. *Business Horizons,* July/August, 65–69.

Barbaree, H.E., Marshall, W.L., & Lanthier, R.D. (1979). Deviant sexual arousal in rapists. *Behaviour Research and Therapy, 17,* 215–222.

Barcus, F.E. (1980). The nature of television advertising to children. In E.L. Palmer & A. Dorr (Eds.), *Children and the faces of television: Teaching. violence, and selling* (p. 273–285). New York: Academic Press.

Barcus, F.E. (1983). *Images of life on children's television.* New York: Prager.

Barnett, M.A., Klassen, M., McMinimy, V., & Schwarz, L. (1987). The role of self- and other-oriented motivation in the organ donation decision. In M. Wallendorf & P. Anderson (Eds.), *Advances in consumer research* (pp. 335–337). Vol XIV. Provo, UT: Association for Consumer Research.

Baron, R.A. (1979). Heightened sexual arousal and physical aggression: An extension to females. *Journal of Research in Personality, 13,* 91–102.

Beagles-Roos, J., & Gat, I. (1983). Specific impact of radio and television on children's story comprehension. *Journal of Educational Psychology, 75,* 128–137.

Beeman, W.O. (1984). The cultural role of the media in Iran: The revolution of 1978–79 and after. In A. Arno & W. Dissayanake (Eds.), *The news media and national and international conflict* (pp. 147–165). Boulder, CO: Westview Press.

Berelson, B. (1942). The effects of print on public opinion. In D. Waples (Ed.), *Print, radio, and film in a democracy* (pp. 41–64). Chicago: University of Chicago Press.

Berelson, B.R., Lazarsfeld, P.F., & McPhee, W.N. (1954). *Voting.* Chicago: University of Chicago Press.

Berkowitz, L. (1965). Some aspects of observed aggression. *Journal of Personality and Social Psychology, 2,* 359–369.

Berkowitz, L. (1984). Some effects of thoughts on anti- and prosocial influences of media events: A cognitive neoassociation analysis. *Psychological Bulletin, 95,* 410–427.

Berry, G.L. (1980). Television and Afro-Americans: Past legacy and present portrayals.

In S.B. Withey & R.P. Abeles (Eds.), *Television and social behavior* (pp. 231–247). Hillsdale, NJ: Lawrence Erlbaum Associates.

Beuf, A. (1974). Doctor, lawyer, household drudge. *Journal of Communication, 24*(2), 142–145.

Bever, T., Smith, M., Bengen, B., & Johnson, T. (1975). Young viewers' troubling responses to TV ads. *Harvard Business Review, 53*(6), 109–120.

Blackman, J.A., & Hornstein, H.A. (1977). Newscasts and the social actuary. *Public Opinion Quarterly, 41*, 295–313.

Blatt, J., Spencer, L., & Ward, S. (1972). A cognitive developmental study of children's reactions to television advertising. In E.A. Rubinstein, G.A. Comstock, & J.P. Murray (Eds.), *Television and social behavior. Vol. IV.: Television in everyday life: Patterns of use* (pp. 452–467). Washington, DC: U.S. Government Printing Office.

Block, C. (1972). White backlash to Negro ads: Fact or fantasy? *Journalism Quarterly, 49*(2), 253–262.

Bloom, P.N., & Novelli, W.D. (1981). Problems and challenges in social marketing. *Journal of Marketing, 45*(2), 79–88.

Blumler, J.G., (1979). The role of theory in uses and gratifications research. *Communication Research, 6*, 9–36.

Blumler, J.G., & Katz, E. (Eds.) (1974). *The uses of mass communications: Current perspectives on gratifications research.* Beverly Hills: Sage.

Blumler, J.G., & McQuail, D. (1969). *Television in politics: its uses and influences.* Chicago: University of Chicago Press.

Bogart, L. (1980). Television news as entertainment. In P.H. Tannenbaum (Ed.), *The entertainment functions of television* (pp. 209–249). Hillsdale, NJ: Lawrence Erlbaum Associates.

Bogatz, G.A., & Ball, S. (1971). *The second year of Sesame Street: A continuing evaluation.* Princeton, NJ: Educational Testing Service.

Bogle, D. (1973). *Toms, coons, mulattoes, and bucks: An interpretive history of blacks in American films.* New York: Viking.

Bollen, K.A., & Phillips, D.P. (1982). Imitative suicides: A national study of the effects of television news stories. *American Sociological Review, 47*, 802–809.

Bower, G.H., Black, J.B., & Turner, T.J. (1979). Scripts in memory for text. *Cognitive Psychology, 11*, 177–220.

Bowes, J.E., & Strentz, H. (1978). Candidate images: Stereotyping and the 1976 debates. In B.D. Ruben (Ed.), *Communication yearbook 2* (pp. 391–406). New Brunswick, NJ: Transaction.

Breslow, L. (1978). Risk factor intervention for health maintenance. *Science, 200*, 908–912.

Brewer, W.F., & Nakamura, G.V. (1984). The nature and functions of schemas. In R.S. Wyer & T.K. Srull (Eds.), *Handbook of social cognition* (pp. 119–160). Hillsdale, NJ: Lawrence Erlbaum Associates.

Brockhoff, W. (1988, February). Magazine not negligent in running ad. *KSU Collegian*, p. 4.

Brown, D., & Bryant, J. (1983). Humor in mass media. In P.E. McGhee & J.H. Goldstein (Eds.), *Handbook of humor research*, Vol II. (p. 141–172). Springer-Verlag.

Brown, J.D., & Campbell, K. (1986). Race and gender in music videos: The same beat but a different drummer. *Journal of Communication, 36*(1), 94–106.

Bruno, K.J., & Harris, R.J. (1980). The effect of repetition on the discrimination of asserted and implied claims in advertising. *Applied Psycholinguistics, 1*, 307–321.

Bryant, J., Alexander, A.F., & Brown, D. (1983). Learning from educational television programs. In M.J.A. Howe (Ed.). *Learning from television: Psychological and educational research* (pp. 1–30). London: Academic Press.

Buerkel-Rothfuss, N.L., & Mayes, S. (1981). Soap opera viewing: The cultivation effect. *Journal of Communication, 31,* 108–115.

Burke, R.R., DeSarbo, W.S., Oliver, R.L., & Robertson, T.S. (1988). Deception by implication: An experimental investigation. *Journal of Consumer Research, 14,* 483–494.

Caird, W., & Wincze, J.P. (1977). *Sex therapy: A behavioral approach.* New York: Harper and Row.

Campbell, A., Gurin, G., & Miller, W.E. (1954). *The voter decides.* Evanston, IL: Row, Peterson.

Cantor, J., & Sparks, G.G. (1984). Children's fear responses to mass media: Testing some Piagetian predictions. *Journal of Communication, 34,* 90–103.

Cantor, J., & Venus, P. (1980). The effect of humor on recall of a radio advertisement. *Journal of Broadcasting, 24*(1), 13–22.

Cantor, M.G., & Cantor, J.M. (1986). American television in the international marketplace. *Communication Research, 13,* 509–520.

Canzoneri, V. (1984, January 28). TV's feminine mistake. *TV Guide,* 14–15.

Carveth, R., & Alexander, A. (1985). Soap opera viewing motivations and the cultivation process. *Journal of Broadcasting & Electronic Media, 29,* 259–273.

Cassata, B., Anderson, P., & Skill, T. (1980). The older adult in daytime serial drama. *Journal of Communication, 30,* 48–49.

Chaffee, S.H., & Choe, S.Y. (1980). Times of decision and media use during the Ford-Carter campaign. *Public Opinion Quarterly, 44,* 53–69.

Chandler, J.M. (1977, April). TV and sports: Wedded with a golden hoop. *Psychology Today,* 64–66, 75–76.

Check, J.V.P. (1985). *The effects of violent and nonviolent pornography.* Ottawa: Department of Justice for Canada.

Christensen, P.G., & Roberts, D.F. (1983). The role of television in the formation of children's social attitudes. In M.J.A. Howe (Ed.). *Learning from television: Psychological and educational research* (pp. 79–99). London: Academic Press.

Churchill, W., & Vander Wall, J. (1987). The FBI takes AIM: the FBI's secret war against the American Indian Movement. *The Other Side, 23*(5), 14–29.

Clark, C. (1969). Television and social controls: Some observation of the portrayal of ethnic minorities. *Television Quarterly, 8*(2), 18–22.

Clarke, G. (1988, July 4). A reluctance to play gay. *Time,* p. 61.

Colfax, D., & Steinberg, S. (1972). The perpetuation of racial stereotypes: Blacks in mass circulation magazine advertisements. *Public Opinion Quarterly, 35,* 8–18.

Comstock, G. (1985). Television and film violence. In S.J. Apter & A.P. Goldstein (Eds.), *Youth violence: Programs and prospects.* New York: Pergamon Press.

Comstock, G., Chaffee, S., Katzman, N., McCombs, M., & Roberts, D. (1978). *Television and human behavior.* New York: Columbia University Press.

Cook, T.D., Appleton, H., Conner, R.F., Shaffer, A., Tabkin, G.., & Weber, J.S. (1975). *Sesame Street revisited.* New York: Russell Sage.

Corcoran, F. (1986). KAL 007 and the evil empire: Mediated disaster and forms of rationalization. *Critical Studies in Mass Communication, 3,* 297–316.

Corder-Bolz, C.R. (1980). Mediation: The role of significant others. *Journal of Communication, 30,* 106–118.

Corliss, R. (1988, July 11). Born in East L.A. *Time,* p. 6–67.

Court, J.H. (1977). Pornography and sex crimes: A re-evaluation in the light of recent trends around the world. *International Journal of Criminology and Penology, 5,* 129–157.

Court, J.H. (1982). Rape trends in New South Wales: A discussion of conflicting evidence. *Australian Journal of Social Issues, 17,* 202–206.

Court, J.H. (1984). Sex and violence: A ripple effect. In N.M. Malamuth & E. Donnerstein (Eds.), *Pornography and sexual aggression* (pp. 143–172). Orlando: Academic Press.

Courtney, A.E., & Whipple, T.W. (1983). *Sex steroetyping in advertising.* Lexington, MA: D.C. Heath.

Culley, J.D., & Bennett, R. (1976). Selling women, selling blacks. *Journal of Communication, 26*(4), 160–174.

Cuperfain, R., & Clarke, T.K. (1985). A new perspective on subliminal perception. *Journal of Advertising, 14*(1), 36–41.

Davis, D.K. & Baran, S.J. (1981). *Mass communication and everyday life: A perspective on theory and effect.* Belmont, CA: Wadsworth.

Davis, M.H., Hull, J.G., Young, R.D., & Warren, G.G. (1987). Emotional reactions to dramatic film stimuli: The influence of cognitive and emotional empathy. *Journal of Personality and Social Psychology, 52,* 126–133.

Davis, R.H. (1983). Television health messages: What are they telling us? *Generations, 3*(5), 43–45.

Davis, R.H., & Davis, J.A. (1985). *TV's image of the elderly.* Lexington, MA: Lexington Books/D.C. Heath.

Dermer, M., & Pyszczynski, T.A. (1978). Effects of erotica upon men's loving and liking responses. *Journal of Personality and Social Psychology, 36,* 1302–1309.

Dershowitz, A. (1985, May 25). These cops are all guilty. *TV Guide,* 4–7.

Devlin, L.P. (1987). Campaign commercials. In A.A. Berger (Ed.), *Television in society* (pp. 17–28). New Brunswick, NJ: Transaction Books.

Diamond, D. (1987, June 13). Is the toy business taking over kids' TV? *TV Guide,* pp. 4–8.

Diamond, E., & Noglows, P. (1987, June 20). When network news pulls its punches. *TV Guide,* 2–9.

Diaz-Guerrero, R., Reyes-Lagunes, I., Witzke, D.B., & Holtzman, W.H. (1976). *Plaza Sesamo* in Mexico: An evaluation. *Journal of Communication, 26,* 109–123.

Diener, E., & DeFour, D. (1978). Does television violence enhance program popularity? *Journal of Personality and Social Psychology, 36,* 333–341.

Dietz, P.E., & Evans, B. (1982). Pornographic imagery and prevalence of paraphilia. *American Journal of Psychiatry, 139,* 1493–1495.

Dietz, P.E., Harry, B., & Hazelwood, R.R. (1986). Detective magazines: Pornography for the sexual sadist? *Journal of Forensic Sciences, 31*(1), 197–211.

Dominick, J.R., & Rauch, G.E. (1972). The image of women in network TV commercials. *Journal of Broadcasting, 16,* 259–265.

Donnerstein, E. (1980). Aggressive erotica and violence against women. *Journal of Personality and Social Psychology, 39,* 269–277.

Donnerstein, E. (1984). Pornography: Its effect on violence against women. In N.M. Malamuth & E. Donnerstein (Eds.), *Pornography and sexual aggression* (pp. 53–81). Orlando: Academic Press.

Donnerstein, E., & Berkowitz, L. (1981). Victim reactions in aggressive erotic films as a factor in violence against women. *Journal of Personality and Social Psychology, 41,* 710–724.

Donnerstein, E., Donnerstein, M., & Evans, R. (1975). Erotic stimuli and aggression: Facilitation or inhibition? *Journal of Personality and Social Psychology, 32,* 237–244.

Donnerstein, E., & Hallam, J. (1978). Facilitating effects of erotica on aggression against women. *Journal of Personality and Social Psychology, 36,* 1270–1277.

Donnerstein, E., Linz, D., & Penrod, S. (1987). *The question of pornography: Research findings and policy implications.* New York: Free Press.

Doob, A.N., & Macdonald, G.E. (1979). Television viewing and fear of victimization: Is the relationship causal? *Journal of Personality and Social Psychology, 37,* 170–179.

Dorr, A. (1980). When I was a child I thought as a child. In S.B. Withey & R.P. Abeles (Eds.), *Television and social behavior* (pp. 191–229). Hillsdale, NJ: Lawrence Erlbaum Associates.

Dorr, A. (1982). Television and the socialization of the minority child. In G.L. Berry & C. Mitchell-Kernan (Eds.), *Television and the socialization of the minority child.* New York: Academic Press.

Dorr, A., Graves, S.B., & Phelps, E. (1980). Television literacy for young children. *Journal of Communication, 30,* 71–83.

Dorr, A., & Kovaric, P. (1980). Some of the people some of the time—but which people? Televised violence and its effects. In E. Palmer and A. Dorr (Eds.), *Children and the faces of television* (pp. 183–199). New York: Academic Press.

Dorris, M. (1988, May 28). Why Mister Ed still talks good horse sense. *TV Guide,* 34–36.

Drabman, R.S., & Thomas, M.H. (1974). Does media violence increase children's toleration of real-life aggression? *Developmental Psychology, 10,* 418–421.

Drabman, R.S., & Thomas, M.H. (1976). Does watching violence on television cause apathy? *Pediatrics, 57,* 329–331.

Dunwoody, S. (1986). When science writers cover the social sciences. In J. H. Goldstein, (Ed.), *Reporting science: The case of aggression* (pp. 67–81). Hillsdale, NJ: Lawrence Erlbaum Associates.

Eastman, H., & Liss, M. (1980). Ethnicity and children's preferences. *Journalism Quarterly, 57*(2), 277–280.

Eban, A. (1983). *The new diplomacy: International affairs in the modern age.* New York: Random House.

Egly, M. (1973). Teleniger. *Dossiers Psychologiques, 1,* 2–5.

Einsiedel, E.F. (1988). The British, Canadian, and U.S. pornography commissions and their use of social science research. *Journal of Communication, 38*(2), 108–121.

Eron, L. D., Huesmann, L.R., Lefkowitz, M.M., & Walder, L.O. (1972). Does television violence cause aggression? *American Psychologist, 27,* 253–263.

Esslin, M. (1982). *The age of television.* San Francisco: Freeman.

Evans, J.S.B. (1982). *The psychology of deductive reasoning.* London: Routledge & Kegan Paul.

Eysenck, H.J., & Nias, D.K.B. (1978) *Sex violence and the media.* New York: Harper.

Fellner, C.H., & Marshall, J.R. (1981). Kidney donors revisited. In J.P. Rushton & R.M. Sorrentino (Eds.), *Altruism and helping behavior* (pp. –). Hillsdale, NJ: Lawrence Erlbaum Associates.

Fenigstein, A., & Heyduk, R.G. (1985). Thought and action as determinants of media exposure. In D. Zillmann & J. Bryant (Eds.). *Selective exposure to communication* (p. 113–139). Hillsdale, NJ: Erlbaum.

Fernandes, M. (1978). Um dia de cao [One bad day]. In M. Fernandes, *Nova fabulas fabulosas* (pp. 21–22). (2nd Ed.) Rio de Janeiro: Nordica.

Fernandez-Collado, C., & Greenberg, B.S. (1978). Sexual intimacy and drug use in TV series. *Journal of Communication, 28*(3), 30–37.

Ferrante, C.L., Haynes, A.M., & Kingsley, S.M. (1988). Image of women in television advertising. *Journal of Broadcasting & Electronic Media, 32,* 231–237.

Feshbach, S. (1955). The drive-reducing function of fantasy behavior. *Journal of Abnormal and Social Psychology, 50,* 3–11.

Feshbach, S. (1976). The role of fantasy in the response to television. *Journal of Social Issues, 32,* 71–85.

Feshbach, S., & Singer, R. (1971). *Television and aggression.* San Francisco: Jossey-Bass.

Final report of the attorney general's commission on pornography. (1986). Nashville, TN: Rutledge Hill Press.

Findahl, O., & Hoijer, B. (1981). Media content and human comprehension. In K.E. Rosengren (Ed.), *Advances in content analysis.* Beverly Hills, CA: Sage.

Findahl, O., & Hoijer, B. (1982). The problem of comprehension and recall of broadcast news. In J.F. LeNy and W. Kintsch (Eds.), *Language and comprehension* (p. 261–272). Amsterdam: North-Holland.

Fiske, J. (1987). *Television culture.* London: Methuen.

Foote, J. (1988, January 9). If it's air time, the anchor must be wearing his fur coat and mittens. *TV Guide,* 10–11.

Ford, G.T., & Calfee, J.E. (1986). Recent developments in FTC policy on deception. *Journal of Marketing, 50,* 82–103.

Freedman, J.L. (1984). Effects of television violence on aggressiveness. *Psychological Bulletin, 96,* 227–246.

Freedman, J.L. (1986). Television violence and aggression: A rejoinder. *Psychological Bulletin, 100,* 372–378.

Freuh, T., & McGhee, P.E. (1975). Traditional sex-role development and time spent watching television. *Developmental Psychology, 11*(1), 109.

Friedrich, O. (1987, August 17). Edging the government out of TV. *Time,* p. 58.

Friedrich-Cofer, L., & Huston, A.C. (1986). Television violence and aggression: The debate continues. *Psychological Bulletin, 100,* 364–371.

Fuchs, D.A. (1966). Election-day radio-television and Western voting. *Public Opinion Quarterly, 30,* 226–236.

Gans, H. (1979). *Deciding what's news.* New York: Pantheon.

Gardner, M.P., & Houston, M.J. (1986). The effects of verbal and visual components of retail communications. *Journal of Retailing, 62,* 64–78.

Garelik, G. (1985, April). The weather peddlers. *Discover,* 18–29.

Gebhard, P. (1977). The acquisition of basic sex information. *Journal of Sex Research, 13,* 148–169.

Geen, R.G., & Quanty, M.B. (1977). The catharsis of aggression: An evaluation of a hypothesis. In L. Berkowitz (Ed.), *Advances in experimental social psychology,* Vol. 10 (pp. 1–37). New York: Academic Press.

Geis, F., Brown, V., Jennings, J., & Porter, N. (1984). TV commercials as achievement scripts for women. *Sex Roles, 10*(7/8), 513–525.

Geis, M.L. (1982). *The language of television advertising.* New York: Academic Press.

Gelb, B.D.., & Zinkhan, G.M. (1985). The effect of repetition on humor in a radio advertising study. *Journal of Advertising, 14*(4), 13–20.

Gerbner, G., & Gross, L. (1980). The violent face of television and its lessons. In E. Palmer & A. Dorr (Eds.), *Children and the faces of television: Teaching, violence, selling* (pp. 149–162). New York: Academic Press.

Gerbner, G., Gross, L., Morgan, M., & Signiorelli, N. (1980). The mainstreaming of America: Violence profile No. 11. *Journal of Communication, 30*(3), 10–29.

Gerbner, G., Gross, L., Morgan, M., & Signiorelli, N. (1981a). Health and medicine on television. *New England Journal of Medicine, 305*(15), 901–904.

Gerbner, G., Gross, L., Morgan, M., & Signiorelli, N. (1981b). Scientists on the TV screen. *Society, 18*(4), 41–44.

Gerbner, G., Gross, L., Morgan, M., & Signiorelli, N. (1982). Charting the mainstream: Television's contributions to political orientations. *Journal of Communication, 32*(2), 100–127.

Gerbner, G., Gross, L., Morgan, M., & Signiorelli, N. (1984). Political correlates of television viewing. *Public Opinion Quarterly, 48,* 283–300.

Gerbner, G., Gross, L., Morgan, M., & Signiorelli, N. (1986). Living with television: The dynamics of the cultivation process. In J. Bryant & D. Zillman (Eds.), *Perspectives on media effects* (pp. 17–40). Hillsdale, NJ: Lawrence Erlbaum Associates.

Gerbner, G., Gross, L., Signiorelli, N., & Morgan, M. (1980). Aging with television: Images on television drama and conception of social reality. Journal of Communication, 30(1), 37–47.

Gerbner, G., Gross, L., Signiorelli, N., Morgan, M., & Jackson-Beeck, M. (1979). The demonstration of power: Violence profile No. 10. *Journal of Communication, 29*(3), 177–195.

Gerbner, G., Gross, L., Signiorelli, N., Morgan, M. (1986, September). Television's mean world: Violence profile No. 14-15. University of Pennsylvania Annenberg School of Communications report.

Gerbner, G., & Signiorelli, N. (1979). Women and minorities in television drama (1969-1978). Philadelphia: Annenberg School of Communication, University of Pennsylvania.

Goldberg, M. (1988, February 20). Take two doses for Kildare and Casey and don't call me in the morning. *TV Guide,* 12–13.

Goldstein, J. H. (ed.) (1986). *Reporting science: The case of aggression.* Hillsdale, NJ: Lawrence Erlbaum Associates.

Goldstein, J.H., & Arms, R.L. (1971). Effects of observing athletic contests on hostility. *Sociometry, 34,* 83–90.

Goldstein, S., & Ibaraki, T. (1983). Japan: Aggression and aggression control in Japanese society. In A. Goldstein & M. Segall (Eds.), *Aggression in global perspective.* (pp. –). New York: Pergamon Press.

Gorn, G.I., Goldberg, M.E., & Kanungo, R.N. (1976). The role of educational television in changing intergroup attitudes of children. *Child Development, 47,* 277–280.

Graves, S.B. (1980). Psychological effects of black portrayals on television. In S.B. Withey & R.P. Abeles (Eds.), *Television and social behavior.* (p. 259–289). Hillsdale, NJ: Lawrence Erlbaum Associates.

Gray, H. (1986). Television and the new black man: Black male images in prime-time situation comedy. *Media, Culture and Society, 8,* 223–242.

Greeley, A.M. (1988, July 9). In defense of TV evangelism. *TV Guide,* 4–7.

Greenberg, B..S. (1980). *Life on television.* Norwood, NJ: Ablex.

Greenberg, B.S. (1982). Television and role socialization. In D. Pearl, L. Bouthilet, & J. Lazar, (Eds.), *Television and behavior: Ten years of scientific progress and implications for the eighties. Vol. 2. Technical Reviews.* Rockville, MD: NIMH.

Greenberg, B.S. (1986). Minorities and the mass media. In J. Bryant & D. Zillman (Eds.), *Perspectives on media effects* (pp. 165–188). Hillsdale, NJ: Erlbaum.

Greenberg, B.S., Abelman, R., & Neuendorf, U. (1981). Sex on the soap operas: Afternoon intimacy. *Journal of Communication, 31*(3).

Greenberg, B.S., & Atkin, C. (1982). Learning about minorities from television: A research agenda. In G. Berry & C. Mitchell-Kernan (Eds.), *Television and the socialization of the minority child* (pp. 215–243). New York: Academic Press.

Greenberg, B.S., Heeter, C., Graef, D., Doctor, K., Burgoon, J.K., Burgoon, M., &

Korzenny, F. (1983). Mass communication and Mexican Americans. In B.S. Greenberg, M. Burgoon, J.K. Burgoon, & F. Korzenny (Eds.), *Mexican Americans and the mass media* (pp. 7–34). Norwood, NJ: Ablex.

Greenberg, B.S., Korzenny, F., & Atkin, C. (1979). The portrayal of the aging: Trends on commercial television. *Research on Aging, 1,* 319–334.

Greenberg, B.S., Neuendorf, K., Buerkel-Rothfuss, N., & Henderson, L. (1982). The soaps: What's on and who cares? *Journal of Broadcasting, 26*(2), 519–535.

Greenfield, J. (1985, March 2). Rich is in—and we may be the poorer for it. *TV Guide,* 2–5.

Greenfield, P.M. (1984). *Mind and media.* Cambridge MA: Harvard University Press.

Greenfield, P., & Beagles-Roos, J. (1988). Radio vs. television: The cognitive impact on children of different socioeconomic and ethnic groups. *Journal of Communication, 38*(2), 31–92.

Greenfield, P., Farrar, D., & Beagles-Roos, J. (1986). Is the medium the message? An experimental comparison of the effects of radio and television on imagination. *Journal of Applied Developmental Psychology, 7,* 201–218.

Gross, L. (1984). The cultivation of intolerance: Television, blacks, and gays. In G. Melischek, K.E. Rosengren, & J. Stappers (Eds.), *Cultural indicators: An international symposium* (pp. 345–364). Vienna: Austrian Academy of Sciences.

Gumpert, G. (1987). *Talking tombstones and other tales of the media age.* New York: Oxford University Press.

Gunter, B. (1985). *Dimensions of television violence.* New York: St. Martin's Press.

Gunter, B. (1987). Poor reception: Misunderstanding and forgetting broadcast news. Hillsdale, NJ: Lawrence Erlbaum Associates.

Gunter, B., Berry, C., & Clifford, B. (1982). Remembering broadcast news: The implications of experimental research for production technique. *Human Learning, 1,* 13–29.

Gunter, B., & Levy, M.R. (1987). Social contexts of video use. *American Behavioral Scientist, 30,* 486–494.

Gunter, B., & Svennevig, M. (1987). *Behind and in front of the screen: Television's involvement with family life.* London: Libbey.

Guttman, A. (1986). *Sports spectators.* New York: Columbia University Press.

Handler, D. (1987, April 18). TV finished first, friends second, helping others third. *TV Guide,* 20–21.

Hanratty, M.A., O'Neal, E., & Sulzer, J.L. (1972). The effect of frustration upon imitation of aggression. *Journal of Personality and Social Psychology, 21,* 30–34.

Hardaway, F. (1979). The language of popular culture: Daytime television as a transmitter of values. *College English, 40*(5), 517–521.

Harris, A., & Feinberg, J. (1977). Television and aging: Is what you see what you get? *Gerontologist, 17,* 464–468,

Harris, R.J. (1977). Comprehension of pragmatic implications in advertising. *Journal of Applied Psychology, 62,* 603–608.

Harris, R.J. (1981). Inferences in information processing. In G.H. Bower (Ed.), *The psychology of learning and motivation* (pp. 82–128). Vol 15. New York: Academic Press.

Harris, R.J., Dubitsky, T.M., & Bruno, K.J. (1983). Psycholinguistic studies of misleading advertising. In R.J. Harris (Ed.), *Information processing research in advertising* (p. 241–262). Hillsdale, NJ: Lawrence Erlbaum Associates.

Harris, R.J., McCoy, S.J., Foster, T.R., Krenke, N., & Bechtold, J.I. (1988). An experimental test of the relationship of advertising language to the strength of inferences drawn about product claims. In M.T. Henderson (Ed.), *Proceedings of the 22nd annual Mid-America Linguistics Conference.* Lawrence KS: University of Kansas.

Harris, R.J., Schoen, L.M., & Hensley, D. (in opress). A cross-cultural study of story memory. *Journal of Cross-cultural Psychology.*

Harris, R.J., Sturm, R.E., Klassen, M.L., & Bechtold, J.I. (1986). Language in advertising: A psycholinguistic approach. *Current Issues and Research in Advertising, 9,* 1–26.

Harris, R.J., Trusty, M.L., Bechtold, J.I., & Wasinger, L. (in press). Memory for implied versus directly asserted advertising claims. *Psychology & Marketing.*

Hartmann, D.P. (1969). Influence of symbolically modelled instrumental aggression and pain cues on aggressive behavior. *Journal of Personality and Social Psychology, 11,* 280–288.

Harvey, M., & Rothe, J. (1986). Videocassette recorders: Their impact on viewers and advertisers. *Journal of Advertising Research, 25*(6), 19–27.

Hass, R.G. (1981). Effects of source characteristics on cognitive responses and persuasion. In R.E. Petty, T.M. Ostrom, & T.C. Brock (Eds.), *Cognitive responses in persuasion* (pp. 141–172). Hillsdale, NJ: Lawrence Erlbaum Associates.

Hawkins, R.P., (1977). The dimensional structure of children's perceptions of television reality. *Communication Research, 4,* 299–320.

Hawkins, R.P., & Pingree, S. (1981). Uniform messages and habitual viewing: Unnecessary assumptions in social reality effects. *Human Communication Research, 7,* 291–301.

Hayes, D., & Birnbaum, D.W. (1980). Preschoolers' retention of televised events: Is a picture worth a thousand words? *Developmental Psychology, 16,* 410–416.

Heeter, C., Greenberg, B., Mendelson, B., Burgoon, J., Burgoon, M., & Korzenny, F. (1983). Cross media coverage of local Hispanic American news. *Journal of Broadcasting, 27*(4), 395–402.

Heiby, E., & Becker, J.D. (1980). Effect of filmed modeling on the self-reported frequency of masturbation. *Archives of Sexual Behavior, 9,* 115–121.

Heiman, J., LoPiccolo, L., & LoPiccolo, J. (1976). *Becoming orgasmic: A sexual growth program for women.* Englewood Cliffs, NJ: Prentice-Hall.

Heller, M.S., & Polsky, S. (1975). *Studies in violence and television.* New York: American Broadcasting Companies.

Heritage, J. (1985). Analyzing news interviews: Aspects of the production of talk for an overhearing audience. In T.A. Van Dijk (Ed.). *Handbook of discourse analysis* (pp. 95–117). Vol 3. London: Academic Press.

Hersch, P. (1988, October). Thirtysomething therapy. *Psychology of Today,* pp.62–64.

Hessing, D.J., & Elffers, H. (1986). Attitude toward death, fear on being declared dead too soon, and donation of organs after death. *Omega, 17*(2), 115–126.

Hickey, N. (1988, January 2). It's upbeat TV—or else! *TV Guide,* 36–39.

Hickey, N. (1988, March 19). The verdict on VCRs (so far). *TV Guide,* 12–14.

Hicks, D.J. (1965). Imitation and retention of film-mediated aggressive peer and adult models. *Journal of Personality and Social Psychology, 2,* 97–100.

Hicks, D.J. (1968). Short- and long-term retention of affectively varied modeled behavior. *Psychonomic Science, 11,* 369–370.

Hiebert, E., & Reuss, C. (Eds.) (1985). *Impact of mass media: Current issues.* White Plains, NJ: Longman.

Hill, C., Davis, H., Holman, R., & Nelson, G. (1984). *Video violence and children.* London: Report of a Parliamentary Group Video Enquiry.

Himmelweit, H. (1978). Youth, television, and experimentation. In *Cultural role of broadcasting.* Tokyo: Hoso-Bunka Foundation.

Hirsch, P.M. (1980). The "scary world" of the nonviewer and other anomalies: A reanalysis of Gerbner et al.'s findings on cultivation analysis, part I. *Communication Research, 7,* 403–456.

Holloway, S.M. & Hornstein, H.A. (1976). How good news makes us good. *Psychology Today, 10*(7), 76–78, 106.

Hornstein, H.A., LaKind, E., Frankel, G., & Manne, S. (1975). The effects of knowledge about remote social events on prosocial behavior, social conception, and mood. *Journal of Personality and Social Psychology, 32,* 1038–1046.

Howitt, D. (1982). *Mass media and social problems.* Oxford: Pergamon Press.

Huesmann, L.R., Eron, L.D., Klein, R., Brice, P., & Fischer,P. (1983). Mitigating the imitation of aggressive behaviors by changing children's attitudes about media violence. *Journal of Personality and Social Psychology, 44,* 899–910.

Huesmann, L.R., Eron, L.D., Lefkowitz, M.M., & Walder, L.O. (1984). Stability of aggression over time and generations. *Developmental Psychology, 20,* 1120–1134.

Huesmann, L.R., Lagerspetz, K., & Eron, L.D. (1984). Intervening variables in the TV violence-aggression relation: Evidence from two countries. *Developmental Psychology, 20,* 746–775.

Hughes, M. (1980). The fruits of cultivation analysis: A reexamination of some effects of television watching. *Public Opinion Quarterly, 44,* 287–302.

Husson, W., Stephen, T., Harrison, T.M., & Fehr, B.J. (1988). An interpersonal communication perspective on images of political candidates. *Human Communication Research, 14,* 397–421.

Huston, A.C., & Wright, J.C. (1987). The forms of television and the child viewer. In G.A. Comstock (Ed.), *Public communication and behavior.* Vol. 2. New York: Academic Press.

Jacoby, J., & Hoyer, W.D. (1987). *The comprehension and miscomprehension of print communication: A study of mass media magazines.* Hillsdale, NJ: Lawrence Erlbaum Associates.

Jacoby, J., Hoyer, W.D., & Zimmer, M.R. (1983). To read, view, or listen? A cross-media comparison of comprehension. *Current Issues and Research in Advertising, 6,* 201–218.

Jakes, J. (1985, November 2). What? A successful media campaign without TV spots and Phil Donohue? *TV Guide,* 12–15.

Jamieson, K.H., & Campbell, K.K (1988). *The interplay of influence: Mass media and their publics in news, advertising, politics.* (2nd Ed.) Belmont, CA: Wadsworth.

Janis, I.L. (1980). The influence of television on personal decision making. In S.B. Withey & R.P. Abeles (Eds.), *Television and social behavior* (pp. 161–189). Hillsdale, NJ: Lawrence Erlbaum Associates.

Jennings, J., Geis, F., & Brown, V. (1980). Influence of television commercials on women's self-confidence and independent judgment. *Journal of Personality and Social Psychology, 38*(2), 203–210.

Johnson, D.K., & Satow, K. (1978). Consumers' reaction to sex in TV commercials. In H.K. Hunt (Ed.), *Advances in consumer research,* Vol. 5. (pp. 411–414). Chicago: Association for Consumer Research.

Johnsson-Smaragdi, U. (1983). *TV use and social interaction in adolescence: A longitudinal study.* Stockholm: Almqvist & Wiskell International.

Johnston, J., & Ettema, J. (1982). *Positive images: Breaking stereotypes with children's television.* Beverly Hills, CA: Sage.

Johnston, J., & Ettema, J.S. (1986). Using television to best advantage: Research for prosocial television. In J. Bryant & D. Zillmann (Eds.), *Perspectives on media effects* (pp. 143–164). Hillsdale, NJ: Lawrence Erlbaum Associates.

Joy, L.A., Kimball, M.M., & Zabrack, M.L. (1986). Television and children's aggressive behavior. In T.M. Williams (Ed.), *The impact of television: A natural experiment in three communities* (pp. 303–360). Orlando: Academic Press.

Joyce, E.M. (1986). Reporting of hostage crises: Who's in charge of television? *SAIS Review, 6*(1), 169–176.

Kalter, J. (1985, November 23). Let's run birth control ads during *Dallas* and *Dynasty. TV Guide,* 30–31.

Kalter, J. (1986, May 24). The untold stories of Africa: Why TV is missing some big ones. *TV Guide,* 2–12.

Kalter, J. (1986, May 11). Disability chic. *TV Guide,* 40–44.

Kalter, J. (1987, May 30). Exposing media myths: TV doesn't affect you as much as you think. *TV Guide,* 2–5.

Kalter, J. (1987, July 11). Guess right—or we'll throw you to the bees! *TV Guide,* 26–28.

Kalter, J. (1988, January 30). What working women want from TV. *TV Guide,* 2–7.

Kalter, J. (1988, June 18). Where TV is as important as school. *TV Guide,* 18–22.

Kalter, J. (1988, July 23). How TV is shaking up the American family. *TV Guide,* 4–11.

Karp, W. (1985). Subliminal politics in the evening news: The networks from left to right. In R.E. Hiebert & C. Reuss (Eds.), *Impact of mass media: Current Issues* (pp. 213–221). New York: Longman.

Kassarjian, H (1969). The Negro and American advertising: 1946–1965. *Journal of Marketing Research, 6,* 29–39.

Kelly, H. (1981). Reasoning about realities: Children's evaluations of television and books. In H. Kelly & H. Gardner (Eds.), *Viewing children through television.* San Francisco: Jossey-Bass.

Kendall, K.E., & Yum, J.O. (1984). Persuading the blue-collar voter: Issues, images, and homophily. In R.N. Bostrom (Ed.), *Communication yearbook 8* (pp. 707–722). Beverly Hills, CA: Sage.

Kenner, H. (1973, July 29). Review of E. Carpenter, *Oh, what a blow that phantom gave me. New York Times Book Review,* p. 7.

Key, W.B. (1981). *The clam-plate orgy.* New York: Signet.

Key, W.B. (1976). *Media sexploitation.* New York: Signet.

Key, W.B. (1974). *Subliminal seduction.* New York: Signet.

Kilbourne, W.E., Painton, S., & Ridley, D. (1985). The effect of sexual embedding on responses to magazine advertisements. *Journal of Advertising, 14*(2), 48–56.

Kimball, M.M. (1986). Television and sex-role attitudes. In T.M. Williams (Ed.). *The impact of television: A natural experiment in three communities* (pp. 265–302). Orlando: Academic Press.

Kintsch, W. (1977). On comprehending stories. In P. Carpenter & M. Just (Eds.), *Cognitive processes in comprehension.* Hillsdale, NJ: Lawrence Erlbaum Associates.

Kintsch, W., & van Dijk, T.A. (1978). Toward a model of text comprehension and production. *Psychological Review, 85,* 363–394.

Klapper, J.T. (1960). *The effects of mass communications.* Glencoe, IL: Free Press.

Knill, B.J., Pesch, M., Pursey, G., Gilpin, P., & Perloff, R.M. (1981). Still typecast after all these years? Sex role portrayals in television advertising. *International Journal of Women's Studies, 4,* 497–506.

Kolatch, J. (1986a, May 31). Uprising in the Philippines: Could there have been a revolution without television? *TV Guide,* 4–14.

Kolatch, J. (1986b, June 7). TV and the Philippines: For the first time the people could see what was happening. *TV Guide,* 16–21.

Krafka, C.L. (1985). *Sexually explicit, sexually violent, and violent media: Effects of multiple naturalistic exposures and debriefing on female viewers.* Unpublished doctoral dissertation. Madison: University of Wisconsin.

Kraus, S. (Ed.) (1962). *The great debates.* Bloomington, IN: Indiana University Press.

Kraus, S. (Ed.) (1977). *The great debates: 1976, Ford vs. Carter.* Bloomington, IN: Indiana University Press.

Kraus, S. (1988). *Televised Presidential debates and public policy.* Hillsdale, NJ: Lawrence Erlbaum Associates.

Kubey, R. (1980). Television and aging: Past, present, and future. *Gerontologist, 20,* 16–35.

Kubey, R. (1986). Television use in everyday life: Coping with unstructured time. *Journal of Communication, 36,* 108–123.

Kunkel, D. (1988). Children and host-selling television commercials. *Communication Research, 15*(1), 71–92.

Kutchinsky, B. (1973). The effect of easy availability of pornography on the incidence of sex crimes: The Danish experience. *Journal of Social Issues, 29*(3), 163–181.

Lambert, W.E., & Klineberg, O. (1967). *Children's views of foreign peoples: A cross-national study.* New York: Appleton-Century-Crofts.

Lang, G.E., & Lang, K. (1984). *Politics and television re-viewed.* Beverly Hills, CA: Sage.

Lang, K., & Lang, G.E. (1968). *Politics and television.* Chicago: Quadrangle Books.

Larsen, S. F. (1983). Text processing and knowledge updating in memory for radio news. *Discourse Processes, 6,* 21–38.

Larson, J.F. (1984). *Television's window on the world: International affairs coverage on the U.S. networks.* Norwood, NJ: Ablex.

Larson, J.F. (1986). Television and U.S. foreign policy: The case of the Iran hostage crisis. *Journal of Communication, 36*(4), 108–130.

Larson, J.F., McAnany, E.G., & Storey, J.D. (1986). News of Latin America on network television, 1972–1981: A northern perspective on the southern hemisphere. *Critical studies in mass communication, 3,* 169–183.

Lasswell, H.D. (1935). *World politics and personal insecurity: A contribution to political psychiatry.* New York: McGraw-Hill.

Lazarsfeld, P.F. (1941). Remarks on administrative and critical communications research. *Studies in Philosophy of Social Science, 9,* 2–16.

Lazarsfeld, P.F., Berelson, B., & Guadet, H. (1948). *The people's choice.* New York: Columbia University Press.

Leahy, M. (1987). Our cities are big bad places—if you believe TV. *TV Guide,.*

Lee, C.C (1980). *Media imperialism reconsidered.* Beverly Hills, CA: Sage.

Lefkowitz, M.M, Eron, L.D., Walder, L.O., & Huesmann, L.R. (1977). *Growing up to be violent: A longitudinal study of the development of aggression.* New York: Pergamon.

Lemar, J. (1977). Women and blacks on prime-time television. *Journal of Communication, 27,* 70–80.

Levy, M.R. (1980). Program playback preferences in VCR households. *Journal of Broadcasting, 24,* 327–336.

Levy, M.R. (1982). Watching TV news as para-social interaction. In G. Gumpert & R. Cathcart (Eds.), *Inter/media.* (2nd ed.) (pp. 177–187). New York: Oxford University Press.

Levy, M.R. (1987). Some problems of VCR research. *American Behavioral Scientist, 30,* 461–470.

Levy, M.R., & Windahl, S. (1984). Audience activity and gratifications: A conceptual clarification and exploration. *Communication Research, 11,* 51–78.

Lewy, G. (1978). Vietnam: New light on the question of American guilt. *Commentary, 65,* 29–49.

Leyens, J., Camino, L., Parke, R., & Berkowitz, L. (1975). The effects of movie violence on aggression in a field setting as a function of group dominance and cohesion. *Journal of Personality and Social Psychology, 32,* 346–360.

Liebert, R.M., & Sprafkin, J.N. (1988). *The early window: Effects of television on children and youth.* (3rd ed.) New York: Pergamon.

Linz, D. (1985). *Sexual violence in the mass media: Effects on male viewers and implications for society.* Unpublished doctoral dissertation. Madison University of Wisconsin.

Linz, D., & Donnerstein, E. (1988). The methods and merits of pornography research. *Journal of Communication, 38*(2), 180–184.

Linz, D. Donnerstein, E., & Penrod, S. (1984). The effects of multiple exposures to filmed violence against women. *Journal of Communication, 34*(3), 130–147.

Linz, D. Donnerstein, E., & Penrod, S. (1987). The findings and recommendations of the Attorney General's Commission on Pornography: Do the psychological "facts" fit the political fury? *American Psychologist, 42,* 946–953.

Linz, D., Donnerstein, E., Bross, M., & Chapin, M. (1986). Mitigating the influence of violence on television and sexual violence in the media. In R. Blanchard (Ed.), *Advances in the study of aggression.* Vol. 2. Orlando, FL: Academic Press, (p. 165–194).

Linz, D., Turner, C.W., Hesse, B.W., & Penrod, S.D. (1984). Bases of liability for injuries produced by media portrayals of violent pornography. In N.M. Malamuth & E. Donnerstein (Eds.), *Pornography and sexual aggression* (p. 277–304). Orlando: Academic Press.

Lippmann, W. (1922). *Public opinion.* New York: Harcourt Brace and World.

Littwin, S. (1988, April 9). How TV Americanizes immigrants—for better or for worse. *TV Guide,* 4–10.

Loftus, E.F., & Burns, T.E. (1982). Mental shock can produce retrograde amnesia. *Memory & Cognition, 10,* 318–323.

Long, D.L., & Graesser, A.C. (1988). Wit and humor in discourse processing. *Discourse Processes, 11,* 35–60.

Longford, L. (Ed.) (1972). *Pornography: The Longford Report.* London: Coronet.

Lovaas, O.I. (1961). Effect of exposure to symbolic aggression on aggressive behavior. *Child Development, 32,* 37–44.

Lowery, S., & DeFleur, M.L. (1983). *Milestones in mass communication research.* New York: Longman.

Lowry, D.T., Love, G., & Kirby, M. (1981). Sex on the soap operas: Patterns of intimacy. *Journal of Communication, 31,* 90–96.

Loy, J.W., McPherson, B.D., & Kenyon, G. (1978). *Sport and social systems: A guide to the analysis, problems, and literature.* Reading MA: Addison-Wesley.

Maccoby, N., & Farquhar, J.W. (1977). Reducing the risk of cardiovascular disease: Effects of a community-based campaign on knowledge and behavior. *Journal of Community Health, 3*(2), 100–102.

Maccoby, N., & Solomon, D.S. (1981). The Stanford community studies in heart disease prevention. In R. Rice and W. Paisley (Eds.), *Public communication campaigns* (pp. –). Beverly Hills, CA: Sage.

Madden, T.J., & Weinberger, M.G. (1982). The effects of humor on attention in magazine advertising. *Journal of Advertising, 11*(3), 8–14.

Madden, T.J., & Weinberger, M.G. (1984). Humor in advertising: A practitioner view. *Journal of Advertising Research, 24*(4), 23–29.

Magnuson, E. (1988, March 7). Search and seizure on Capitol Hill. *Time,* p.23.

Malamuth, N.M. (1981). Rape fantasies as a function of exposure to violent sexual stimuli. *Archives of Sexual Behavior, 10,* 33–47.

Malamuth, N.M. (1983). Factors associated with rape as predictors of laboratory aggression against women. *Journal of Personality and Social Psychology, 45,* 432–442.

Malamuth, N.M. (1984). Aggression against women: Cultural and individual causes. In N.M. Malamuth & E. Donnerstein (Eds.), *Pornography and sexual aggression* (pp. 19–52). Orlando: Academic Press.

Malamuth, N.M., & Check, J.V.P. (1980a). Penile tumescence and perceptual responses to rape as a function of victim's perceived reaction. *Journal of Applied Social Psychology, 10,* 528–547.

Malamuth, N.M., & Check, J.V.P. (1980b). Sexual arousal to rape and consenting depictions: The importance of the woman's arousal. *Journal of Abnormal Psychology, 89,* 763–766.

Malamuth, N.M., & Check, J.V.P. (1983). Sexual arousal to rape depictions: Individual differences. *Journal of Abnormal Psychology, 92,* 55–67.

Malamuth, N.M., Feshbach, S., & Heim, M. (1980). Ethical issues and exposure to rape stimuli: A reply to Sherif. *Journal of Personality and Social Psychology, 38,* 413–415.

Malamuth, N.M., Haber, S., & Feshbach, S. (1980). Testing hypotheses regarding rape: Exposure to sexual violence, sex differences, and the "normality" of rapists. *Journal of Research in Personality, 14,* 121–137.

Malamuth, N.M., Heim, M., & Feshbach, S. (1980). Sexual responsiveness of college students to rape depictions: Inhibitory and disinhibitory effects. *Journal of Personality and Social Psychology, 38,* 399–408.

Malamuth, N.M., & Spinner, B. (1980). A longitudinal content analysis of sexual violence in the best-selling erotica magazines. *Journal of Sex Research, 16,* 226–237.

Manhattan Mercury, (1987, May 4). Ivory Coast television, p. 5. (AP wire story)

Mankiewicz, F., & Swerdlow, J. (1978). *Remote control: Television and the manipulation of American life.* New York: Ballantine.

Marty, M. (1983, December 24). We need more religion in our sitcoms. *TV Guide,* 2–8.

Maslin, J. (1982, November 11). Bloodbaths debase movies and audiences. *New York Times.*

Massing, H.H. (1987). Decoding "Dallas": Comparing American and German viewers. In A.A. Berger (Ed.), *Television in society* (p. 96–103). New Brunswick, NJ: Transaction Books.

Maynard, J. (1987, May 9). Raising kids and having a career is a snap. *TV Guide,* 4–7.

Mayo, J.K., Hornik, R.C., & McAnany, E.G. (1976). *Educational reform with television: The El Salvador experience.* Stanford: Stanford University Press.

McAnany, E.G. (1983). Television and crisis: Ten years of network news coverage of Central America, 1972–1981. *Media, culture and society,* 5(2), 199–212.

McCombs, M.E. (1981). The agenda-setting approach. In D.D Nimmo & K.R. Sanders (Eds.), *Handbook of political communication* (pp. 121–140). Beverly Hills: Sage.

McDermott, S., & Greenberg, B. (1985). Parents, peers, and television as determinants of black children's esteem. In R. Bostrom (Ed.), *Communication yearbook* (Vol. 8). Beverly Hills CA: Sage.

McGhee, P. (1979). *Humor: Its origin and development.* San Francisco: Freeman.

McGuire, W.J. (1974). Psychological motives and communication gratification. In Blumler, J.G., & Katz, E. (Eds.). *The uses of mass communications: Current perspectives on gratifications research* (p. 167–196). Beverly Hills: Sage.

McGuire, W. J. (1985). Attitudes and attitude change. In G. Lindzey & E. Aronson (Eds.), *Handbook of social psychology.* (3rd ed.). Reading MA: Addison-Wesley.

McGuire, W.J. (1985). The myth of massive media impact: Savagings and salvagings. In G. Comstock (Ed.), *Public communication and behavior.* Vol. 1. New York: Academic Press.

McIntyre, P., Hosch, H.M., Harris, R.J., & Norvell, D.W. (1986). Effects of sex and attitudes toward women on the processing of television commercials. *Psychology and Marketing, 3,* 181–190.

Mele, M. (1987, October). Joint TV programming. *World Press Review,* 57.

Mendelsohn. H.A. (1966). Election-day broadcasts and terminal voting decisions. *Public Opinion Quarterly, 30,* 212–225.

Mendelsohn, H.A., & O'Keefe, G.J. (1976). *The people choose a President: Influences on voter decision making.* New York: Praeger.

Merikle, P.M. & Cheesman, J. (1987). Current status of research on subliminal advertising. In M. Wallendorf & P. Anderson (Eds.), *Advances in Consumer Research. Vol. XIV.* (p. 298–302). Provo, UT: Association for Consumer Research.

Meyrowitz, J. (1985). *No sense of place: The impact of electronic media on social behavior.* New York: Oxford University Press.

Michaels, J. (1988, March). Soap dollars. *World Press Review,* p. 51.

Mielke, K.W., & Chen, M. (1983). Formative research for *3-2-1 Contact:* Methods and insights. In M.J.A. Howe (Ed.), *Learning from television: Psychological and educational research* (p. 31–55). London: Academic Press.

Milavsky, J.R., Kessler, R., Stipp, H., & Rubens, W. (1982). Television and aggression: Results of a panel study. In D. Pearl, L. Bouthilet, & J. Lazar (Eds.), *Television and behavior: Ten years of scientific progress and implications for the eighties* (p. 138–157). Vol 2. Washington: U.S. Government Printing Office.

Moore, T.E. (1982). What you see is what you get. *Journal of Marketing, 46*(2), 38–47.

Morgan, M. (1982). Television and adolescents' sex-role stereotypes: A longitudinal study. *Journal of Personality and Social Psychology, 43*(5), 947–955.

Morgan, M., & Gerbner, G. (1982). TV professions and adolescent career choices. In M. Schwarz (Ed.), *TV and teens: Experts look at the issues* (pp. 121–126). Reading, MA: Addison-Wesley.

Morley, D. (1986). *Family television: Cultural power and domestic leisure.* London: Comedia.

Morris, L.A., Brinberg, D., Klimberg, R. Rivera, C., & Millstein, L.G. (1986). Miscomprehension rates for prescription drug advertisements. *Current Issues and Research in Advertising, 9,* 93–118.

Mowlana, H. (1984). The role of the media in the U.S.–Iranian conflict. In A. Arno & W. Dissayanake (Eds.), *The news media in national and international conflict* (p. 71–99). Boulder, CO: Westview Press.

Murphy, M. (1986, June 21). Let Clare Huxtable—just once—break down and cry. *TV Guide,* 10–13.

Murray, J.P. (1980). *Television and youth: Twenty-five years of research and controversy.* Boys Town, NE: Boys Town Center for the Study of Youth Development.

Nelson, J.P., Gelfand, D.M., & Hartmann, D.P. (1969). Children's aggression following competition and exposure to an aggressive model. *Child Development, 40,* 1085–1097.

Newsweek, (1981, September 28). Soap operas, p .

Nias, D.K.B. (1983). The effects of televised sex and pornography. In M.J.A. Howe (Ed.), *Learning from television: Psychological and educational implications* (p.179–192). London: Academic Press.

Nimmo, D., & Savage, R.L. (1976). *Candidates and their images.* Pacific Palisades, CA: Goodyear.

Northcott, H.C. (1975). Too young, too old: Aging in the world of television. *The Gerontologist, 15,* 184–186.

O'Bryant, S.L., & Corder-Bolz, C.R. (1978). The effects of television on children's stereotyping of women's work roles. *Journal of Vocational Behavior, 12,* 233–244.

Olweus, D. (1979). The stability of aggressive reaction patterns in human males: A review. *Psychological Bulletin, 85*, 852–875.

Paletz, D.L. (1988). Pornography, politics, and the press: The U.S. attorney general's commission on pornography. *Journal of Communication, 38*(2), 122–136.

Palmgreen, P. (1984). Uses and gratifications: A theoretical perspective. In R.N. Bostrom (Ed.), *Communication yearbook 8* (pp. 20–55). Newbury Park, CA: Sage.

Panitt, M. (1988, June 4). In India, they'll trash a station . . . or worship an actor. *TV Guide*, 44–45.

Parke, R., Berkowitz, L., Leyens, J., West, S., & Sebastian, R. (1977). Some effects of violent and non-violent movies on the behavior of juvenile delinquents. In L. Berkowitz (Ed.), *Advances in social psychology*, Vol. 10, New York: Academic Press.

Patterson, T.E. & McClure, R.D. (1976). *The unseeing eye: The myth of television power in national politics.* New York: Putnam.

Patton, G.W.R. (1978). Effect of party affiliation of student voters on the image of presidential candidates. *Psychological Reports, 43*, 343–347.

Penrod, S., & Linz, D. (1984). Using psychological research on violent pornography to inform legal change. In N.M. Malamuth, & E. Donnerstein (Eds.), *Pornography and sexual aggression* (pp. 247–275). Orlando: Academic Press.

Percy, L., & Rossiter, J.R. (1983). Mediating effects of visual and verbal elements in print advertising upon belief, attitude, and intention responses. In L. Percy & A. Woodside (Eds.), *Advertising and consumer psychology* (pp. 171–186). Lexington MA: Lexington Books.

Perse, E.M. (1986). Soap opera viewing patterns of college students and cultivation. *Journal of Broadcasting & Electronic Media, 30*, 175–193.

Pezdek, K., & Hartman, E.F. (1983). Children's television viewing: Attention and comprehension of auditory versus visual information. *Child Development, 54*, 1015–1023.

Pezdek, K., Lehrer, A., & Simon, S. (1984). The relationship between reading and cognitive processing of television and radio. *Child Development, 55*, 2072–2082.

Pezdek, K., & Stevens, E. (1984). Children's memory for auditory and visual information on television. *Developmental Psychology, 20*, 212–218.

Phillips, D.P. (1977). Motor vehicle increase just after publicized suicide stories. *Science, 196*, 1464–1465.

Phillips, D.P. (1984). Teenage and adult temporal fluctuations in suicide and auto fatalities. In H.S. Sudak, A.B. Ford, & N.B. Rushforth (Eds.), *Suicide in the young* (pp. 69–80). Boston: John Wright.

Phillips, D.P., & Carstensen, L.L. (1986). Clustering of teenage suicides after TV news stories about suicides. *New England Journal of Medicine, 315*, 685–689.

Pierce, C.M. (1980). Social trace contaminants: Subtle indicators of racism in TV. In S.B. Withey & R.P. Abeles (Eds.), *Television and social behavior* (p. 249–257). Hillsdale, NJ: Lawrence Erlbaum Associates.

Pierre, E. (1973). La communication class-écran: Une relation d'apprentissage [Student-to-TV communication: A relationship of learning] *Dossiers Pedagogiques, 1*, 6–11.

Pingree, S., & Hawkins, R. (1981). U.S. programs on Australian television: The cultivation effect. *Journal of Communication, 31*(1), 97–105.

Pitkanen-Pulkkinen, L. (1981). Concurrent and predictive validity of self-reported aggressiveness. *Aggressive Behavior, 7*, 97–110.

Poindexter, P.M. & Stroman, C. (1981). Blacks and television: A review of the research literature. *Journal of Broadcasting, 25*(2), 103–122.

Postman, N. (1985). *Amusing ourselves to death.* New York: Viking Penguin, 1985.

Potter, W.J. (1986). Perceived reality and the cultivation hypothesis. *Journal of Broadcasting & Electronic Media, 30,* 159–174.

Potter, W.J. (1988). Perceived reality in television effects research. *Journal of Braodcasting & Electronic Media, 32,* 23–41.

Powell, L. (1977). Voting intention and the complexity of political images: A pilot study. *Psychological Reports, 40,* 243–246.

Powers, R. (1984). *Supertube: The rise of television sports.* New York: Coward-McCann.

Preston, I.L. (1975). *The great American blow-up: Puffery in advertising and selling.* Madison: University of Wisconsin Press.

Preston, I.L., & Richards, J.I. (1986). Consumer miscomprehension as a challenge to FTC prosecutions of deceptive advertising. *The John Marshall Law Review, 19,* 605–635.

Prottas, J.M. (1983). Encouraging altruism: Public attitudes and the marketing of organ donation. *Health and Society, 61*(2), 278–306.

Quinsey, V.L., & Marshall, W. (1983). Procedures for reducing inappropriate sexual arousal: An evaluation review. In J.G. Greer & I. Stuart (Eds.), *The sexual aggressor: Current perspectives on treatment.* New York: Van Nostrand Reinhold.

Rabinovitch, M.S., McLean, M.S., Markham, J.W., & Talbott, A.D. (1972). Children's violence perception as a function of television violence. In G.A. Comstock, E.A. Rubinstein, & J.P. Murray (Eds.), *Television and social behavior, Vol. 5. Television's effects: Further explorations.* Washington DC: U.S. Government Printing Office.

Rachman, S. (1966). Sexual fetishism: An experimental analogue. *Psychological Record, 16,* 293–296.

Rachman, S., & Hodgson, R.J. (1968). Experimentally-induced 'sexual fetishism:' Replication and development. *Psychological Record, 18,* 25–27.

Radecki, T. (1984). Deerhunter continues to kill, 35th victim—31 dead. *NCTV News, 5*(3–4), 3.

Rader, B.G. (1984). *In its own image: How television has transformed sports.* New York: The Free Press.

Read, W.H. (1976). *Americans mass media merchants.* Baltimore: John Hopkins University Press.

Reid, P.T. (1979). Racial stereotyping on television: A comparison of the behavior of black and white television characters. *Journal of Applied Psychology, 64*(5). 465–489.

Report of Special Committee on Pornography and Prostitution. Vol. 1. (1985). Ottawa: Minister of Supply and Services.

Rivera, G. (1987, April 18). There's Lt. Castillo, Sifuentes . . . and little else. *TV Guide,* 40–43.

Roberts, D.F., & Maccoby, N. (1985). Effects of mass communication. In G. Lindzey & E. Aronson (Eds.), *Handbook of social psychology* (3rd ed.). New York: Random House.

Robertson, T.S., Rossiter, J.R., & Gleason, T.C. (1979). *Televised medicine advertising and children.* New York: Praeger.

Rogers, E. (1988). Video is here to stay. *Media & Values, 42,* 4–5.

Rosencrans, M.A., & Hartup, W.W. (1967). Imitative influences of consistent and inconsistent response consequences to a model on aggressive behavior in children. *Journal of Personality and Social Psychology, 7,* 429–434.

Rotfeld, H.J.(1988). Fear appeals and persuasion: Assumptions and errors in advertising research. *Current Issues and Research in Advertising, 11.*

Rubin, A.M., (1981). An examination of television viewing motivations. *Communication Research, 8,* 141–165.

Rubin, A.M., (1983). Television uses and gratifications: The interactions of viewing patterns and motivations. *Journal of Broadcasting, 27,* 37–51.

Rubin, A.M. (1984). Ritualized and instrumental television viewing. *Journal of Communication, 34*(3), 67–77.

Rubin, A.M. (1986). Uses, gratifications, and media effects effects research. In J. Bryant & D. Zillmann (Eds.), *Perspectives on media effects* (p. 281–301). Hillsdale, NJ: Lawrence Erlbaum Associates.

Rubin, A.M., & McHugh, M.P. (1987). Development of parasocial interaction relationships. *Journal of Broadcasting & Electronic Media, 31,* 279–292.

Rubin, A.M., & Perse, E.M. (1987). Audience activity and television news gratifications. *Communication Research, 14,* 58–84.

Rubin, A.M., & Perse, E.M. (1988). Audience activity and soap opera involvement. *Human Communication Research, 14,* 246–268.

Rubin, A.M., & Perse, E.M., & Powell, R.A. (1985). Loneliness, parasocial interaction, and local television news viewing. *Human Communication Research, 12,* 155–180.

Rubin, A.M., Perse, E.M., & Taylor, D.S. (1988). A methodological examination of cultivation. *Communication Research, 15,* 107–134.

Rumelhart, D.E. (1980). Schemata: Building blocks of cognition. In R.J. Spiro, B.C. Bruce, & W.F. Brewer (Eds.), *Theoretical issues in reading comprehension* (p. 33–58). Hillsdale, NJ: Lawrence Erlbaum Associates.

Russo, J.E., Metcalf, B.L., & Stevens, D. (1981). Identifying misleading advertising. *Journal of Consumer Research, 8,* 119–131.

Saegert, J. (1987). Why marketing should quit giving subliminal advertising the benefit of the doubt. *Psychology and Marketing, 4,* 107–120.

Salomon, G. (1979). *Interaction of media, cognition, and learning.* San Francisco: Jossey-Bass.

Salomon, G. (1983). Television watching and mental effort: A social psychological view. In J. Bryant & D. Anderson (Eds.), *Children's understanding of television* (p. 181–198). New York: Academic Press.

Sapolsky, B.S. (1984). Arousal, affect, and the aggression-moderating effect of erotica. In N.M. Malamuth & E. Donnerstein (Eds.), *Pornography and sexual aggression* (p. 85–113). Orlando: Academic Press.

Savitsky, J.C., Rogers, R.W., Izard, C.E., & Liebert, R.M. (1971). Role of frustration and anger in the imitation of filmed aggression against a human victim. *Psychological Reports, 29,* 807–810.

Schachter, S., & Singer, J.E. (1962). Cognitive, social, and physiological determinants of emotional state. *Psychological Review, 69,* 379–399.

Schank, R., & Abelson, R. (1977). *Scripts plans goals and understanding.* Hillsdale, NJ: Lawrence Erlbaum Associates.

Schement, J.R., Gonzalez, I.N., Lum, P., & Valencia, R. (1984). The international flow of television programs. *Communication Research, 11,* 163–182.

Schlesinger, P. (1978). *Putting "reality" together: BBC news.* London: Methuen.

Schlesinger, P. (1987). Ten years on. Introductory essay in reissue of Schlesinger, P. (1978). *Putting "reality" together: BBC news.* London: Methuen.

Schlinger, M.J. (1976). The role of mass communications in promoting public health. In B.B. Anderson (Ed.), *Advances in consumer research,* Vol. III (pp. 302–305). Association for Consumer Research.

Schlinger, M.J., & Plummer, J. (1972). Advertising in black and white. *Journal of Marketing Research, 9,* 149–153.

Schneider, J.A. (1987). Networks hold the line. In A.A. Berger (Ed.), *Television in society* (p. 163–172). New Brunswick, NJ: Transaction Books.

Schneider, K.C., & Schneider, S.B. (1979). Trends in sex roles in television commercials. *Journal of Marketing, 43*(3), 79–84.

Scholfield, J., & Pavelchak, M. (1985). *The Day After:* The impact of a media event. *American Psychologist, 40,* 542–548.

Schramm, W. (1977). *Big media, little media.* Beverly Hills, CA: Sage.

Schuman, H., & Presser, S. (1981). *Questions and answers in attitude surveys: Experiments on question form, wording, and context.* New York: Academic Press.

Schwartz, T. (1981). *Media: The second god.* New York: Random House.

Seefeldt, C. (1977). Young and old together. *Children Today, 6*(1), 22.

Seggar, J.F., Hafen, J., & Hannonen-Gladden, H. (1981). Television's portrayal of minorities and women in drama and comedy drama, 1971–1980. *Journal of Broadcasting, 25*(3), 277–288.

Seifart, H. (1984). Sport and economy: The commercialization of Olympic sport by the media. *International Review for the Sociology of Sport, 19,* 305–315.

Shaheen, J. G. (1984a). *The TV Arab.* Bowling Green, OH: Bowling Green State University Popular Press.

Shaheen, J. G. (1984b). Arabs—TV's villains of choice. *Channels,* March—April, 52–53.

Shaheen, J. G. (1984c, November 23). The Arabs and the moviemakers. *Middle East International,* 15–16.

Shaheen, J. G. (1987). The Hollywood Arab (1984–1986). *Journal of Popular Film and Television,* 148–157.

Shanteau, J. (1988). Consumer impression formation: The integration of visual and verbal information. In S. Hecker & D.W. Stewart (Eds.), *Nonverbal communication in advertising* (pp. 43–57). Lexington MA: Lexington Books.

Sheikh, A.A., Prasad, V.K., & Rao, T.R. (1974). Children's TV commercials: A review of research. *Journal of Communication, 24*(4), 126–136.

Sherman, B.L., & Dominick, J.R. (1986). Violence and sex in music videos: TV and rock 'n' roll. *Journal of Communication, 36*(1), 79–93.

Shevchenko, A.N. (1986, Aug. 9) Danger: The networks are misreading the Russians. *TV Guide,* 3–8.

Shimp, T. A., & Gresham, L.G. (1983). An informative-processing perspective on recent advertising literature. *Current Issues and Research in Advertising 6,* 39–75.

Siegel, A.N. (1956). Film-mediated fantasy aggression and strength of aggressive drive. *Child Development. 27,* 365–378.

Signiorelli, N., Gross, L., & Morgan, M. (1982). Violence in television programs: Ten years later. In *Television and behavior: Ten years of scientific progress and implications for the 80s.* Washington DC: U.S. Government Printing Office.

Simon, H.A., & Stern, F. (1955). The effect of television upon voting behavior in Iowa in the 1952 Presidential election. *American Political Science Review, 49,* 470–477.

Simon, R. (1985, July 13). What's red, white, and blue—and makes Madison Avenue see green? *TV Guide,* 36–37.

Simon, R.J., & Fejes, F. (1987). Real police on television supercops. In A.A. Berger (Ed.), *Television in society* (pp. 63–69). New Brunswick, NJ: Transaction Books.

Singer, D.G., & Singer, J.L. (1983). Learning how to be intelligent consumers of television. In M.J.A. Howe (Ed.), *Learning from television: Psychological and educational research* (pp. 203–222). London: Academic Press.

Singer, D.G., Singer, J.L., & Zuckerman, D.M. (1981). *Getting the most out of TV.* Santa Monica, CA: Goodyear Publishing Co.

Singer, D.G., Zuckerman, D.M., & Singer, J.L. (1980). Helping elementary school children learn about TV. *Journal of Communication, 30*(3), 84–93.

Singer, J.L., & Singer, D.G. (1976). Can TV stimulate imaginative play? *Journal of Communication, 26*, 74–80.

Singer, J.L., & Singer, D.G. (1981). *Television, imagination, and aggression: A study of preschoolers.* Hillsdale, NJ: Lawrence Erlbaum Associates.

Singer, M. (1984). Inferences in reading comprehension. In M. Daneman & P.A. Carpenter (Eds.), *Reading research: Advances in theory and practice*, Vol. 6. New York: Academic Press.

Sintchak, G., & Geer, J. (1975). A vaginal plethysymograph system. *Psychophysiology, 12*, 113–115.

Slater, D., & Elliott, W.R. (1982). Television's influence on social reality. *Quarterly Journal of Speech, 68*, 69–79.

Soley, L. (1983). The effect of black models on magazine ad readership. *Journalism Quarterly, 60*(4), 686–690.

Solomon, D.S., & Cardillo, B.A. (1985). The elements and process of communication campaigns. In T.A. van Dijk (Ed.), *Discourse and communication* (p. 60–68). Berlin: de Gruyter.

Sparks, G.G. (1986). Developmental differences in children's reports of fear induced by the mass media. *Child Study Journal. 16*(1), 55–66.

Sprafkin, J.N., & Silverman, L.T. (1981). Update: Physically intimate and sexual behavior on prime-time television 1978-79. *Journal of Communication, 31*(1), 34–40.

Stein, B. (1979). *The view from Sunset Boulevard.* New York: Basic Books.

Stein, B. (1987). Fantasy and culture on television. In A.A. Berger (Ed.), *Television in society* (p. 215–228). New Brunswick, NJ: Transaction Books.

Stempel, G. (1971). Visibility of blacks in news and news picture magazines. *Journalism Quarterly, 48*(2), 337–339.

Stern, B.L., & Harmon, R.R. (1984). Disclaimers in children's advertising. *Journal of Advertising, 13*, 12–16.

Sternthal, B., & Craig, S. (1973). Humor in advertising. *Journal of Marketing, 37*(4), 12–18.

Stewart, L. (1988, February 18). For ABC, it's been all downhill in Winter Olympics. *Manhattan Mercury, (L.A. Times* wire) p. B4.

Surlin, S.H. (1974). Bigotry on air and in life: The Archie Bunker case. *Public Telecommunications Review, 212*, 34–41.

Sutton, S.R. (1982). Fear-arousing communications: A critical examination of theory and research. In R. Eiser (Ed.), *Social psychology and behavioral medicine* (pp. 303–337). London: John Wiley & Sons.

Tan, A.S. (1986). Social learning of aggression from television. In J. Bryant & D. Zillman (Eds.), *Perspectives on media effects* (pp.41–55). Hillsdale, NJ: Lawrence Erlbaum Associates.

Tan, A.S., Li, S., & Simpson, C. (1986). American TV and social stereotypes of Americans in Taiwan and Mexico. *Journalism Quarterly, 63*, 809–814.

Tannenbaum, P.H. (1971). Emotional arousal as a mediator of communication effects. *Technical reports of the Commission on Obscenity and Pornography*, Vol. 8. Washington DC: U.S. Government Printing Office.

Tannenbaum, P.H. (1980). Entertainment as vicarious emotional experience. In P.H. Tannenbaum (Ed.), *The entertainment functions of television* (p.107–131). Hillsdale, NJ: Lawrence Erlbaum Associates.

Tate, E., & Surlin, S. (1976). Agreement with opinionated TV characters across culture. *Journalism Quarterly, 53*(2), 199–203.

Tavris, C. (1986). How to publicize science: A case study. In J. H. Goldstein, (Ed.), *Reporting science: The case of aggression* (p. 23–32). Hillsdale, NJ: Lawrence Erlbaum Associates.

Taylor, S. (1982). The availability bias in social perception and interaction. In D. Kahneman, P. Slovic, & A. Tversky (Eds.), *Judgment under uncertainty: Heuristics and biases* (pp. 190–200). Cambridge: Cambridge University Press.

Thomas, S., & Callahan, B.P. (1982). Allocating happiness: TV families and social class. *Journal of Communication, 32,* 184–190.

Thorndyke, P.W. (1984). Applications of schema theory in cognitive research. In J.R. Anderson & S.M. Kosslyn (Eds.), *Tutorials in learning and memory* (pp. 167–192). San Francisco: Freeman.

Time. (1987, June 1). Child's play: Violent videos lure the young, p. 31.

Time. (1988, June 6). Television: For gold or for broke? 59.

Tower, R.B., Singer, D.G., & Singer, J.L. (1979). Differential effects of television programming on preschoolers' cognition, imagination, and social play. *American Journal of Orthopsychiatry, 49,* 265–281.

Townley, R. (1988, February 27). Daniel Striped Tiger . . . Meet Stepashka the brash rabbit. *TV Guide,* 12–17.

Trenaman, J., & McQuail, D. (1961). *Television and the political image: A study of the impact of television on the 1959 general election.* London: Methuen.

Tuchman, G. (1978). *Making news: A study in the construction of reality.* New York: Free Press.

Tuchman, G. (1987). Mass media values. In A.A. Berger (Ed.)., *Television in society* (pp. 195–202). New Brunswick, NJ: Transaction Books.

Tuchman, S., & Coffin, T.E. (1971). The influence of election nights television broadcasts in a close election. *Public Opinion Quarterly, 35,* 315–326.

Tunstall, J. (1977). *The media are American.* New York: Columbia University Press.

Tversky, A., & Kahneman, D. (1973). Availability: A heuristic for judging frequency and probability. *Cognitive Psychology, 5,* 201–232.

Tversky, A., & Kahneman, D. (1974). Judgment under uncertainty: Heuristics and biases. *Science, 185,* 1124–1131.

U.S. Commission on Obscenity and Pornography (1970). *The report of the commission on obscenity and pornography.* New York: Bantam.

Van der Voort, T.H.A. (1986). *Television violence: A child's eye view.* Amsterdam: North-Holland.

Van Dijk, T.A. (Ed.) (1985a). *Discourse and communication.* Berlin: De Gruyter.

Van Dijk, T.A. (1985b). Introduction: Discourse analysis in (mass) communication research. In T.A. Van Dijk (Ed.), *Discourse and communication* (pp. 1–9). Berlin: De Gruyter.

Vidmar, N., & Rokeach, M. (1974). Archie Bunker's bigotry: A study in selective perception and exposure. *Journal of Communication, 24*(1), 35–47.

Vokey, J.R., & Read, J.D. (1985). Subliminal messages: Between the devil and the media. *American Psychologist, 40,* 1231–1239.

Volgy, T.J., & Schwarz, J.E. (1980). TV entertainment programming and sociopolitical attitudes. *Journalism Quarterly, 57,* 150–155.

Walters, R.H., & Willows, D.C. (1968). Imitative behavior of disturbed and nondisturbed children following exposure to aggressive and nonaggressive models. *Child Development, 39,* 79–89.

Ward, S., Wackman, D., & Wartella, E. (1977). *How children learn to buy: The development of consumer information-processing skills.* Beverly Hills, CA: Sage.

Wartella, E. (1980). Individual differences in children's responses to television advertising. In E.L. Palmer & A. Dorr (Eds.), *Children and the faces of television: Teaching, violence, and selling* (pp. 307–322). New York: Academic Press.

Wason, P.C., & Johnson-Laird, P.N. (1972). *Psychology of reasoning.* Cambridge, MA: Harvard University Press.

Waters, H.F., & Huck, J. (1988, January 25). TV's new racial hue. *Newsweek,* 52–54.

Watkins, B. (1988). Children's representations of television and real-life stories. *Communication Research, 15,* 159–184.

Watkins, B.A., Huston-Stein, A., & Wright, J.C. (1980). Effects of planned television programming. In E.L. Palmer & A. Dorr (Eds.), *Children and the faces of television* (pp. 49–69). New York: Academic Press.

Weaver, J.B., Masland, J.L., & Zillmann, D. (1984). Effects of erotica on young men's aesthetic perception of their female sexual partners. *Perceptual and Motor Skills, 58,* 929–930.

Weaver, J., & Wakshlag, J. (1986). Perceived vulnerability to crime, criminal victimization experience, and television viewing. *Journal of Broadcasting & Electronic Media, 30,* 141–158.

Webster, J.G., & Wakshlag, J. (1985). Measuring exposure to television. In D. Zillmann and J. Bryant (Eds.). *Selective exposure to communication* (pp. 35–62). Hillsdale, NJ: Lawrence Erlbaum Associates.

Weigel, R.H., Loomis, J., & Soja, M. (1980). Race relations on prime time television. *Journal of Personality and Social Psychology, 39*(5), 884–893.

Weymouth, L. (1981, Jan.-Feb.). Walter Cronkite remembers. *Washington Journalism Review.* p. 23.

White, L.A. (1979). Erotica and aggression: The influence of sexual arousal, positive affect, and negative affect on aggressive behavior. *Journal of Personality and Social Psychology, 37,* 591–601.

Whitman, W., & Quinsey, V.L. (1981). Heterosexual skills training for institutionalized rapists and child molesters. *Canadian Journal of Behavioral Science, 13,* 105–114.

Wilcox, B.L. (1987). Pornography, social science, and politics: When research and ideology collide. *American Psychologist, 42,* 941–943.

Wilhoit, G.C. & de Bock, H. (1976). All in the Family in Holland. *Journal of Communication, 26*(1), 75–84.

Will, E. (1987). Women in media. *The Other Side, 23*(4), 44–46.

Williams, B. (1979). *Report of the Committee on Obscenity and Film Censorship.* London: Her Majesty's Stationery Office. Command 7772.

Williams, F., Phillips, A., & Lum, P. (1985). Gratifications associated with new communication technologies. In K. Rosengren, L. Wenner, & P. Palmgreen (Eds.), *Media gratifications research: New perspectives.* Beverly Hills, CA: Sage.

Williams, T.M. (Ed.). (1986). *The impact of television.* Orlando: Academic Press.

Wilson, B.J. (1987). Reducing children's emotional reactions to mass media through rehearsed explanation and exposure to a replica of a fear object. *Human Communication Research, 14,* 3–26.

Wilson, B.J., & Cantor, J. (1987). Reducig fear reactions to mass media: Effects of visual exposure and verbal explanation. In M. McLaughlin (Ed.), *Communication yearbook 10* (pp. 553–573). Newbury Park, CA: Sage.

Wilson, B.J., Hoffner, C., & Cantor, J. (1987). Children's perceptions of the effectiveness of techniques to reduce fear from mass media. *Journal of Applied Developmental Psychology, 8,* 39–52.

Windahl, S. (1981). Uses and gratifications at the crossroads. In G.C. Wilhoit & H. de Bock (Eds.), *Mass communication review yearbook,* Vol. 2. (pp. 174–185). Newbury Park, CA: Sage.

Winn, M. (1977). *The plug-in drug: Television, children, and the family.* New York: Viking Penguin.

Wober, J.M. (1978). Televised violence and paranoid perception: The view from Great Britain. *Public Opinion Quarterly, 42,* 315–321.

Wober, J.M. (1986). The lens of television and the prism of personality. In J. Bryant & D. Zillmann (Eds.), *Perspectives on media effects* (pp. 205–231). Hillsdale, NJ: Lawrence Erlbaum Associates.

Wober, J.M. (1988). *The use and abuse of television: A social psychological analysis of the changing screen.* Hillsdale, NJ: Lawrence Erlbaum Associates.

Wober, J.M., & Gunter, B. (1986). Television audience research at Britain's Independent Broadcasting Authority, 1974–1984. *Journal of Broadcasting & Electronic Media, 30,* 15–31.

Wurtzel, A., & Lometti, G. (1987a). Researching television violence. In A.A. Berger (Ed.), *Television in society* (pp. 117–131). New Brunswick, NJ: Transaction Books. Pp. 117–131. (a)

Wurtzel, A., & Lometti, G. (1987b). Smoking out the critics. In A.A. Berger (Ed.), *Television in society* (pp. 143–151). New Brunswick, NJ: Transaction Books.

Yorke, D., & Kitchen, P. (1985). Channel flickers and video speeders. *Journal of Advertising Research, 25*(2), 21–25.

Zillmann, D. (1971). Excitation transfer in communication-mediated aggressive behavior. *Journal of Experimental Social Psychology, 7,* 419–434.

Zillmann, D. (1978). Attribution and mis-attribution of excitatory reactions. In J.H. Harvey, W.J. Ickes, & R.F. Kidd (Eds.), *New directions in attribution research,* Vol. 2. Hillsdale, NJ: Lawrence Erlbaum Associates.

Zillmann, D. (1979). *Hostility and aggression.* Hillsdale, NJ: Lawrence Erlbaum Associates.

Zillmann, D. (1980). Anatomy of suspense. In P.H. Tannenbaum (Ed.), *The entertainment functions of television* (pp. 133–163). Hillsdale, NJ: Lawrence Erlbaum Associates.

Zillmann, D. (1983). Transfer of excitation in emotional behavior. In J.T. Cacioppo & R.E. Petty (Eds.), *Social psychophysiology* (pp. 215–240). New York: Guilford Press.

Zillmann, D. (1984). *Connections between sex and aggression.* Hillsdale, NJ: Lawrence Erlbaum Associates.

Zillmann, D., & Bryant. J. (1982). Pornography, sexual callousness, and the trivialization of rape. *Journal of Communication, 32*(4), 10–21.

Zillmann, D., & Bryant, J. (1983). Selective-exposure phenomena. In D. Zillmann and J. Bryant (Eds.), *Selective exposure to communication* (pp. 1–10). Hillsdale, NJ: Lawrence Erlbaum Associates.

Zillmann, D., & Bryant, J. (1984). Effects of massive exposure to pornography. In N.M. Malamuth, & E. Donnerstein (Eds.), *Pornography and sexual aggression* (pp. 115–141). Orlando: Academic Press.

Zillmann, D., & Bryant, J. (1985). Pornography's impact on sexual satisfaction. *Journal of Applied Social Psychology. 18,* 438–453.

Zillmann, D., & Bryant, J. (1988). A response to Linz and Donnerstein. *Journal of Communication, 38*(2), 185–192.

REFERENCES **271**

Zillmann, D., & Bryant, J. (in press). Effects of prolonged consumption of pornography on family values. *Journal of Family Issues.*

Zillmann, D., Bryant, J., Comisky, P.W., & Medoff, N.J. (1981). Excitation and hedonic valence in the effect of erotica on motivated intermale aggression. *European Journal of Social Psychology, 11,* 233–252.

Zillmann, D., Bryant, J., & Sapolsky, B.S. (1979). The enjoyment of watching sport contests. In J.H. Goldstein (Ed.). *Sports, games and play: Social and psychological viewpoints* (pp. 297–335). Hillsdale, NJ: Lawrence Erlbaum Associates.

Zillmann, D., Weaver, J.B., Mundorf, N., & Aust, C.F. (1986). Effects of opposite-gender companion's affect to horror on distress, delight, and attraction. *Journal of Personality and Social Psychology, 51,* 586–594.

Zoglin, R. (1988, July 11). Awaiting a gringo crumb. *Time,* 76.

Zoglin, R. (1988, May 30). Heady days again for cable. *Time,* 52–53.

Zohoori, A.R. (1988). A cross-cultural analysis of children's TV use. *Journal of Broadcasting & Electronic Media, 32*(1), 105–113.

Zuckerman, D., Singer, D., & Singer, J. (1980). Children's television viewing, racial, and sex role attitudes. *Journal of Applied Social Psychology, 10*(4), 281–294.

Author Index

Subject Index